DATE DUE

Social Cognition and
Individual Change

SAGE SOURCEBOOKS FOR THE HUMAN SERVICES SERIES

Series Editors: ARMAND LAUFFER and CHARLES GARVIN

Social Cognition and Individual Change

Current Theory and Counseling Guidelines

AARON M. BROWER
PAULA S. NURIUS

Sage Sourcebooks for
the Human Services Series
26

SAGE Publications
International Educational and Professional Publisher
Newbury Park   London   New Delhi
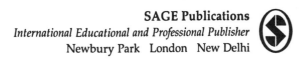

For information address:

SAGE Publications, Inc.
2455 Teller Road
Newbury Park, California 91320

SAGE Publications Ltd.
6 Bonhill Street
London EC2A 4PU
United Kingdom

SAGE Publications India Pvt. Ltd.
M-32 Market
Greater Kailash I
New Delhi 110 048 India

Printed in the United States of America

Library of Congress Cataloging-in-Publication Data

Brower, Aaron M.
    Social cognition and individual change: Current theory and counseling guidelines / Aaron M. Brower, Paula S. Nurius.
        p.   cm.—(Sage sourcebooks for the human services series; v. 26)
    Includes bibliographical references and index.
    ISBN 0-8039-3883-7 (cl).—ISBN 0-8039-3884-5 (pb)
    1. Social service—Psychological aspects.   2. Social perception.
3. Counseling.   I. Nurius, Paula.   II. Title.   III. Series.
HV41.B693   1993   93-29475
362.3′2—dc20   CIP

93 94 95 96   10 9 8 7 6 5 4 3 2 1

Sage Production Editor: Judith L. Hunter

CONTENTS

ACKNOWLEDGMENTS

Writing this book has been the culmination of many years of intellectual fermentation and development, and many people deserve recognition. We wish to thank, first and foremost, Charles Garvin for his encouragement and support as Series Editor and friend. Marquita Fleming, our editor at Sage, skillfully guided us from concept to completion. Nancy Cantor and Hazel Markus were important influences in the early development of the work reflected in this book. The Schools of Social Work at the Universities of Wisconsin and Washington provided needed resources to help us complete this project. Special thanks go to the wonderfully patient and supportive staffs who unfailingly aided us in overcoming the technological headaches of long distance collaboration. Many years of students and colleagues provided challenge and feedback to us as the ideas and techniques in these chapters took shape. We wish to thank the following in particular: Mary Lou Balassone, Sharon Berlin, John Gibson, Mary Gilfus, John Longres, Sheldon Rose, and Suzanne Staudenmaier.

A note of acknowledgment to one another is in order. It has been a long road since 1983 when we submitted our first joint conference abstract on this topic. We recognized then, as we do now, that our differences are what make the sum greater than the individual parts, and we value the special friendship and collegial commitment that allows us to weave our differences into a coherent whole.

Finally, we dedicate this book to our families: Nancy, Jacob, and Nathaniel Brower, and Michael and Noisette Nurius; and to our ohana— our families without blood ties. They are what made it worth doing.

FOREWORD

For a long time, it has seemed to me that understanding how memory works is essential to understanding personal change. Understanding how we remember who we are and what we are supposed to do in particular circumstances seems absolutely basic to figuring out how to develop new memories that are more satisfying and adaptive. With *Social Cognition and Individual Change,* Aaron Brower and Paula Nurius provide this basic knowledge and explain exactly what it has to do with accomplishing change within the context of direct human service practice. They go on to explore the concept of the ecological niche and to explicitly map out the interrelatedness of cognitive processes and environmental situations, the ways that people understand and then act upon and react to their social circumstances.

In this era of the cognitive revolution, books that address the use of cognitive techniques to facilitate personal change are abundant. None, however, match the conceptual depth and clarity offered by Brower and Nurius. These authors synthesize the best available knowledge from social and personality psychology to explain how the mind works and to explain how to help clients change their minds and their immediate social circumstances.

A cognitive intervention tool is only a tool, but a solid conceptual framework that provides critical information about how people come to think, feel, and act as they do, allows practitioners and clients to generate additional ways to guide these same processes. With this gift of an empirically supported conceptual framework, Brower and Nurius also give new, more explicit, and more useful meaning to a range of familiar ideas such as empowerment, self-concept, goal setting, problem solving, and evaluating client progress. For example, their detailed discussion of the motivational properties of personal goals builds upon and adds new conceptual and procedural dimension to goal-oriented intervention models such as Task-Centered Treatment (Epstein, 1992; Reid, 1992). As the authors explain, it is the detailed vision of how things could be better that sustains and guides our efforts to consider, practice, and experience positive differences.

Despite the theoretical bent to this book, Brower and Nurius couldn't be clearer about how to apply the concepts they present. I have already used their explanation of the differences between declarative knowledge (knowing about) and procedural knowledge (knowing how) to help refocus a client who has been irritated that her insights into the nature of her difficulties don't cause her to do anything about them. She is relieved to understand that her repetition of old patterns, despite knowing better, is not a matter of spinelessness. While she has had the *idea* that something else would be better, she hasn't really known *how* to act outside of the old habit patterns. It is this knowing how that we need to work on.

In the preface to this book, Brower and Nurius describe themselves as "hybrids, of a sort." Their formal training is in social work and social and personality psychology. They have experienced the human service enterprise from all sides. And it must be this breadth of experience and commitment that accounts for the remarkable inclusiveness and balance of their book. Never compromising depth, Brower and Nurius appreciate and weave together disciplinary theory, research findings, explicit value choices, and their first-hand experiences as teachers, practitioners, and fellow humans.

As fellow humans ourselves, we are familiar with the difficulties inherent in trying to experience and represent ourselves differently— the difficulties of noticing opportunities to think, feel, and act differently; of maintaining mindfulness of troublesome thought-feeling patterns; and of awkwardly practicing other perspectives. Given that all of us are shaped and constrained by what we know, tend to hang on to prior conceptions, and hardly ever fully and permanently transcend beliefs about our vulnerabilities, the cognitive-ecological model takes on a kind of "we are all in this together" tone. In laying out a normative model of human memory and social functioning, Brower and Nurius depathologize client problems. They explain how adaptive and dysfunctional patterns often stem from the same normative processes. They also describe how the same kinds of cognitive processes that make it hard for clients to move beyond their expectations also interfere with practitioners altering their preconceptions in order to be more helpful in their professional roles.

Overall, the material Brower and Nurius present is sophisticated and complex, but they also manage to make it highly accessible. By using clear conceptual descriptions, chapter introductions, and capsule summaries, Brower and Nurius deftly follow their own prescriptions about how to capture attention, prime associations, and facilitate recall.

I read this manuscript with genuine pleasure because it seemed clear to me that Brower and Nurius have significantly advanced our ability to understand and accomplish personal change.

Sharon B. Berlin, Ph.D.
Professor
The University of Chicago
School of Social Service Administration

PREFACE

The Sage Sourcebook Series serves as a starting place for those of us involved in human service practice, education, and research who are searching for theoretical and empirical updates that bear upon our work. Communicating and translating results reported in the academic journals often suffers from time lags. This is particularly true with respect to translating research findings from allied disciplines into a consumable form applicable to human services. This book fits squarely into this objective. This book is not intended to be a comprehensive primer on direct human service practice. There are a number of useful books available to meet that need. Rather, the strength of this book is the bridge that it helps form to some of the recent cutting-edge findings in the area of social and personality psychology—and social cognition in particular—that are of considerable interest and utility to the human service practitioner.

Much like our work, we, the authors, are hybrids of a sort: We have been trained both as social workers and as social and personality psychologists, and have worked as practitioners, educators, and researchers. This hybridization will be apparent in the integrative perspective that we offer. Consistent with this, our overall aim is to contribute to a more integrative model that practitioners can use to conceptualize their work with clients, one that will help them more fully articulate their thinking and actions in cognitive and ecological directions throughout the helping process.

In recent years, there have been some enormously useful and clarifying developments in the area of social cognition. Social cognition is a body of work that describes the ways in which people perceive, interpret, manipulate, and remember social stimuli. Social cognition emphasizes the role played by social, cultural, and affective forces that influence these cognitive processes, along with the behavioral and interpersonal consequences of them. Although social transactions and processes of perceptual "meaning-making" have long been recognized as critical for the helping professional, they have also been among the fuzziest and, consequently, among the more difficult to adequately assess and use for intervention.

As we work with any given individual client or client group, we become exquisitely aware of the need for a solid conceptual knowledge base in order to understand how and why people think, feel, and act as they do—both in the normal sense as well as when things go wrong. We need a solid conceptual base from which we can assess which factors to focus on, among the myriad of factors that influence every person in every situation, in problem development and problem management. Because of the importance of this conceptual grounding to inform and guide intervention techniques, the practice framework that we offer will contain three parts: (a) a model of how people normatively live and function in everyday life; (b) a model of how and why things go wrong (i.e., a view and explanation of problems in daily life); and (c) a model of intervention that builds upon this backdrop of social cognitions and social transactions. We also note that the helping process itself is a social context and relationship. Thus, we will also discuss how social cognitive factors influence human service practitioners in their helping role, and ways to best manage these normative processes.

The first section—Chapters 1 through 4—will focus on the theoretical underpinnings of the cognitive-ecological model: its strengths and limitations, as well as a detailed discussion of its key components. The concepts and terms used throughout the book will be introduced and explained in these first four chapters. Chapter 1 will first briefly describe the ecological perspective and how a cognitive-ecological one builds upon and extends prior work. Here we identify four core themes that help organize our approach in this book and the ways in which social-cognitive theory and research help to refine many of the central features of the ecological perspective. Chapter 2 builds upon this introduction by outlining in detail the assumptions and features underlying the cognitive-ecological model.

In Chapter 3, two features of the cognitive-ecological model will be isolated and described further—the niche and the self-system. These two features describe the processes and concepts particularly relevant to individual change efforts. The niche focuses on the subset of forces in an individual's environment that significantly influences development of a life story, social routines, and problem-solving patterns. The self-system focuses more on intrapersonal factors involved in these undertaking, including processes of developing, sustaining, and changing personal identity. In detailing the concepts of the niche and the self-system, the following concepts are introduced and discussed: the self-concept, the working self, possible selves, possible niches, and components of memory (declarative and procedural memory, short-term or working memory, and the sensory-perceptual system). Chapter 4 focuses on the role of life goals in daily life, and the relationship between possible selves and possible niches to life goals. This chapter concludes with discussion of when things go wrong, and the interrelationships among processes of normative functioning and those involved in several types of dysfunction.

Chapter 5 shifts focus from clients and their natural environment to the practitioner and the environment (the context and relationship) of formal helping efforts. Here we describe ways in which normative affective, cognitive, and social functioning serve both as potential assets and handicaps for practitioners in their efforts to understand and intervene with their clients. The same factors that influence normative observation, inference, reasoning, and judgment—both positively and negatively—influence helping or intervention-related observation, inference, reasoning, and judgment—both positively and negatively. We will discuss some of the most prevalent pitfalls and vulnerabilities, as well as ways to guard against bias and ways to enhance effectiveness.

In the second section of this book—Chapters 6 through 9—the emphasis will be on applying the cognitive-ecological model to the phases of counseling and clinical practice. Chapter 6 will describe a cognitive-ecological perspective on assessment, focusing on more clearly assessing the client's daily life, presenting problems, and characteristic cognitive and affective processes, all within the context of the client's niche. Assessment also initiates the helping relationship—the in vivo social interactions that can serve to solidify effective client change.

Chapter 7 describes the processes of goal setting and contracting, practices that create the structure for the ongoing helping relationship and for lasting change. The process of determining goals and making a contract also serves to demystify the professional practice role and the problem-solving framework, which in turn helps to foster change.

Emphasized in this chapter are how possible selves and possible niches are developed as life goals, and then how life goals are translated into specific behavior-change goals pursued in the helping relationship. Chapter 8 focuses on intervention planning and implementation. Consistent with our desire for practitioners to model and train clients to become their own counselors, this chapter focuses on principles of planning, tailoring, and implementing interventions that foster mindfulness, self-efficacy, and durable change.

Chapter 9 focuses on the feedback and evaluation of client-directed change that guides intervention and follow-through: how to help clients maintain desired changes in their lives; how to use feedback aids and social supports to shape their niches and self-systems in more long-lasting and functional ways; and how to develop monitoring systems to help clients keep themselves on track.

In the Epilogue we discuss aspects of cognitive-ecological practice that continue to need further development, as well as ways to actively collaborate in this developing professional base.

Because of the dual focus here on updating the theoretical foundation of ecological practice with social cognitive advances, and on translating these into practical applications, this book will be appropriate for courses on human behavior in the social environment, for courses on practice methods, and for elective courses focusing on self-development and change within a dynamic social environment. The book is intended primarily for students; however, it is also suited for human service practitioners who would like a single, updated resource to fill the gap in their social psychological training as it relates to their helping efforts.

The process of updating and refining our practice models is continuous. We do not mean for this book to serve as a comprehensive reference that contains all the practice guidelines a practitioner will ever need. Rather, we are offering a set of ideas that we hope will serve as impetus for discussion and further development of person-environment models of human interaction and counseling. We have first focused on gaps in the conceptual canvas of ecological thinking that selected advances from the social-cognitive arena help fill. We then concentrated on specifying bridges, or translations, of theory to practice principles and method.

We hope to present person-environment interactive processes with sufficient detail to allow others to test the application of these processes in a wide range of practice settings. We offer numerous examples throughout this book to illustrate cognitive-ecological concepts and principles. While many of the examples describe only a subset of the kinds of problems clients bring to us (for example, the majority of our examples are of voluntary clients), our students have used the cognitive-ecological model with clients across varied settings and helping situations.

The notion of a sourcebook reflects the ongoing nature of revision and change. We have attempted here to synthesize innovative theory and research that support the practice tasks familiar to most human service practitioners. We have turned to our own practice experience and those of others (very much including our students) in this effort. Your perspective as the readers will be crucial in the further development of our work to develop good, solid practice theory. We welcome your comments and suggestions.

Chapter 1

INTRODUCTION

Matt is a 12-year-old boy, the oldest of three kids (one year older than his brother, Michael, and 5 years older than a sister, Kristen). Matt's mother, Joan, called the clinic in a panic, unable to handle her kids, particularly her oldest, whom she thought was the ringleader, and who was becoming increasingly out of control. A single mother with limited financial resources, Joan has returned to college and has recently moved to cramped family housing at the university. She hopes to become the first of her family to advance beyond a high school education. For Joan, college offers a ticket into the good life: financial stability, stimulating work, and the opportunity to be someone others would respect.

Matt, Michael, and Kristen's constant fighting was escalating. Joan was particularly worried since Kristen's complaints about Matt began to include descriptions of teasing of a sexual nature. Joan was beginning to feel like she was "losing it," and being new to the area, did not know where to turn.

How should a helping practitioner approach this family's multiple problems? Where does one begin to understand the complex dynamics in this family, and what are the best ways to help them? One often wishes for a solid theory base to use when working with clients: one that will guide assessments, highlight the appropriate behaviors that lead naturally to effective interventions, and structure the counseling relationship to allow clients to maintain their healthy gains. With moves toward theoretical rapprochement (see Goldfried, 1982; Kanfer, 1984; Maddux, Stoltenberg, & Rosenwein, 1987; Strean, 1982), ecological frameworks, those highlighting person-environment interactions, are gaining quickly in popularity.

Ecological models are founded on the principle of reciprocal influence of individuals with other people and with other systems in the environment. Individual behaviors are seen as products of a myriad of forces, and problems are best understood within the interactions between the perceptions, needs, and resources of people and their environments. Furthermore, rather than mere reactors to environmental forces, individuals are highly active in constructing and shaping their social and physical environments.

As conceptually appealing as these ideas might sound, the utility of ecological models in practice settings has been constrained by the ideas remaining at too high a level of abstraction. For example, other than in the most general sense, what does it mean to say that we shape our environment? Or, when practitioners are encouraged to use this approach, what are we using? Are we rallying behind ecological approaches as a philosophical and value orientation, yet continuing to assess and intervene in a person-focused manner? In what ways can we operationalize this theory into practice methods?

Answers to questions such as these serve as important bridges between the theory and the conduct of ecological practice. In recent years there have been increasing efforts to encourage and guide practitioners and researchers to look at the whole of the person's life and the problems in living that trouble him or her. It would be unfair to say that progress has not been made to form bridges between values and theory on the one hand, and action guidelines on the other. Yet those bridges are better defined in some arenas than in others (e.g., working with people with disabilities; see Mackelprang & Hepworth, 1987). And significant gaps remain.

In this book we will focus on some of these gaps. As the title suggests, our thrust will be on recent advances in the understanding of cognition as a pivotal mediating factor in how the person and the environment mutually influence each other. The past 15 years in particular have seen an explosion of research and thinking in the area of social cognition. This involves study that explores how people perceive, interpret, act, and receive feedback in interpersonal situations. Much of this work can be applied directly to specify interactive elements of an ecological model, and particularly to better operationalize some of the processes describing how people shape their environments and their social interactions. With the contribution of this work from social and cognitive science, we will present what we refer to as a *cognitive-ecological* model. This approach is *ecological* in that we view people in situation, viewing behavior as being a product of person-situation interaction. It is *cognitive* in recognizing that people shape their environment by constructing an understanding of that environment, and then responding within that framework. (And, of course, individuals' efforts in these initial and ongoing cognitive constructions emerge within cultural contexts that provide a framework of meaning.)

Yet, this model is not meant to explain everything. It is meant to help move ecological practice an increment forward by more fully integrating recent social science findings with social service objectives. In this book, we work to integrate recent findings regarding social-cognitive dynamics of human behavior in the social environment with direct practice assessment and intervention. In service of this goal, we purposefully overemphasize cognitive and affective perceptual processes in order to highlight refinements in this arena and to stimulate subsequent additions and refinements.

FOUR CORE THEMES

Four core themes organize our approach in this book. The broadest is that of bridging between theory and practice as we assess particular clients' situations and generate intervention responses appropriate to their needs. This involves an understanding of normative social cognitions and social transactions as the backdrop for understanding our clients' presenting problems and for developing change strategies that will positively build upon these normative processes. Therefore, rather than searching for pathology per se to define and understand problems, one must look first at normative processes that may function toward negative ends. Individuals do indeed encounter experiences and behave in ways that greatly undermine well-being. But the fundamental processes through which individuals come to understand and interact with their environment are essentially the same, whether they are adaptive or maladaptive. In this sense, we will illustrate ways that a cognitive-ecological model can help us cross traditional schisms in theoretical orientations toward a more integrative or unified perspective.

A second theme of this book revolves around the notion of social construction. In an interpretive and experiential sense, we live among multiple realities. Although there can be considerable consensus among people about a given aspect of a shared reality, we are constantly engaged in an individual process of selectively noticing things, of inference and interpretation, of evaluation and prediction, and of how we emotionally, psychologically, and physically experience phenomena. This is not to argue that there are not clear external targets in need of change (such as poverty or otherwise oppressive environments). Rather, it is to underscore that an understanding of any given individual's problem requires an effort to understand the interpretive construction that person is operating from. In this book, we will be focusing on individuals' constructions related to personal identity and to their life niche.

A third core theme running through this book is that human behavior is best understood as our best efforts to solve problems or tasks, or strive for goals in our lives. We are doing the best we can, given what we know about ourselves and our world. Viewing behavior as problem solving, however, does not mean that we always know what problems we are attempting to address, or that we are attempting to solve problems in ways that are desirable or effective. As we will discuss in subsequent chapters, we all often grapple with problems or goals that we have not articulated to ourselves, and we very often react to situations in "mindless" or automatic ways. Nevertheless, we will argue in this book that a very fruitful way to understand any given behavior (from the spontaneous reaction of surprise that serves to alert us to incoming stimuli, to the more thoughtful and conscious planning involved in solving problems at work) is to understand it as our attempt to solve problems and strive to achieve goals in our lives. We will use the term *everyday problem solving* to refer to the everyday "juice" that motivates our daily behavior, and to refer to the processes that embed that behavior within our daily life.

Finally, the fourth theme in this book has to do with mindfulness and intentionality, with the goal being to enhance awareness and informed choice for practitioners and clients alike. This theme is consistent with empowerment goals of supporting conscious awareness and preparation for client self-determination. It also speaks to practitioners' responsibility to build checks and balances into their practice to safeguard against the risks of unintended bias and undue influence.

The counseling relationship is ultimately a business relationship—practitioners should be *humanely businesslike,* to use Reid's term (1978). Clients hire us—either directly or through third-party sources—because of our skills and knowledge, to assist them with specific problems they are facing. We are not our clients' friends, relatives, gurus, or lovers; we are certainly not the final arbiters nor experts in their lives. Every action we take, and every question we have, should be expressed explicitly for the client's benefit. Our role, therefore, takes a strong educational focus as we train clients—through modeling of our own behavior, through specific psycho-educational methods, and through assistance in mobilizing or obtaining needed resources—to understand their own and others' behavior within the context of their life course and to understand how to help themselves become more "mindful" and creative in their everyday problem solving and striving for goals.

We are presenting a perspective of practice and of better understanding the seemingly murky aspects of social-cognitive transactions between people and their environments. It is our hope that this perspective will help practitioners better help their clients, that decisions and assessments in their practice will be more well-informed because the reader is on firmer theoretical and empirical ground. As we survey the field of direct human service practice, we are impressed with the seemingly endless number of intervention packages, techniques, and technologies available. Yet unless practitioners work from a clear and verifiable practice theory—one that helps make sense of "normal" behaviors as well as those that are problematic—it is impossible to make valid choices among these techniques. We therefore focus this book on practice theory and the thoughtful translation of theory into well-suited action rather than on techniques.

Before we begin our discussion of the cognitive-ecological model in the next chapter, we devote the remainder of this one to a broad description of how systems, or person-environment interactive, approaches have been applied to practice settings.

WHAT IS THE PERSON-ENVIRONMENT INTERACTION?

There have been numerous approaches to answering this question, from the early period of formal human services to contemporary times.[1] This has taken somewhat different forms across disciplines: being associated with a value premise of empowerment in social work, with statistical interaction formulations in psychology, and with role-based symbolic interactionism in sociology (Balgopal & Vassil, 1983; Magnusson, 1981; Maluccio, 1981). In its simplest form, the *person-environment interaction* refers to making central the role of joint influences on behavior. People act in certain ways not only because of the situation they are in but also because of who they are. It is inappropriate, inaccurate even, to isolate the effects of the person from the effects of the situation. Behaviors must be seen as the product of the unique person-situation interaction, rather than solely as a function of either one or the other.

Looking back to the case presented at the beginning of this chapter, is Joan worried about her kids' behaviors because she needs to spend less time with them now (so their behaviors have not really changed, but she has school work to do in the evening and less time to spend with them)? Or maybe the children's behaviors have changed: such as acting out in order to get her attention. Possibly Matt's burgeoning sexuality, coupled with his poor social skills and aggressive tendencies, is responsible for his change in behavior. Or maybe the problem is none of these, but instead Joan is hearing complaints from her upstairs neighbors. Perhaps the family roles and boundaries that were adaptive at one time are beginning to break down as a result of the changes in living situation and Joan's additional responsibilities. From an ecological perspective, all of these factors, and more, must be considered to be the cause of the problems. And none of them by itself is a complete answer.

Efforts to date have reckoned with the notion of finding a "fit" between people and their environments, such as finding a fit or balance between environmental demands and personal capacity, or between personal need and environmental resources (e.g., Gould, 1987; Milner, 1987). This has included linking people with community resources to help them better meet personal needs (e.g., Guterman & Blythe, 1986; Whittaker, Schinke, & Gilchrist, 1986).

While these are reasonable applications of an ecological approach to practice, we instead argue in this book that the fit notion only exploits one part of this approach. We will focus on the social-cognitive and social-ecological processes that mediate interactions between people and their environments. As we will discuss below, a fit notion implies that the person-environment interaction is one of piecing together parts of a puzzle, with a static person finding his or her place within a static environment. Instead, we hope to conceptualize the processes by which people and environments interact in much more dynamic terms; the person shapes the environment through his or her presence while at the same time being shaped by it.

This book can be seen as the latest evolution of a series of works that have taken a person-environment interaction approach to practice (see Berlin & Marsh, 1993; Germain, 1991; Germain & Gitterman, 1980; Maluccio, 1981; Meyer, 1983; Perlman, 1957; Pincus & Minahan, 1973). Yet, despite the plethora of theoretical models of the person-environment interaction, what has lagged behind are methods to take full advantage of these models in human service practice (Kahle, 1979). In other words, how can professional practitioners use an ecological model in their face-to-face meetings with their clients?

According to Germain and Gitterman (1980), the ecological model serves as a metaphor for human interaction and human behavior. Through the principle of ecology we seek to understand the reciprocal relations between organisms and environments: how species maintain themselves by using the environment, shaping it to their needs without destroying it; and how such adaptive processes increase the environment's diversity and enhance its life-supporting properties. In healthy ecological systems, there is a balance, often a delicate one, wherein both the species' and the environment's (which includes other species) needs and capacities operate in interdependence.

We shape our surroundings to help ourselves fit into them, while at the same time we shape our behaviors to fit into our surroundings. This does not suggest that the individual does all the shaping. The environment includes other people and social forces (in addition to its physical aspects) that very definitely exert influence on the individual. It is, however, rare that environmental influences on individuals are direct. That is, there is nearly always some kind of communication, interpretation, and decision making going on, even if on a fairly rudimentary level, that constitutes what we refer to as a mediated influence.

From an ecological framework, cause and effect are not linear. Instead, events are the result of, and at the same time impact on, a field of forces. Thus, Meyer (1983) notes that in the problem of truancy, a practitioner can work, for example, with the child or with the teacher (or both) to effect the same outcome of keeping the child in school. Rather than assuming that the cause-effect chain flows in one direction, leading to the repeated specification of one target or type of intervention, an ecological perspective suggests tailoring intervention choices to an ecological assessment of the problem. For example, different interventions oriented toward the child, the teacher, or a host of other targets (e.g., the child's family) might result in the same desired effect. As will be discussed in a subsequent chapter, interventions are selected because of the client's priorities, the practitioner's perspective, the leverages for change that exist in the system, and the guidance that the professional knowledge base offers regarding what works well with whom. It is rare that interventions are selected because one causal factor stands out as the one right answer.

In the truancy example above, no matter where one begins to work with the system, be it the child, the teacher, or the family, the intervention will impact other closely related factors, which themselves will reverberate to changes in the system as a whole. Sometimes the interventions will start chain reactions that have effects that are desired: helping the teacher to accommodate the child's idiosyncratic needs allows the child to be more focused and successful in class, which takes the heat off the child at home and reduces tensions with her parents. In other instances, however, interventions that appear appropriate in their direct effect make matters worse: helping the teacher accommodate the child's idiosyncratic needs serves to scapegoat the child with her peers, which makes school an even more painful experiences, exacerbating tensions at home. In both examples, the same principle is demonstrated: that a change in one part of the system will necessitate a change in other parts of the system.

As the professional knowledge base has evolved, so too has the model. With recent theoretical and empirical advances in the social and cognitive sciences, the assumptions and features of an ecological approach can be extended and more clearly developed into what we are calling the cognitive-ecological model. In the following chapter we will detail the basic assumptions and characteristics that constitute a cognitive-ecological model of practice.

NOTE

1. For example, see Bartlett, 1970; Germain, 1973; Glasser, Sarri, & Vinter, 1974; Goldstein, 1973; Gordon & Schutz, 1977; Hollis, 1972; Meyer, 1970; Morris & Anderson, 1975; Perlman, 1957; Richmond, 1917; Simon, 1970; and Tropp, 1977.

Chapter 2

CHARACTERISTICS OF A COGNITIVE-ECOLOGICAL MODEL

The previous chapter outlined the four core themes that carry through the cognitive-ecological model of practice: that we must understand clients' normative cognitive and affective processes in order to understand their daily life and presenting problems; that we take a social constructionism perspective to understanding human behavior; that behaviors are clients' best efforts to respond to situations; and that one practice objective is to enhance clients' mindfulness. In this chapter, we build on these four themes to describe the basic features of the cognitive-ecological model.

FEATURES OF THE COGNITIVE-ECOLOGICAL MODEL

One of the obstacles to making more full use of an ecological approach in practice has been the difficulty in operationalizing its basic features. This chapter will do just that: introduce basic concepts and characteristics of the cognitive-ecological model that will be used throughout this book. In Chapter 3 we discuss how the model functions to describe normal or everyday behavior. Chapter 4 extends this model further, focusing on life goals and how these same processes can be understood to operate in several types of dysfunction. To describe and develop the cognitive-ecological model, research and theory in cognitive social science will be used to explicate processes implied, but not operationalized, in earlier applications of ecological practice.

Surviving as a Function of Interdependence on the Environment

First, the cognitive-ecological model makes the assumption that the fundamental motivation for human beings is to survive in one's environment. Based on this need to survive, we are motivated to adapt to our surroundings—to shape ourselves to be able to adapt in order to survive, and to mold our surroundings to enable us to find what we need. At the same time, the ecological model emphasizes that the effects of this shaping change the surroundings and ourselves so that we are intricately connected to our surroundings for our survival. Moreover, the various parts of our surroundings are likewise intricately linked together in a network that maintains a state of homeostasis.

To take a macro-level example, when we build hydroelectric power plants on rivers to take advantage of the water current, we change the ecology of the river itself. If a number of power plants use the same river for their source of energy, the river's current itself is appreciably decreased, and the power generated is lessened (to say nothing of the devastation to the original inhabitants of the river ecosystem). To output the same power levels, the plants must then either work harder to squeeze more power from the decreased flow of the river, or cooperate with one another to minimize their interference with one another's flow.

To take a more micro-level example, when grade school teachers expect more from their students, the students tend to respond with higher performances (Frank, 1941). Then when the teachers see these higher performances, the tendency is to reinforce the performance and to further raise the level of expectation. This iterative process continues until a balance is stabilized between the teachers' expectations and the students' performances.

Even our perceptions are likewise linked to our environments. Imagine how a 50° day feels in early fall versus late winter. When it comes in September, it marks for us the beginning of the cold, and we bundle up with sweaters and scarfs. When it comes in March, we throw off our heavy coats and hats and are heartened by the coming of spring. Not only do we feel different emotionally, but the temperature feels physically different to us, because of not only our physical adaptation to the weather that preceded this 50° day but also our psychological associations with the season to come.

To have survived as a species, then, we have learned to become extremely sensitive to the changes around us at the physical, social, and even biological levels of existence. Our drive to survive—and to survive as pleasantly as possible—has necessitated that we adapt to our surroundings and manage them to provide us with what we need. Most of us do not live at the edge in terms of physical survival, though we certainly will confront clients for whom this is a daily occurrence. However, the point we wish to make concerning the cognitive-ecological perspective is that our cognitive and affective processes have also evolved to facilitate our survival: We use our perceptions and feelings both to adapt to our environments and to shape our experience of them.

Our Evolutionary Need to Manage Our Environment

Based on our survival motive, the second feature made explicit in the cognitive-ecological model is that it is evolutionarily adaptive for us to manage both our physical and our social environments. George Herbert Mead described this process in the 1930s when he was outlining his tenets of *symbolic interactionism* (Mead, 1934). Symbolic interactionism says that we survive as a species because of our ability to manage our environments through the use of symbols. A *symbol* is defined as a culturally agreed upon representation of a physical or mental object. We use symbols as cultural shorthand to enable us to communicate in rich and complex ways, while doing so in a "quick and dirty" manner. A specific chair, for instance, is simply a chair, but when the symbol *chair* is used in a phrase, it carries with it figurative and affective meaning. We say "pull up a chair" to communicate our interest in someone or our desire to spend time with him. We say "take a load off" (which in itself implies the use of the chair symbol) to let someone know it is okay to relax. We say "sit up straight in your chair" to tell someone to pay attention or to get busy. The symbol carries with it the richness of the language that is the basis for communication in a culture.

Creating and communicating in symbolic language require considerable cognitive skill. When we say "pull up a chair," we intend it to be loaded with meaning, that is, loaded with emotional and cognitive messages directed at the receiver. Complimentarily, when we are the receiver of this phrase, we must decode its message to hear the phrase as it was intended. Thus, to communicate with others, we must imbue incoming information with meaning. Cognitive science tells us that we are never passive receivers of information, but instead we actively make sense of any incoming stimulus by attaching affective and cognitive meanings to it. Making sense out of the world—reading into messages received, and picking and choosing which messages to read in the first place—is essential for our survival. Why is it important to communicate in symbols instead of using a more presentational language? One prevailing explanation is that it was evolutionarily adaptive to develop this ability; it enabled us to survive better (Chomsky, 1972). The use of symbols allows us to communicate quickly and efficiently: We can say to our clients "pull up a chair" to indicate our readiness to begin the session, rather than go through a lengthy explanation each time that we are prepared to listen, that we remember where the work ended last time, that the client can go on to tell whatever is important from the previous week, and so forth.

Lauer and Handel (1983) list a number of reasons why it is so important for us to make sense out of our world:

1. We need to believe we live in a "just world" where rules apply so that we are rewarded when we do what is right, and punished when we do wrong; we need to believe that our world works according to logical rules rather than seeing that events happen capriciously or randomly.

2. We need to feel we have some measure of control over our world, that it is predictable and that we are masters of our lives.

3. In order to further our sense of control, we need to construct a coherent "life story" from the (often) random events that shaped our lives and (often) disconnected or uninformed choices we made.

4. We need to act on our natural curiosity, to discover how things work.

Note that it is not necessary to posit that human beings strive to grow or develop in order to act on our survival needs. Growth-oriented striving is, of course, an important aspect of life, and some of the reasons identified by Lauer and Handel play a role in such striving (e.g., our curiosity). But, most fundamentally, we will first strive to establish a status quo, or a sense of stability that enables us to survive within our ever-changing world.[1] Upon this bedrock, we can contemplate growth, although we will sometimes experience growth and stability as being in conflict with each other.

This feature of the cognitive-ecological model, that we are driven to make sense of our world in order to satisfy our survival motive, is related to the classic determinism versus free will debates in the social sciences. Do we make real choices in our lives, or are we passive victims to internal and external stimuli? (Interestingly, Wachtel [1977] argues that both psychoanalytic and behavioral perspectives assume that behavior is generated deterministically.) From a cognitive-ecological point of view, this debate is better cast as one where we either passively receive meanings from our surroundings and then respond to this stimuli, or actively make sense out of our surroundings—imbuing them with meaning—and then use the meaning to structure our responses.

In this book, we take the position that human beings are active construers of meaning: We pick and choose the cues in our environment, we put these cues together to make sense of situations, and then we respond to situations based on our understanding of them. This is not to say that we always act as masters of our destiny, nor do we always appear to make decisions in this kind of deliberate, willful constructionism. As will be discussed more fully below, we often act in an automatic or mindless manner in response to internal and external cues (and this is often functional for us). And, particularly in novel situations, we are enormously influenced by our environments (e.g., as models and guides, as sources of affirmation and reinforcement). Yet we have the capacity to respond in novel ways to situations because we have the capacity to imbue situations with novel meanings.

The Development of Life Stories, Based in Schematic Knowledge

One of the results of our need to make sense of our world, and therefore a third explicit feature of a cognitive-ecological model, is that we develop a coherent story from our history of experiences. These life stories form the basis of how we understand the world, ourselves, and particularly ourselves within the world. Much research documents the importance of these stories to our lives. The literature on reminiscence, for example, demonstrates both the importance of having a life story to support mental health and self-esteem, as well as the importance of being able to update our stories by integrating new events that we encounter (Atchley, 1989). Lerner's (1980) work on the "belief in the just world" demonstrates that we work extraordinarily hard to find explanations for random or capricious events that allow them to fit into our life stories and to make us feel less vulnerable.

In one sense, our life story can be viewed as the human analogue to General System Theory's description of *steady state* (von Bertalanffy, 1969). We create life stories in order to maintain a sense of coherence and consistency in our lives. We create a life course much as a natural system strives for continuity through its steady state processes.

When we say we have learned from our experiences, we are referring to our ability to extract meaning from our interactions with our environment and apply that understanding in the future. Extracting meaning results directly from our ability to link the event to the current knowledge we have about ourselves and the world (Cantor & Kihlstrom, 1987), that is, to our ever-revised life story. We extract and retain information because it is useful to us; we discard information when it is no longer useful (and we take great license in how we edit our stories). Current research on social cognition finds that we store this knowledge in the form of *schemas,* which are cognitive representations of events, objects, and concepts (Cohen, 1981).

Schemas are mental images that allow us to catalog a lot of information in a small package. In part, we abstract information from a variety of observations and experiences in the form of prototypic features. Again, if we picture a chair in our minds, we most likely see something with legs to support itself, a seat to support the user, and often a back to support the user. It may or may not have arms and/or padding and may be made out of any number of materials. The "chair" schema is flexible enough to allow us to recognize different chairs when we see them, from traditional wooden straight-backed schoolroom chairs, to sleek dining room chairs, to beanbag chairs. We can recognize all of these as a version of chair since we recognize that each supports itself, and supports its users. One notes that this definition of the chair schema implicitly contains not only concrete features, such as a seat and legs, but also contains a message as to the function of the chair: Chairs are what we use to sit on.

Social schemas work the same way: They contain features and functions in a prototypic image that we store in our minds, as well as containing a collection of specific examples that have been encountered. Our "reliable person" schema tells us that such a person can be trusted to complete assigned tasks on time, and will be honest (among other things). Saying that schemas are mental images is not to suggest that only visual or semantic information is included; all sensory inputs can be encoded as part of this representation. We attach emotions directly to schemas. If we attach feelings of friendliness and openness to our reliable person schema, then we will tend to feel friendly and open to someone we view as reliable. Similarly, if we are feeling friendly and open, it is easier to judge a person to be reliable, versus when our feelings are contradictory to openness and friendliness.

Schemas allow us to interpret events, and respond to them, based on our past experiences (although our schemas are not necessarily accurate or consistent with others' schemas of the same thing). Our ability to call up schemas when we either anticipate or enter situations is the basis of our ability to imbue meaning into situations. When we enter a restaurant, we call up our "restaurant" schema, which allows us to know how to act and what to expect. Similarly, when we enter new intimate relationships, we call up schemas based on past observations and experiences with intimate relationships, which may or may not be well informed, well rounded, or adaptive, but which will nevertheless shape how we will judge and respond to the new relationship.

Social schemas incline us to categorize people in a very short amount of time. Upon meeting others, we tend to call up schemas that we use to allow us to make sense of our first impressions. We attribute a whole host of thoughts and feelings to the person, and then anchor subsequent interpretations in line with our initial impressions. On the positive side, social schemas allow us to click with, or understand, others after having met them for only a short time. On the negative side, our use of schemas allows us to be fooled by situations and by others, and it fosters stereotyping. We may, and often do, call up schemas inappropriate to the situation or the person, and thus begin traveling down a road of anticipating and interpreting events based on erroneous early impressions.

Schemas fill our lives with meaning. They allow us to understand ourselves, others, and our surroundings within a context that is broader than what is immediately present. When we feel angry at a boss for not fully recognizing our accomplishments, this feeling may become intensified as we experience memories of other such instances that have been stored as part of an "unappreciated self" schema, one that we have called up (unconsciously or not) and thus made salient. When a friend is in trouble and we drop everything in order to help, our priorities may be clarified because we have attached the present situation to a "loyal friend" schema that we hold dear about ourselves, which has become active in our thoughts and feelings of the moment. When we learn that a national politician gets paid very large speaking engagement fees after being indicted for misusing his office, our initial dismay turns to cynicism when social schemas, such as those about power and glamour (that people are foolishly impressed and influenced), become activated and used to interpret and evaluate what we see and feel.

Separately, the schemas that we develop and maintain contain the concepts and rules that we use to understand ourselves and our surroundings when we step into specific situations. Together, our schemas become the threads that we use to create the tapestry of our life stories. If we associate an unappreciated self-schema with other schemas having to do with competence, dedication, institutional prejudice, and power brokering, we are presented with a different understanding of ourselves and others than if we associate this same unappreciated self-schema with schemas having to do with duty, self-sacrifice, timidity, and insensitivity of others. By calling up and remembering specific memories attached to these schemas, we are presented with a rich conceptual and emotional landscape of our unique social learning history. When we put these self-schemas together with our schemas about the world, such as with our power and glamour schema, we are presented with a rich—although neither necessarily accurate nor healthy—picture of how the world works, or at least how we conceive it to work. We learn higher-order, or more complex and broadly generalizable, concepts and rules when we attach schemas together that were derived from different sources.

Our life story, therefore, contains the rules and concepts that we use to live. It contains the rules and concepts that we use to make sense of our surroundings, and that we use to make sense of our own thoughts, feelings, and actions. We create our life stories whenever we describe them in any kind of coherent manner, either to ourselves or to others— that is, whenever we weave our schemas together to tell ourselves or others about ourselves. We will discuss more about how we weave our schemas together in the next chapter when we discuss the building blocks of memory. Understanding the links between what we know and how we construct and revise our life stories in both positive and negative ways is important to adequate assessment, goal setting, and intervention planning.

We are constantly refining and updating our life stories, since we are constantly encountering new situations that test our schemas' ability to help us respond appropriately and in functional ways. This is not to say that we fabricate our lives. From a cognitive-ecological perspective, while the act of responding to our surroundings is a distortion in the sense that we see in situations what we believe them to contain, it is also true that distorting situations for the purpose of understanding them is a requirement for living and interacting with others.

Ideally, this is a functional process: Social learning theory tells us that we learn and retain what works for us and discard what does not work (including memories, which undergo considerable rewriting over the course of our lives). At the same time, we will see in subsequent chapters of this book that problems arise when we are reluctant to discard cherished or highly familiar concepts and rules that no longer seem to apply, when we are unable to call up appropriate schemas in given situations, or when we overgeneralize our knowledge by applying existing schemas to new situations.

The Anomie of Situations

The cognitive-ecological model makes an assumption about situations themselves, which is the fourth feature of this model. In order for situations to be as amenable to interpretation as they are described here, they must in and of themselves be malleable, that is, lend themselves to multiple meaning. This view of situations is similar to the sociological concept of *anomie*. Durkheim (1951) defined anomie as a crisis state in which a society's goals and norms no longer exert social control over its members; where individuals determine for themselves what goals should be sought and by what means.

To apply this idea to situations is to say that actors in a situation determine for themselves what goals should be sought and by what means. The actors determine for themselves the situation's meaning, with the dominant culture determining the range of norms for how to interpret and behave (Merton, 1957). It is not the situation, per se, that tells us what to do. It is instead the schemas we have developed, depicting norms of the dominant culture, that do so. The current situation itself is therefore inherently anomic, in and of itself neither requiring specific responses from individuals nor containing specific goals to accomplish.

But this is not how people typically experience situations. For the most part, we see our selves as understanding situations by perceiving the appropriate goals and behaviors required. We feel as if particular situations present us with the cues for how to respond, or that the appropriate response is obvious. Social cognition research argues that we have learned to impose a structure onto the situation that directs our attention and dictates a range of behaviors appropriate to the setting.

For example, entering a restaurant is an event so familiar and routine in American culture that we can be seen to follow a clear "restaurant script" (Abelson, 1978): Our actions and decisions are so automatic as to appear functionally unconscious. One can easily imagine, however, that if one were entering a restaurant for the first time, the multitude of unfamiliar sights and sounds would appear quite chaotic. Does one stand around at the door or find one's own seat? What does one do with one's coat? How does one find out what food is available, and then how does one get it? We learn to pick out the appropriate cues to answer these questions based on our accumulated experience with situations of this type. This is not to say that cues are never obvious nor presented unambiguously. For example, seeing a coat rack in a corner with numerous coats on it, and then watching a person placing his on it, is not a completely unambiguous answer to the question of what to do with one's coat.

Nevertheless, one cannot be completely certain that this rack is for customers' coats, and not just for employees of the restaurant, or whether one pays for the use of the rack.

Deciphering situational cues becomes even more difficult when the cues are more social or interactional. For example, is one to interpret anger in the voice of the man taking sandwich orders behind the counter at a New York deli? Should one respond angrily in kind? Or what do the stares from a waitress and other customers mean when you order a cup of coffee at the counter and then sit down at the nearest table to drink it? In terms of this latter example, one of the authors learned the hard way that different cultures have different price structures, implied by ordering at different locations in the restaurant. If one buys at the counter, the social norm is that one drinks at the counter. And if instead one sits at a table, one signals to others one's ignorance and outsider status, or worse, one's arrogance of trying to get more than what was paid for.

The cognitive-ecological model takes the position that the general process at work here is that situations do not inherently contain a given meaning, but instead are amenable to the meaning that we place on them. At the same time, the extent to which situations are viewed commonly within a culture is the extent to which the culture can agree on the meaning we place on it. As a culture, we may agree so completely about the range of appropriate responses to some situations that it may appear as if the situations do contain a given meaning. For other situations, social consensus is so loose that the situations themselves appear as very ambiguous. Clients may find situations at both ends of this continuum problematic, though for different reasons. When high social consensus exists, what constitutes deviant behavior is clearly defined and not often tolerated. When low consensus exists, many people find themselves "at sea" and flooded with self-doubt, as they are paralyzed by their confusion and inability to know how to act. Our ability to help our clients will depend on our assessment of situations as much as our assessment of individuals. For example, does the client lack schemas necessary for understanding and effectively responding to certain situations? Is the situation deviant in the sense of imposing non-normative demands? Are there competing cues in the environment that render it difficult to read? These and related questions will be taken up in later chapters.

At the same time that situations are themselves anomic, it is also true that we confront real limitations in our abilities (e.g., physical, psychological, economic, political) to manipulate and control our environments. Yalom (1980) has discussed this in his descriptions of four basic "existential realities" that we must live with as humans: death, freedom, isolation, and meaninglessness. He uses these four realities as an organizing scheme to understand the psychological issues involved when humans confront that which they cannot change. We also encounter physical and sociological realities as well. We are limited in our physical strength and intelligence, in our abilities to exert power over others, in our abilities to access resources in the environment. Accurately assessing and working within these realities is important in our professional role with clients, to avoid blaming clients for actions beyond their control or capacity. In Chapters 6 through 9 we discuss how to assess clients, how to set goals and plan interventions, and how to help them maintain their gains—all within the framework of clients' realities of life. In Chapter 5 we discuss ways to help ourselves as practitioners become more aware of our own assumptions and "realities," and ways to avoid potential pitfalls of our cognitive processes.

The Importance of Shared Schemas

If situations are inherently anomic, and if individuals interpret situations in individual ways, how then do we ever interact? Are we not all living in our own worlds, separated by our subjectivity?

In its extreme, the previous discussion of how individuals create schemas and imbue situations with meaning does posit that we each have our own idiosyncratically constructed understandings of given events, situations, or people that may or may not bear much resemblance to reality or to the social consensus of reality. A fifth feature of the cognitive-ecological model is that the extent to which we can sustain a conversation or an interaction within a situation is the extent to which we can share our constructions of the situation.

It is our ability to share our schemas through social interaction that is the basis of communication and human relationships. We articulate our schemas to each other—either directly when we have heart-to-heart talks to share our life stories, or indirectly when we observe how others respond in various situations. The depth and strength of our relationships are based on our ability to articulate our schemas to others, and to respond to others' schemas by finding ourselves in them (that is, finding parts or whole schemas shared by others). When we feel understood by others, we mean that we feel that others understand our schemas (e.g., about who we are, how things are, and what is important), and the bidirectional process of this sharing is a large part of how new schemas are born and existing ones are elaborated or challenged.

Relationships are built on the process of developing shared schemas. Consider this example (taken from Brower, 1988). Imagine a person, John, who has a "committee meeting" social schema that represents meetings as opportunities to impress people with his wit, to take a break from "real" work, to relax, and to tell loud, off-color jokes. In most meetings John has attended in the past, others have responded favorably, thus elaborating and reinforcing his schema and his expectation of similar responses in the future.

The committee meeting schema of another member of this office, Sarah, is also characterized by a view that these times are an opportunity to impress people. For her, however, the schema is represented as an opportunity to impress superiors with her intelligence and ability to get the job done. For Sarah, these meetings are where real work takes place, where the real decisions are made. She takes them seriously, and particularly hates loud obnoxious people who waste her time (i.e., obstruct her goal for the situation). Sarah's colleagues know this about her and have come to invite her to meetings specifically for her input. Sarah, too, has learned to expect this reinforcement of her schema and her role in the social process.

There is no problem, in the abstract, with both of these schemas of committee meetings existing simultaneously, except when Sarah and John are present at the same one. In that situation, almost at the moment the meeting begins, they will both be jarred by the unreality of this situation. John will think Sarah needs to lighten up; Sarah will be dismayed by John's disruptiveness.

Sarah and John are now faced with two choices. They can either remove themselves, graciously or not, from the setting, thereby keeping their respective committee meeting schemas intact. Alternatively, they can try to engage one another, painfully struggling to either change the other or to find some sort of common ground between them. In either case, an important implication about interacting appropriately in social situations can be made: Social interaction requires that the participants in the situation communicate their schemas of it to one another and create some measure of a common schema.[2]

In the above illustration, Sarah's and John's investment to interact will be directly proportional to their goals for the meeting. If neither one of them has a high investment in this meeting, the amount of shared schema developed needs only to be sufficient to allow both of them to make this meeting as painless as possible. But, in the case in which they both have high investments, as members of an ongoing policy-making committee for example, the development and articulation of a shared schema will necessarily need to be greater. (And, of course, the extent to which either John or Sarah bends his or her schema to the other will also depend on their formal and informal roles within the workplace—if one is more senior to the other, it is likely that the junior member will adapt his or her schema to suit the senior member.)

The processes described here concerning the difficulties of sharing schemas can very often describe the problems presented to us. For example, when parents and teens argue over things such as household responsibilities and rights, and when parents argue about proper limit-setting and discipline for their young children, we can understand their struggles as problems with clashing schemas. It is often the case that families will have developed shared, though tacit, understandings of family roles that prescribe the rights and responsibilities of each member. When children reach adolescence, however, it is a normal part of maturation for them to begin challenging their prescribed role in the family and to request (and sometimes demand) new and expanded rights and privileges, such as access to the car. (See Eccles, Midgley, Wigfield, Buchanan, Reuman, Flanagan, & Mac Iver, 1993, for a review of this perspective.) Based on these new demands and requests, the parents may then require that the son or daughter take on new responsibilities, such as making sure the gas tank is filled, and that homework is done before leaving the house. One way to understand these negotiations, then, is that each member is presenting his or her own schema of family rights and responsibilities. When both parties are flexible and open to the discussion, the shared schemas develop relatively smoothly. When either party is less flexible or open, which is more common, conflicts erupt. Each party leaves the interaction very often experiencing shock, dismay, anger, and hurt that the other person does not get it, that one does not understand what is perfectly clear to the other.

Two Basic Activities Involved in Shaping Our Environments

The sixth feature of the cognitive-ecological model is that it provides a conceptualization of how we shape our environments. Based on the discussions above, shaping our environment can be seen to include two basic activities in which we engage: manipulating our physical environment, and psychologically and emotionally imbuing situations with personal meaning. Examples of the first activity are plentiful. Humans have developed farming and agricultural methods that have allowed them to work the land to produce food, clothing, and shelter; and since the industrial revolution, our ability to manipulate our physical environments has increased exponentially. We manipulate our social environment similarly; in fact, most interventions directed toward targets other than the individual client could be considered a manipulation of the environment. Consider the special forms of manipulation that the physically, sensory, and learning impaired need to live their daily life. Consider how certain welfare programs (such as food stamps, subsidized housing, and so on) have significantly manipulated the environment (in both good and bad ways) for many. More generally, consider the ways in which we manipulate our social environments through our use of clothing, furniture, speech patterns, and so forth.

The second type of environment-shaping activity, that of imbuing meaning into our surroundings, is also easy to imagine. When two people walk into the same 10-year high school class reunion, they enter with different expectations in mind, different memories of their high school years, and different self-perceptions. One person feels comfortable with her current place in her life, and sees the reunion as a chance to catch up with people she has not seen in a while. The other person, before he even walks into the room, begins to feel the same social pressures and insecurities that plagued him in high school.

These differences in perception and emotion will cause these two people to actually see this social gathering differently. When both enter through the door at the same time, Ann will scan the room for familiar faces, see her good friend Rebecca, and hurry over to her. Bill, on the other hand, will only see that others are staring at him. He will recognize that the same people are hanging out in the same cliques, feel their stares as validating that nothing has changed in terms of his social worth in the past 10 years. Not immediately seeing anyone he feels comfortable approaching, he'll likely edge his way to the periphery of the activity and wonder why he came.

Both Ann's and Bill's experiences are probably familiar to us all; both are clearly within the range of our normal, everyday experiences. In another social situation, or under different circumstances, it might even be the case that Ann and Bill will switch their experiences. What is important in this example is that their preexisting beliefs and expectations about themselves and others will influence their perceptions of the situation and their response to it. They will look for and notice environmental and interpersonal cues consistent with their mood and schemas, and this stream of perceptual activity will greatly influence how they will relate to others (Showers & Cantor, 1985). This, in turn, will influence how others will relate to them, most often in ways that confirm Ann's and Bill's initial perceptions (Snyder, 1980).

Ann and Bill will have entered the same physical situation, and yet their experience of it will be wholly different. The shaping that created these differences will be particularly strong in this case since the store of interactive memories, roles, and patterns is so strong at a class reunion. Ann and Bill will each have a wealth of prior memories from which to draw as they survey the room and interpret what they see. Moreover, the same can be said for each of the other people attending the reunion. It will be very easy for both of them to slip into old relationships, patterns, and feelings, some of which they will not have experienced since high school graduation. This is, in fact, what can make attending class reunions difficult for some of us, particularly if those high school years are remembered as negative or if the individuals have changed since then and relate to these earlier roles and patterns in negative terms.

Knowing that primary modes of shaping our surroundings are through physical manipulation and through cognitive and affective processes allows the practitioner a fuller understanding of clients' patterns of interaction with their environment. Are clients particularly rigid in their perceptions of situations, drawing upon the same set of schemas and scripts without attention to differences in the moment? Are their expectations about certain types of situations so negative that they avoid those situations and never encounter opportunities to have flawed schemas challenged or changed? Or are clients needing to manipulate features that are beyond their individual control, suggesting the need for environmental change? Having a clear understanding of the nature of our clients' interactions with the environment will be crucial to a cognitive-ecological view of assessment and intervention planning. This will be taken up again in subsequent chapters.

The Social and Environmental Regulation Process

While our perceptions of situations may initiate our reactions to them, our continued interactions are based on intricate feedback mechanisms. Along the lines of Mead, the process of ongoing social interactions is not analogous to flipping a switch to set an automatic sequence of events in motion, which might be analogous to how a subroutine operates in a computer. The seventh feature of a cognitive-ecological model is that behaviors are regulated according to processes analogous to a feedback model. Like a thermostat, we constantly assess our current state (internal and external) and evaluate it against a goal state. Actions are taken and modified, based on our continual evaluation of the discrepancy between our current state and the goal (Lauer & Handel, 1983; Mead, 1938)

It is natural to search for metaphors to capture phenomena that are difficult to directly observe. These can be very useful, but are nearly always incomplete in one respect or another. For example, a computer analogy is useful to provide a way to operationalize how different information can be taken in, categorized, stored, revised or updated, accessed under certain conditions, and either protected or lost under differing conditions. Here we might see schemas, and particularly scripts, as acting something like subroutines we access and put into motion in response to environmental cues. Thus, in a new job situation, a computer analogy would suggest that we put into motion our "new job subroutine" that tells us to act cheerfully, to circulate to meet new people in the office, to act deferentially to our superiors, and to keep our eyes and ears open for potential political infighting among the office staff.

Yet, to date, our computer models are not as interactive as needed to serve as a very complete metaphor. We are suggesting, in addition, the use of a thermostat analogy: where social interactions are governed by goals and expectations—"end state" or "goal state" images of where we wish to end up. Our daily behaviors (i.e., thoughts, feelings, actions) are then governed by our interactive evaluations of the discrepancy between our current and end states. On the job, then, we are constantly evaluating our current state against the end state, and acting in ways to bring us closer to it. If part of our end state includes job advancement, and we view the road to getting there as one of avoiding office politics, then we will be very sensitive to the loyalties and alliances we observe, and we would make an effort to store this information in order to avoid getting in the middle of in-fights in the future.

Thus, while it is necessary for clients to have appropriate scripts or subroutines in various situations, it is not enough to teach them only these skills and behaviors. We must also assist them in learning how to analyze feedback from the environment (sometimes in small or subtle increments) so they can modify their present behavior states in line with their goal states. This is discussed more fully in subsequent chapters.

Recent research tells us that our personally significant goals or end states are not simply statements, passing thoughts, or abstract ideals. Instead, they can also take the form of envisioning and cognitively representing possible versions of oneself and one's niche, both positively and negatively (Markus & Nurius, 1986). Positive "possible selves" and "possible niches" (i.e., having lots of money and being important in the eyes of others, being surrounded by interesting and caring people) motivate us by being attractive: They present images that we want to emulate or pursue. Negative possible selves and niches (i.e., being rejected and a failure at things we care about, seeing ourselves isolated and depressed) are motivating by presenting images that we wish to avoid or change. In the new job situation used above, the goal or end state might consist of our image of ourselves engaged in the work activities that we would like, interacting with others in various settings, feeling the pride of the position and the respect desired from others, and even wearing the clothes that symbolize the attainment.

Exactly how these images are represented or filled out is extremely important in determining the degree and type of effect they will have on the individual. Possible selves and possible niches that have become detailed and complete have become so through a considerable amount of thinking, observation, practice, and feedback from the environment. We tend to expend considerable energy (cognitive, emotional, and activity) on possibilities that we value and seriously regard. Generally, the more complete an image is, the more compelling is the goal, and the more effort we will put into reaching it. However, the relative balance in how these images are represented makes a big difference. For example, if a possible self is predominantly composed of emotional content (e.g., intense desire to "make it big" or to "not be the kind of parent my father was"), but has little in the way of depicting how to get from here to there, the likely effect of that possible self is to stimulate a great sense of urgency but relatively ineffective behavior, due to the lack of goal-related guidance. We will discuss these issues more fully in Chapters 4 and 7.

Our possible selves and niches change and become increasingly specified in response to our experience and desires. Many small boys and girls see themselves as superheros (Batman or Wonder Woman), but relatively few of them actually train for this profession. In high school and college, many young people today expect to get business degrees in order to pursue high-paying jobs in the business sector. Their images of themselves include making a lot of money, being able to travel to interesting places, and having autonomy in their work. Relatively few of them have had actual experience in business, but instead base their vision of it on the glamour they perceive through newspapers, films, and television.

But when students are required to take accounting or marketing courses, and once they have a summer internship in a business, they realize that the realities of the business world are not necessarily as glamorous and exciting as imagined. Many drop out or change their majors at that time; others shift their future image to include these realities and more mundane responsibilities. Those individuals who do enter the business world then take the now-modified vision of their possible business self and niche, and use it to plan their careers. They hold job opportunities up against their vision, and make career choices by evaluating the discrepancies that exist between them. And this is a very dynamic process: Life goals (i.e., possible selves and niches) are continually modified, based on experiences and expectations, and choices are made by continually comparing one's current state to one's goals.

Although in the following chapter we will discuss the role of possible selves and possible niches as part of the self-system, we would like to anticipate a few issues here. One is the assumption that we have clear goals in mind and that we always behave in a relatively rational, goal-oriented fashion. In fact, we often do not have clearly articulated goals, or we act on goals or images of ourselves that are largely symbolic or emotional in nature. Under these circumstances, we may feel strongly motivated due to the emotional punch of these schemas, yet remain very unsure of how to proceed due to the lack of means-ends guidance embedded in the schema; we then may end up more dependent on the environment for direction.

We also hold diverse goals, some of which may be in conflict at any given moment. For example, in the new job situation above, one set of goals will likely be related to achievement and advancement, whereas an additional set of goals will be related to acceptance and affiliation. We also hold goals across life domains that will converge at some points and diverge at others. Again, taking the new job situation, our goals may be in conflict if we want to both do well in our job and be a full participant with our families. In this case, we will be fighting ourselves whenever work demands cut into time with family. If we are able to reflect upon these two goals, generate alternative pathways, and make conscious decisions about how to establish a plan for meeting both goals, we are in a relatively good position. What is more often the case, however, is to be unaware of one or more of our goals, to not know how to interpret the dissonance we are feeling at the moment, or to have limited creativity at the moment (e.g., to rely on a relatively rigid model of how to approach or avoid certain goal states, rather than being able to try out a variety of formulations). Under such circumstances, we may find ourselves either unable to take any actions because we feel paralyzed by the various pulls in our lives, or acting in ways that sabotage one goal or the other, such as taking on but not completing projects that require long hours away from family, or consistently scheduling weekend meetings during times that the family has made plans.

Finally, only a portion of our knowledge base about ourselves and the world is goal-focused. Within the self-concept, for example, we have schemas of what was, what is, and what could be: who we were, who we are, and who we will be. These self-schemas are by no means independent. Yet at any given moment, we may well experience a tension between maintaining consistency and stability of our known self and pursuing change through the attainment of attractive possible selves (or the avoidance of aversive possible end states). Moreover, the same goal-related schemas will be evaluated and acted upon differently by the individual, depending on the context within which it is momentarily embedded. The goal of becoming highly successful in one's business career will likely be evaluated differently in the company of competitive co-workers, as contrasted to being with friends who value political involvement more highly than financial success, as contrasted to times when the personal costs of dedication to work are particularly acute.

The Mindless Nature of Our Interactions
With Our Environments

One limitation of the thermostat analogy is that it assumes a certain degree of conscious planning and decision making. Within the context of our ordinary activities and interactions in everyday life, however, we typically are not all that aware or deliberate. Thus, an eighth feature of the cognitive-ecological model is that, for much of the time, the perception, interpretation, feedback, and evaluation processes undergirding our meaning making and social interactions take place in a nonconscious and automatic fashion. This has recently been described in terms of *mindlessness,* in the sense of our relative lack of conscious awareness governing our decisions and actions (Langer, 1989). As we will discuss in the next chapter, this is a misnomer in that the mind is still very much involved in these routinized and automatic functions. "Awarelessness" might be a more accurate (though more cumbersome) phrase to use.

This more automatic mode of functioning is essential to us. Imagine if we had to constantly think about every single event we see or take action within. We would be either paralyzed into inactivity, or so consumed by mundane detail and actions as to appear as robots. Thus, as one way of managing the never-ending stream of inputs and demands, our lives become governed to a large extent by routines and patterns. As we will discuss at length in later chapters, these patterned habits are both a blessing and a bane.

Klinger (1977) notes, in fact, that these routines and patterns help give our lives meaning and value. The cognitive-ecological model sees us as attempting to actively and competently resolve the seemingly endless series of routine problems and tasks that make up our daily life. Furthermore, we act on these problems and tasks by evaluating the discrepancies between our current state and a goal state that we hold in our minds. These problems and tasks, and our efforts toward them, can certainly become stressful and burdensome, but they also provide us with our feelings of success, accomplishment, and satisfaction. During times of relative stability, we can rely on our daily routine to guide us in understanding what we encounter, how to act, how to solve problems, and how to plan our activities. Again, this is functional: Imagine having to create anew our routines for how to act, think, and feel whenever we step into a new situation.

At the same time, we can become so accustomed to relying on our routines that we can overlook important information, get stuck in certain routines, or become real experts at negative patterns. Consider, for example, the clinically depressed person who has become extraordinarily sensitive to information related to rejection or failure. He or she will tend to anticipate such experiences or feedback, will no longer see information to the contrary, will tend to have depression-related schemas chronically activated, will tend to interpret events consistent with these expectations, will behave in patterned ways consistent with the foregoing, and, of course, will get at least some feedback that can be construed as consistent with his or her expectations (Beck, Rush, Shaw, & Emery, 1979, provides a good review on this topic). This applies to our professional work as practitioners as well as in our personal lives. We often get stuck in routines with clients, by typecasting them, by oversimplifying our assessments, and by relying on favored intervention strategies irrespective of the client's needs. We will discuss more fully in Chapter 5 the importance of mindful and appropriate use of self within the practitioner role. When people are in a mindless mode of functioning, they are "concept-driven" and not "evidence-driven." When these concepts are adaptive, flexible, and well suited to the environment, this is a tremendous advantage. When they are maladaptive, poorly suited to the environment, or not generalizable to new situations, they pose a formidable barrier. For the practitioner, part of our work needs to focus on helping clients draw the line between where their routines remain functional and where they become restrictive. But this raises an interesting dilemma: Given that our lives are never really static, when do we need to make real changes in our routines in response to gradual shifts in our surroundings? When is it functional and when is it dysfunctional to maintain a steady state?

While ecological theorists have not really addressed this issue, others have critiqued the application of homeostatic models of systems to human interactions. Maruyama (1968) writes that the survival of any living system (that is, any self-sustaining entity) depends on the existence of two processes: *morphostasis* and *morphogenesis.*

Morphostasis is the process by which systems maintain constancy in the face of environmental changes, accomplished through the use of negative feedback—making changes to bring deviations back to stasis. Morphogenesis is the process by which systems change their basic structure, accomplished through positive feedback—making changes that amplify deviations, such as when organisms successfully mutate in response to environmental changes. This overlaps the notions of *assimilation* and *accommodation,* as applied to cognitive structures. Interpreting current experiences in terms of what is already known (i.e., previously established schemas) is assimilation; discovering new facts about experiences and modifying one's understanding (i.e., one's underlying schemas) is accommodation (Piaget, 1968; Zimbardo, 1979). Whereas assimilation modifies or transforms incoming information (the input to the perceiver is shaped by the individual's cognitive structures), accommodation modifies previously developed cognitive structures (the perceiver is changed by the input).

Hoffman (1981) argues that family systems must contain both morphostasis and morphogenesis processes for survival. Families become dysfunctional when they remain too rigidly static in the face of environmental changes (such as when a family does not adapt in response to the first child's leaving home). They also become dysfunctional when they have no constancy of roles, rules, or routines. A system survives, then, when it can balance its ability to change and adapt with its ability to maintain its integrity or character. One set of processes is not inherently advantageous; all are necessary and are intrinsic to human system functioning.

One way that we change our responses to the environment is when the environment's reaction to the response itself changes. For example, if we are interested in getting complimented by our boss, and the typical way to do this has been to prepare for and speak up at meetings, then we will expect this to happen in a new job situation. At a meeting on this new job, if we speak up and do not get the reaction that we expect, we will theoretically change our behavior to better meet our goal—in this case, perhaps agree with the boss rather than present our own opinion. In fact, however, we often attribute unexpected reactions to a host of other causes that keep us from reflecting upon our own role and from changing our own behaviors: The boss was in a bad mood, the others are too stupid to realize the value in our comment, the point we presented was good but was not said clearly enough, we inadvertently said something that put ourselves in the middle of office politics that had not been anticipated, and so forth. Changing our own behaviors is often our last resort, after eliminating all other explanations (Snyder, 1980).[3]

The Creation of Our Niche

The cognitive-ecological model can be used to describe the result of our dynamic equilibrium with our environment. The ninth feature of the cognitive-ecological model is that the result of our patterned interactions with the world is our creating a niche for ourselves within it. This niche defines the routine situations that we enter, and the routine set of assumptions and rules we use to understand ourselves and our world. It is one way to describe the goal state of our striving for stable survival in our ever-changing world. When we commonly say that someone has found a niche, what we mean is that the person has found a place that was previously unused or underused, that makes use of that person's strengths, and that can sustain the person. It represents the unique place in which one fits into the environment, the workplace, or the community. It is the special place within which one feels comfortable; one has made it one's own. According to the cognitive-ecological model, the niche is defined more technically as that portion of the environment with which an individual has regular and routine contact and upon which he or she is interdependent.

Barring abrupt changes in either the person or the environment that would threaten the survival of the whole, the niche maintains itself by adjusting to the continual fluctuations of everyday life. Each component of the niche is dependent upon all others for its survival, and each establishes an intricate relationship to all other components. For the niche to survive, change made in one part necessitates accommodation from all other parts. The niche must maintain a dynamic yet stable status, while remaining in harmony with its surroundings. A tall order indeed.

According to the cognitive-ecological model, the niche is the optimal unit with which to work in practice (Brower, 1988, 1989c). Different types of problems will require different degrees and kinds of change, and thus will require different work with the multiple roles, relationships, habits, and life stories that make up our clients' present niches. Because of its central importance to how people function in everyday life, the idea of the niche will be described in detail in the following chapter.

Our Attempts at a Growth Orientation Within Our Lives

According to the Germain and Gitterman (1980) and Germain (1991) ecological model, our actions are growth oriented; we strive to become better, to improve our ecological niche. The tenth and final feature of the cognitive-ecological model explicates our attempts toward growth and development. Germain and Gitterman note that in biology, accommodation is defined not as passive adjustment to a status quo but as the active efforts of a species and of an individual over its life span to reach and maintain a goodness-of-fit with the environment, thus ensuring continued development and survival. Accommodation is not a static process that ends once one finds a place for oneself; it continues throughout life, as one continually adapts to an ever-changing world.

According to Greif and Lynch (1983), accommodation activities are not simply motivated from a need-reduction model—where the first solution is selected that reduces a felt need before evaluating its relative value against other need-reducing solutions. Instead, people are creative and proactive: They meet their needs intelligently, in the sense that they evaluate solutions according to criteria in addition to those based on immediate gratification or through paths of least resistance.

Accommodation within this framework is seen as a process mediated by the person's internal forces and by forces from the immediate and remote environment (Greif & Lynch, 1983). From this perspective, human beings are viewed as active, goal-seeking, and purposeful—they make decisions and choices, and take actions, guided by the memory of past experiences and anticipating future possibilities. These forces are thus organized into a *developmental history of experience,* acquired through learning from one's interaction with the environment.

Yet we can easily think of examples where this is not the case, when people are not necessarily growth oriented. Instead, it is our contention that we can be seen to attempt to do what is best for ourselves, based on what we know, regardless of whether our actions in fact result in an improvement of our status. A more accurate adaptation of the biological systems model (from which ecological theory draws) is that systems themselves can change to produce novel responses that sometimes lead to evolution and growth, and sometimes do not (Hoffman, 1981). We have the benefit of human intelligence when we import this notion to human systems (niches), and therefore we might be inclined to assume that we evaluate our novel responses according to their appropriateness and functionality. Yet, it is simply not possible to predict how immediate decisions and actions will affect our futures. "Twenty/twenty hindsight" tells us that a decision that seemed correct at the time can later be seen as ill-advised, or even foolish. Moreover, because we are bombarded at all times with demands, expectations, and problems that require different solutions, often in conflict with one another, at best our decisions and actions must be seen as our best guess, given what we know.

Because our goals, values, and life situation change over our life span, what was a reasonable response at one stage in our life can become very problematic at later stages. And, although we are generally goal-directed creatures, our decisions and behaviors are very often not made in a strictly rational manner. To illustrate the point of rationality, let us exaggerate the problem-solving approach: We first enumerate a list of possible solutions to a problem that has been clearly identified and circumscribed. Each possible solution is then evaluated, regarding both its absolute merits (and disadvantages or impediments) as well as its benefits relative to other solutions on our list. Finally, we select the best solution and then perfectly put it into action.

Obviously, even in the most rarefied atmosphere, such a lock-step version of problem solving is rarely followed. Nisbett and Ross (1980) and Tversky and Kahneman (1974) describe how rarely we follow this idealized problem-solving process in everyday life. At every step our emotions and "irrational" beliefs intercede to color our judgments. We often do not spend time to see problems clearly and in their entirety; we seldom list a very diverse set of possible solutions to a problem, or even seriously consider more than one solution; if more than one solution is identified, we rarely evaluate them in any systematic or unbiased fashion; and even if we do happen to select the best solution to a problem, it is virtually impossible to execute it perfectly (i.e., without running into the messiness of life with other people).

Thus, because we are regularly fumbling and stumbling human beings, our most common response to problems is to take the most comfortable or immediately reasonable route: mindlessly executing a response that we have used countless times in the past, meeting the most pressing and immediate concerns in the situation, or being swayed by the strongest emotions (both positive and negative) evoked by the problem. We are creatures of habit above all else, and find comfort in our patterns and routines, even while we know we are not always doing what we should be doing, or acting in the ways we should.

Nevertheless, we contend that this is functional for the large part. Again, if we had to stop and proceed rationally and carefully through the steps of a problem-solving model every time we were faced with a task or problem in our lives, we would be virtually paralyzed.

To a large degree, then, our daily behavior is dictated by routine, by expediency, and by "satisficing": We do what is good enough under the circumstances, and for the most part, our best guess serves us well (Kaplan & Kaplan, 1978). But this book is about an approach to working with clients, and we argue that problems will exist when our routines and best guesses do not serve us well. In later chapters we will describe the problems that this approach creates, and how the cognitive-ecological model can be applied to help solve some of these problems within the practice setting.

SUMMARY

We can now summarize the primary features of a cognitive-ecological model of human behavior as we have discussed them here.

1. We are primarily motivated to survive within our environment. We satisfy this motivation by adapting to our surroundings and by molding our surroundings to allow us to take what we need. Thus, we shape our environment at the same time that we are shaped by it.

2. It is evolutionarily adaptive for us to make sense of our world. It allows us to believe we exert a measure of control and predictability in our lives, it allows us to create a coherent life story from events in our lives, and it satisfies our natural curiosity about how things work.

3. Our need to create coherent life stories that make sense of the events in our lives is an important feature of human existence. These life stories contain the basic concepts that we use to understand the world and ourselves, and the rules that we use to figure out how to behave when we enter various situations. These concepts and rules are stored in organized cognitive and affective structures called schemas. It is the process of weaving these schemas together in a coherent way that forms the basis of our life story, and therefore the basis of our knowledge about ourselves, the world, and ourselves in the world.

4. Because we are able to shape meaning from our surroundings, specific situations themselves must be relatively anomic, or contain little or no intrinsic meaning separate from the people who inhabit them. The extent to which situations are commonly viewed is the extent to which members of society can agree on the meaning that we place on the situations.

5. The extent to which we can communicate our meanings to each other is the extent to which we share schemas, or rules and concepts about the world. The development of shared schemas is an important component in the process of the development of culture (of what is known, common, inside/outside, expected, normal, and so forth).

6. Based on these discussions, the concept of shaping our environment can be seen to consist of the two basic activities of (a) manipulating our environment and (b) psychologically and emotionally imbuing situations with personal meaning. Both of these activities include a variety of subactivities. Those activities used to imbue situations and events with meaning are focused on in this book.

7. Ongoing interactions with the environment can be thought of in part as a computer subroutine process (where we have a variety of potential interpretation frameworks and response strategies that we access under differing conditions) and in part as a thermostat process (where we constantly assess discrepancies between our current states and our goal states and then attempt to make adjustments in desired directions). These goal states take the form of images of ourselves and our surroundings projected into the future (i.e., possible selves and possible niches), and the more complete and emotion-laden these images are, the more compelling and motivating they will be for us.

8. Despite the fact that ongoing interactions are based on a discrepancy-assessment process, for the most part we act in ways that appear to be in a mindless or automatic fashion. If it were otherwise, we would be paralyzed and overwhelmed by the countless tasks and problems that confront us daily. Thus, for the most part, we interact with our environment in routine and patterned ways that provide efficiency and manageability, but also incline us to lose sight of our underlying processes of meaning making and resistance to change.

9. A result of our patterned interactions with the environment is that we create niches for ourselves. Our niche defines the set of environmental and internal forces that are mutually interdependent: Within it we are sustained, and within it we can take advantage of our strengths and allow for our weaknesses. Rather than using a person-environment fit analogy, implying a jigsaw-puzzle process of fitting a static person into a static environment, the development of a niche is better thought of as a fluid, lifelong process, where the person and environment change and accommodate to one another, where each becomes dependent on the other, forming, ideally, a delicate dynamic balance. Niches survive by having the capacity to undergo basic structural changes when necessary, and by having the capacity to maintain structural integrity in the face of environmental variations.

10. While ecological models have traditionally assumed that we are intrinsically growth-striving in our behavior, this is not necessarily the case. It is more accurate to describe ourselves as attempting to do the

best we can, given what we know, regardless of whether the results of our actions in fact improve our status. We make a best guess about how to act, based on our perceptions of ourselves and the situation. In the following chapter, two features of the cognitive-ecological model—the niche and the self-system—will be explored in detail. We will also examine the affective and cognitive processes through which we understand, construct, and seek to exert influence on the environment in general, and the niche in particular.

NOTES

1. As will be discussed below, because our world is everchanging, we never can establish a true balance with our environment. To further disrupt true stability in our lives, we use visions of how we wish our lives to be as goals toward which we strive. In other words, at the point when we reach stable plateaus in our lives, we very often begin to try to make our visions of our possible lives into realities. These goals or visions of possibilities are seldom clear and concrete objectives that we strive for straightforwardly and unambiguously. Instead, they are often undefined and unarticulated future states that guide us by alerting us to when we are on the right or wrong track. These ideas will be discussed below and in the next chapter when we discuss the thermostat metaphor of goals, and when we discuss possible selves and possible niches.

2. This process of creating a common schema, of creating a common perception of social reality, has been elsewhere discussed more fully as the basis of a model of group development. See Brower, 1989a.

3. Explanations for our reluctance to change our behaviors may be due to many processes, including the *fundamental attribution error,* our self-enhancement biases, and our tendency to underassess our own cognitive contributions to understanding situations (see Worchel, Cooper, & Goethals, 1988, for a review of basic social psychological processes affecting social interaction). Yet these processes occur because they operate relatively automatically, or mindlessly. Gaining awareness of these processes in operation is often the first step toward change, with several different kinds of interventions needing to be applied next for sustained change. This will be taken up in later chapters.

Chapter 3

THE NICHE AND THE SELF-SYSTEM *Basic Elements for Working With the Cognitive-Ecological Model in Direct Practice*

The previous chapter enumerated features of the cognitive-ecological model as it applies to professional practice. In this chapter, we focus more narrowly on two components of this model that will help practitioners structure their work with clients. These two features of the cognitive- ecological model—the niche and the self-system—are key links in bridging theory on human behavior in the social environment to direct practice theory and tasks. They also represent portions of the environment and the person, respectively, that are amenable to change, that are applicable to a wide spectrum of types of problems, and that are important to sustaining long-term change.

We will begin this chapter with two figures that will present a conceptualization of the niche and the self-system. Figure 3.1 presents a macro view of how the niche and self-system can be placed within the larger environment; Figure 3.2 presents a micro view of the cognitive and affective problem-solving processes that we use to regulate our perceptions and behaviors. Following a brief discussion of these figures, we present a review and fuller description of the niche and the self-system. We will detail how these factors can be seen as concrete manifestations of the person-environment interaction that operate on different, yet complementary levels of functioning.

Following the discussion of the self-system is a discussion and figure describing the building blocks of human memory functioning: An important premise of this book is that our perceptions and interactions with others are both based on and limited by the processes of human memory.

The reader will note that this chapter continues our attempts to describe with increasingly finer detail the processes that explain our person-environment interactive model of human behavior. In the previous chapter we defined the niche and the self-system to be a critical subset of components for focus within the broader person-environment perspective. In this chapter, we detail processes of the *working self-concept* as a pivotal subset for focus within the broader self-system and niche. We then will describe human memory processes as the building blocks for how the working self-concept operates within the niche.

AN ILLUSTRATION OF THE NICHE/
SELF-SYSTEM INTERACTION

We have described the cognitive-ecological practice model as benefiting from the application of social cognitive theory and research. The notion of individuals bringing meaning to situations, and then responding to what they see, can quite naturally be extended through a variety of practice theories. For example, discussions of how social cognition informs problem-solving processes have been described by writers as diverse as Haley (1976) and D'Zurilla (1986). Similarly, links to coping and adaptation have been considered by such writers as Lazarus and Folkman (1984) and Taylor (1986).

In this section we will present a series of figures and explanations to help conceptualize the social and cognitive processes highlighted by the cognitive-ecological model. We will focus on a distillation that combines the elements of the niche, self-system, and everyday problem solving that reflect our struggles and triumphs in daily life.

The model presented in Figure 3.1, and later in Figure 3.2, distinguishes among the major classes of variables that make up a niche, and the cognitive and affective processes in play when specific situations are faced. We will walk through these figures to discuss them.

Macro-Level Analysis

One of the major points in Figure 3.1 is that the factors that most directly define and govern the niche are *proximal* in nature. That is,

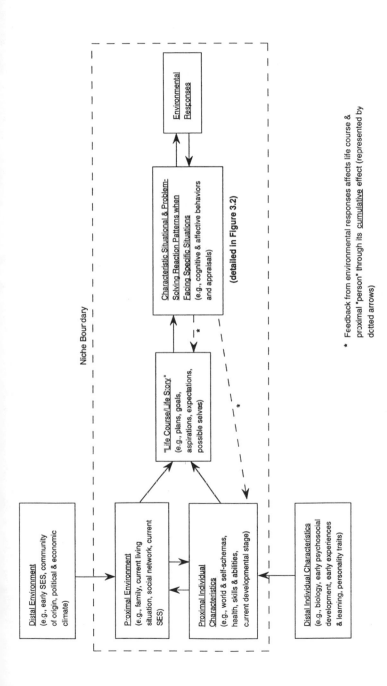

Figure 3.1. Major Classes of Variables Comprising the Niche (Macro-Level Analysis)

while distant environmental and person factors, such as early social class and community of origin on the one hand and biology and early psychosocial development on the other, are important shaping forces, their effect on current functioning is generally indirect, mediated through or moderated by more proximal forces.

We should note that while we have primarily used nonpsychotic examples in our discussions, the cognitive-ecological model applies to psychiatric populations as well. For example, while biochemistry obviously plays a substantial role in schizophrenia, and needs to be included in assessment and intervention planning, clients grappling with this problem are also involved in social learning: People with schizophrenia live within a social niche, hold life goals, and must engage in daily problem-solving tasks (Strauss, 1989). In fact, in 1989, *Schizophrenia Bulletin* published a special issue devoted to the problem of the "person" having become lost in the study and treatment of schizophrenia. The cognitive, affective, and social processes used by these clients will greatly overlap those drawn upon by all of us.

In the figure, we have listed examples of factors that constitute *distal* and *proximal* forces. Due to differences in people's cultures, relationships, and states of physical health (among other things), the amount that any given factor will be proximal or distal will vary. For example, single adults who have minimal contact with their families of origin are not likely to be as influenced by their families as will married adults with children who have sustained ongoing contact with their families of origin. In a similar vein, those with chronic conditions, such as schizophrenia, will be forced to attend to biochemical changes on a more daily basis since their biochemistry is more unpredictable than for most people, and therefore more prominent in daily functioning.

Nevertheless, regardless of the specific factors most prominent across individuals' lives, those environmental and personal factors that affect behavior proximally will themselves interact. In the previous chapter we described how the social environment shapes our schemas about ourselves and our world. On the other hand, these schemas are also powerful influences in their own right as they shape how we present ourselves, how we interact with others, and how we apply meaning and give importance to the social, economic, and physical factors of our environment.

Individuals' constructions of their life stories and of the trajectory of their lives emerge as a product of these cumulative person-environment interactions. Through observing real and imagined possibilities (and dead ends), and through the positive and negative experiences associated with trying out various behaviors, people develop beliefs about what can be expected as consequences of their actions. These beliefs are then used to attach meaning and salience to both feared and hoped-for possible selves and possible niches. These beliefs and possibilities become the foundation of a life course that further filters and dictates the range of situations one enters, and how one characteristically responds to them.

What evolves, then, as the person's characteristic style or approach to interpreting and responding to situations, becomes very pivotal in how one develops one's life course. One's perceptual and interpretive style results from one's life story and the proximal environment and person factors that affect it. Yet one's style also contributes to these prior transactions, as is represented by the dual-directional arrows that indicate two-way relationships in Figure 3.1. With accumulated life experience, we develop routines and stylistic ways of presenting and interacting that are part of our niche development and maintenance.

Finally, the broader environment reacts to us, based on our efforts to solve tasks or problems and achieve goals. Of course, environmental reactions are implicit throughout each of these major classes of variables comprised in the niche. Here we are referring to the outcome of the individual's specific problem-solving and goal-achievement efforts and the (positive or negative) feedback and learning that they provide to the individual. Consistent with the notion of a niche, each of these components becomes patterned or routinized over time (for example, we will come to anticipate and search for certain environmental and social responses to our actions, which are then incorporated into our life course). With significant life changes, commensurate changes in each of the components will be required, which result in modifications to the niche. When all of these forces and counterforces are in balance, we can say that one has established a successful niche within the environment.

Micro-Level Analysis

Let us now look more closely at this pivotal component of characteristic situational and problem-solving reaction patterns. While each component within the niche is a viable target of intervention, these characteristic reaction patterns are often the most accessible in a professional practice setting. That is, they have to do with functioning in the moment of the situations that are of concern for clients (e.g., situations that present challenges or stressors, or situations that present important opportunities).

Figure 3.2 describes more micro-level processes involved in how individuals confront specific situations in their lives. As can be seen in this figure, we incorporate elements involved in both coping and problem solving. For example, Lazarus and Folkman's (1984) stress-appraisal-coping model stipulates that individuals first determine (in primary appraisal) whether a situation is threatening, challenging, or representing a loss, as opposed to being benign. If the answer is not benign, the individual then determines how he or she will deal with it (in secondary appraisal). Problem-solving models argue that when obstacles are perceived, individuals first strive to identify the goals desired, and then identify the tasks necessary to accomplish these goals. Based on these goals and tasks, the individual formulates some type of plan of action (including a plan to escape or avoid the situation) (see D'Zurilla, 1986, for a good review).

Specific situations are perceived uniquely by individuals based on their life course (their plans, goals, fears, and aspirations) and on the broader store of data they have in memory about themselves and their world. Based on these perceptions, a situation-dependent, working self-concept and set of working hypotheses are generated (i.e., working knowledge), as will be described later in this chapter. Thus, in conjunction with the activation of a subset of schemas about oneself and the world, the nature of the particular problems or tasks at hand is identified.

These factors then shape the beginning of problem formulation (e.g., "Can I deal effectively with this situation? What have I done before that did or did not work well?"). Depending on the nature of the schemas present in the working knowledge of the moment, the answers to questions such as these will vary, even if the individual possesses broad knowledge for how to deal with the situation. For example, even if one has the knowledge for how to meet new people, and can undertake this successfully in some contexts, if one's self-view in a particular situation or moment is "awkward and unlikable," the ability to access this social knowledge will be greatly constrained.

In short, what we formulate as plans or reactions is shaped by our current and momentary knowledge about ourselves, and the resources perceived as available in the situation. The plans are acted upon to produce an outcome, and then this outcome is evaluated, based on the individual's expectations for the performance and feedback. Finally, based on perceived discrepancies (according to the thermostat analogy

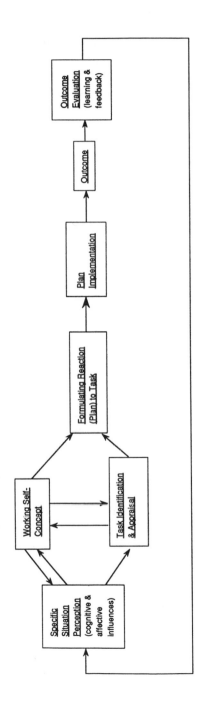

Figure 3.2. Processes Involved in Characteristic Situational and Problem-Solving Reaction Patterns When Facing Specific Situations (Micro-Level Analysis)

discussed in the previous chapter), on the importance of these discrepancies to long- and short-term goals, and on reactions of relevant others and feelings attached to these reactions, the individual makes adjustments to initial goals and aspirations, plans, and perceptions of relevant tasks and problems.

The individual will cycle through this problem-solving sequence again and again until a measure of stability is reached—that is, a niche is established—between the demands on the individual and the problem-solving activities brought to bear to address them. It is at this point that we may view the individual as having established a characteristic or patterned way of interacting with the environment for the problem, task, or goal in question. These patterned responses may be either adaptive or maladaptive in nature; the same processes and categories of variables fuel each. In addition, people often vary in their patterns of response and thus their degree of healthy coping across different domains in their lives. For example, a person can be seen to cope well with one task (such as being a competent employee), while struggling and coping less well with another (such as managing finances, or setting appropriate limits with children). We should also note that what constitutes *adaptive* or healthy patterns does not remain constant. What may have been adaptive at one point in one's life will not necessarily be so later.

Before leaving this section, we should note that balance does not mean complete harmony or the total lack of tension. In fact, being underchallenged represents a form of stress (such as the boredom and vexation a child feels whose learning capacity and needs exceed what she is receiving in her classes). A certain amount of stress in the form of constructive challenge and goals to stretch toward is necessary, healthy, and motivating. Thus, the concept of balance should be understood to be a dynamic one—constantly shifting in magnitude and in configuration across the multiple domains of a person's life (we may encounter challenges in our work setting one day and in our home life the next). With this understanding in mind, we can see that the feeling of being settled into our niche involves establishing a relative balance between the range of task demands on oneself and the activities directed toward meeting them; of evolving routines to govern which situations will be encountered and how they will be responded to, compatible with one's goals and aspirations (see also Buss, 1987).

With these figures in mind, let us now turn to a more complete discussion of the niche and the self-system.

THE NICHE: THE CONNECTION
TO THE ENVIRONMENT

When we think of someone finding a niche, we mean that they have found a place that was previously undiscovered or underused, and that can sustain them. For example, in the early 1980s, Atari found a niche in the computer market between Apple and IBM by marketing their machine as an inexpensive fun machine that ran snazzy applications. They found a spot between IBM's business machines and Apple's market in the school systems. When someone finds a niche in his workplace, it means that he finds a place where he can exhibit, and be appreciated for, his talents and skills.

The word *niche* has a specific definition when used in ecological biology. A niche describes a system of interdependent parts; it develops by evolving over time into a system of intricate relationships, where each component has adapted to each other as changes are encountered, and where each component depends on each other for its survival. The ecological/biological definition of the word also describes the countless micro-level processes that take place to establish the niche. It describes the structural changes that take place within organisms (insects mutating to adapt to DDT) as well as the precise and delicate connections between organisms (the specific odors, colors, and shapes of orchids that have developed to attract specific birds and insects for pollination).

These intra- and inter-organism processes present a number of implications for our social-cognitive use of the word. The different components of the niche can include the target person, the people with whom he or she interacts on a regular basis, and the situations with which he or she comes into contact on a regular basis. Within the person, the processes that connect us to our environment are based both on our innate drive to create meaning from our surroundings, and on our innate drive to manipulate our physical environment (as was discussed in Chapter 2).

Then, to understand how absolutely we are linked to our environments, and how completely we are dependent on our drives to control and predict our world (i.e., how much we live inside our niches), we need to look at the countless micro-level behaviors in which we engage in our daily lives. In our daily lives, our niche takes the phenomenological form of establishing and maintaining routines in our daily behavior: getting up at the same time every day, hitting the snooze button twice before getting out of bed, taking our morning shower, how we go about selecting what to wear, the breakfast table litany of telling our children to stop arguing and to not forget their lunches, and so forth.

One result of activating a set of routines to lead our lives is that our routines can be seen to put us into the same (or similar) situations on a daily basis; by and large, we enter the same kind of work situations, the same kinds of social and recreational activities, and the same kinds of relationships. We normally do not frequent very different parts of the town we live in, or go to parties that are wholly unfamiliar to us, or seek out people who are quite unlike others whom we have become familiar with in the past. In fact, when we enter wholly new situations (parties, work settings, parts of town or parts of the country, engaging in conversations about new topics) we very often treat them as if they were familiar by calling up schemas (mental prototypes of concepts and objects, discussed in Chapter 2) that may only peripherally fit, but which help us make sense of and respond to the situation (Snyder & Swann, 1978). The alternative is to feel "at sea" and somewhat groundless (that is, feeling the situational anomie described in the previous chapter) in trying to make sense of things (Brower, 1988).

It is our contention that every part of our lives is dictated by routine to an extent, and that these routines describe the niche in which we live. At times, of course, we encounter events that are both unexpected and unfamiliar. However, even under novel circumstances, we tend to draw upon what we know best, however adaptive or maladaptive that may prove to be in the end. Our routines themselves are interconnected, and at least to some degree, dependent on each other. This is not to say that if we brush our teeth differently (that is, change our morning routine), we would lose our jobs (by forcing change in our work routines). But it is implying that we rely on routine to a great extent so that we do not have to think about the countless tasks that we perform in order to survive; we can instead focus our energies on those tasks that require more spontaneous and original thought and action.

Imagine how difficult it would be to get through a day if nothing were predictable, if one had no idea what was coming next. This is often the experience of the first day on a new job, the first day and weeks after bringing home a first baby, or being on one's own after separating from a longstanding partner.

This is reported as one of the ongoing stresses experienced by those suffering from thought disorders. That is, they cannot trust their instincts about what is coming next, feeling like they have no control over events in their lives and instead like they are buffeted from one event to the next. This is also the experience of clients who are new to both individual and especially group counseling (Lieberman, Yalom, & Miles, 1973). What should they expect? How should they behave? Clearly, not knowing what to expect and what is expected of us is an anxiety-producing experience. It makes us feel both threatened and inadequate, and places us in a hypervigilant, almost paranoid, mode of functioning.

Establishing a niche for oneself, then, is the product of the human nature. We establish sets of routines and patterned interactions with others and with situations as a result of our attempt to understand ourselves and our world, which itself results from our human need to predict, control, and manipulate our surroundings. Within our niche, we understand the rules, we know what to expect from others, we know what others expect from us, and generally we are afforded some predictability in our lives. We work hard to maintain our niche in order to maintain our sense of control and predictability in our lives, and to maintain our ability to take what we need from our surroundings.

In a stable, successful (i.e., surviving) niche, each component has accommodated to every other to a larger or lesser extent. Each component has changed in substantial ways, based on all other components of the niche. A change in any one component will require change or adaptation in other components.

Examples of this are easy to find in work settings where a group of individuals must depend on one another to develop a product. For the work group to survive and be successful, each member must develop a role that is both unique and functional vis-à-vis the roles of the other members. Each member's niche within that group, and the group as a whole, is successful if it develops completely. That is, its members take on all roles necessary to see a prospect through to a finished product. We see parallels in other groupings, such as families, gangs, and friendship networks, as well as the ways in which changes in any one component reverberate throughout the niche.

At the same time, a niche does not have to contain other people, at least not in a directly interactive way. We can imagine an individual who has little direct interaction with others, and who has created a niche that allows him to meet all of his living needs. An elderly widow, for example, who spends much of her day reading and watching television, leads a relatively solitary existence. Assuming that her Social Security and pension checks pay her bills, and that she is comfortable with her life, her niche can be deemed stable and successful for her, even if it is not the life that we might choose for ourselves. And imagine how difficult it may be to provide home-based services to this woman as her physical health begins to deteriorate and she is not able to adequately care for herself. Students working in these settings very often report their elderly clients as having absolutely no interest in the services and assistance that they have been trained to provide.

In this case, the components of this person's niche would include herself, her home, her telephone and television, her books, and so on. We could describe her niche even more precisely by describing her daily routines: how she gets up and prepares for the day, what she eats for breakfast, which books she reads (and which chair she reads in), which television programs she watches, whom she talks to on the phone, and so forth. Even more precisely, we might be able to describe the specific cognitive and affective processes and constructs that she uses to make sense of what she reads and watches, those that help her understand herself and the world—both within her house and outside of it.

However, even for the person remote from direct social interactions, the influence of the social environment is far from absent. In this example, the widow is still shaped on an ongoing basis by the selection of television programs and books available to her, by the occasional interpersonal contacts she has with friends and family who call on her, by the incidental contacts when packages and groceries are delivered, and through the many cultural messages and social norms that touch virtually all of our behavior. We make this point to highlight the ubiquitous and sometimes subtle forms of influence that the environment has on behavior. Even those cognitive and affective processes that might be considered to exist "in the head" are connected to the environment through the individual's niche (Kaplan & Kaplan, 1978). For any thought, feeling, or behavior to be sustained, it must be reinforced by the niche.

We described a successful niche as one that survives. This does not imply that because it is successful in this survival sense, it is necessarily healthful or adaptive over the long run. In fact, part of what makes some dysfunctional aspects of one's niche so difficult to change is that the survival impulse must be overcome to create change. Often this entails a change that poses a very fundamental threat to the individual's sense of equilibrium, and to that of her or his most intimate social environment. Again, imagine how the widow described above reacts to her gradual deterioration in her health, and how she reacts to the well-meaning family and social service workers who try to provide her with assistance and companionship. Here we can see how a normal and typically advantageous feature of human behavior—the tenacity of our understandings of the world and our niche within it—can become maladaptive and can seriously undermine both well-being and change efforts. We will be discussing these distinctions further later in this chapter and in subsequent chapters.

Niches will vary in their capacity to adapt to change, to incorporate new elements or lose existing elements. This capacity has important implications for well-being. Even when the events are happy ones, the niche must adjust to change, which sometimes places quite a lot of strain on its members. Different families will adapt to the same event differently, often explainable through their ability to develop and to tolerate new routines of behavior, interdependent roles, and patterns of communication. The *reverberation effects* that ripple through a family are evident in changes that follow events such as the birth of a child, promotions or relocations, and children leaving for college. Significant adjustments are necessary, often under conditions where strains are confusing ("How can I be wishing this baby wasn't here? I must be a terrible parent."), and where supports are scarce (few people come to the aid of those in the flush of positive life events). Events that are not so happy—deaths, divorces, losing one's job, serious illness—are of course easier to imagine as difficult to cope with.

It should be noted, however, that a balance must be struck between the readiness to change (to accommodate forces) and the resistance to change (to protect the integrity of the system). Either in the extreme will prove unhealthy in the long run. At any given juncture, however, it is not always clear where to strike the balance between flexibility and tenacity. This balance can be visualized by thinking about the size of one's niche: One's niche should not become too large—referring to the range of situations one routinely enters and tries to accommodate to—lest one becomes overtaxed by environmental demands (i.e., trying to do too much or spreading oneself too thin). Likewise, the niche created cannot be too small, or rigidly defined, since the individual then becomes too vulnerable to slight changes internally or in the environment (as is sometimes the case for people with obsessive-compulsive disorders).

The cognitive-ecological model's description of the niche predicts that we strive, more or less, for stability and routine in our lives (Nisbett & Ross, 1980; Snyder & Swann, 1978). It is not that our lives are in fact all that stable or routine. Instead, it is that we strive for that state—or at least our perception of that state—as a goal. In the normal course of daily living we encounter many challenges, obstacles, and opportunities that we have not planned for. Thus, one's daily routine is determined both by planful and spontaneous activity, and is adjusted to address the tasks and problems in the situations at hand. One's niche must continually change shape and size to remain adaptive to one's ever-changing surroundings as new situations are encountered and old ones are left behind. One's niche must remain in a reciprocal and fluid state of dynamic balance with the broader environment.

Based on this description, many questions arise that are important to how niches both reflect and influence how individuals function in daily life. For example, what are the costs of living without a niche? Such as, what costs do refugees and the recent homeless bear in being stripped of routines important to their lives? What balance exists between allowing routines to help us focus our energies versus allowing them to take over our lives (e.g., becoming stuck in a rut, or being overly rigid in our behaviors and interactions with others)? And, specifically, what is the influence of the individual's sense of personal identity, goals, competency, and vulnerability in developing and sustaining his or her niche?

We will address such questions in subsequent chapters, but it is to the last question that we turn next. That is, what is the role of the self in these efforts to create and sustain a niche? As we move to this next section, we will be shifting our level of analysis. The niche speaks primarily to the social environment and the individual goals and patterns that motivate and influence many of the social transactions between individuals and significant others. To complement this more environment-based component of human behavior in the social environment, we now turn to a closer analysis of a more person-based component: the self-system. Here we will also discuss the relation of the self-system to the niche and the central organizing and regulating influence the self-system exerts over the individual's social ecology.

THE SELF-SYSTEM: A CENTRAL REGULATOR
IN THE COGNITIVE-ECOLOGICAL SYSTEM

When we speak of fundamental life tasks, establishing a niche for oneself and developing a life course, it is hardly surprising that the self-system will play a central orchestrating and regulating role. But, what exactly do we mean by the *self-system*? One core component, certainly, is the self-concept, but then what really does this mean?

Even though self-concept has long been held to be among the most critical factors to well-being by philosophers and clinicians alike, its definition has remained remarkably fuzzy. Most people feel they have a strong impression of what they mean by self-concept, but typically blur important distinctions (for example, by equating self-esteem and self-concept). This vagueness of definition has not been without cost: Wylie (1979) and others (Gecas, 1982) have catalogued the inconsistencies and failures of efforts to study and to effect real change in the self-concept. These lackings are understandable in light of the enormous complexity of the self-concept and the larger self-system, and the constrained means of studying these factors. However, we now have additional analysis tools to sharpen our focus on the murky notions of self-concept and self-system, and to strengthen change efforts.

In this part of the chapter, we will highlight some of the most recent theory and research on the self-concept that bears upon clinical work, for example, assessment, change-oriented intervention, and sustaining change. Recent work on human memory has advanced our understanding of the self-concept and the broader self-system. Consistent with the focus of this book, we will be focusing on a social cognitive analysis of the self and how these factors participate in and influence social transactions between the individual and the outside world.

Building Blocks Within the Self-System

Since the 1970s we have witnessed an explosion of attention to the cognitive features of human decision making, coping, and social transactions, as well as to the importance of cognitive constructs and processes in clinical assessment and treatment. These efforts have helped to underscore the extent to which the self-concept serves as a pivotal referent point, and as a central mediating filter, for processing information relevant to the individual (e.g., in constructing an understanding of one's world, in creating a niche to live within, and in regulating one's behavior and life course).

Efforts to define the self-concept have spanned many years and have traversed multiple disciplines—psychology, sociology, social work, anthropology, philosophy. Recent years have seen a focus on self-referent thoughts and feelings. Work on this focus has been pursued in terms of an individual's "self-talk" concerning self-evaluations and self-expectations with respect to a particular domain of functioning (e.g., work or school competence, friendships, parenting). Current research and practice goals now involve even more fine-grained questions, such as: What are the sources of self-conceptions, and what form do they take? How can we explain our sense of a coherent identity while exhibiting a remarkable range in situational self-concepts (i.e., still feeling like the same person while acting one way in one situation and another way in another situation)? How does the self-concept undergo change, and what effects do these changes have on immediate and delayed behaviors?

These types of questions put greater emphasis on the basic building blocks of cognition—that is, the repertoire of cognitive structures individuals have stored in memory, and the cognitive processes that influence which structures are made most salient, and are pulled on-line to interpret and regulate behavior in specific situations (see Greenwald & Pratkanis, 1984; Markus & Wurf, 1987; McGuire & McGuire, 1988; Winfrey & Goldfried, 1986, for overviews of some of these developments). By *cognitive structure* we are referring to memories, beliefs, and feelings about the self that are stored in memory in an organized and durable form. These memories, beliefs, and feelings are organized in memory so we can activate them when necessary to help us make sense of situational cues, and also so we can modify and update them when appropriate. For example, from early childhood we quickly begin to develop a concept of what it means to be female or male; we each create what might be called a "male concept" and a "female concept" that we use to understand ourselves and the world. These conceptions are not static. They undergo continual change through our physical and psychosocial development, through general messages about what constitutes appropriate gender-specific behavior, and through specific messages about us as males or females.

The self-concept, then, can be thought of operationally as the set of schemas (memories, beliefs, feelings) that we hold about ourselves. *The self-concept is really a misnomer, then, as we have numerous self-concepts that we use to understand ourselves and to act in various situations. These multiple concepts themselves are connected as a system—into a self-system—that includes the activities we use to govern how messages about our self are received, interpreted, stored, retrieved, and applied in various situations.

The cognitive schema concept has proven particularly useful in this regard. As was discussed in Chapter 2, schemas refer to the manner by which bits of information are organized into meaningful wholes and stored in memory, and thus are a type of cognitive structure. These bits of information take many different forms, for example, words, symbols, images, and other sensory traces (smells, sounds, bodily experiences). The *organized wholes* (i.e., schemas) refers to the fact that these bits of information fit together to form knowledge about the world and about oneself as that information is interpreted as knowledge by the individual. *Self-schemas* refer specifically to our schemas that are self-referent. For example, our schema of an "outgoing person" might contain images of someone who is friendly, who always knows the right things to say, who is a real take-charge person. Our self-schema of being outgoing would contain memories of specific situations in which we were friendly and knew the right thing to say; it would contain memories of how we felt and what feedback we received when we were outgoing. Schemas generally, and self-schemas specifically, vary in how positive or negative they are to us, and in how central or peripheral they are to our values, functioning, and personal sense of identity.

Schemas also contain representations of an individual's extensions in time. That is, we know that we retain self-schemas from childhood (and, in fact, are chagrined to find them pop out during extended visits with our families). And we obviously hold a variety of self-schemas related to our present life. But equally important, we also have schemas that reflect our images of what might happen to us in the future. By this, we are not referring to periodic daydreams or transient images of ourselves, but rather to the future or possible selves (both hoped for and feared) that we focus on repeatedly. We give substantial form to our future or possible selves through observation, discussion, and reflection.

Self-schemas are involved in virtually every aspect of information processing since they are involved any time stimuli is experienced as personally relevant (including our perceptions of others; see Markus, 1983). Schemas have been likened to a blueprint or map. That is, they are both a plan of action (an organized recording of what we or others have been or done in the past) as well as a plan for action (orienting our attention in certain directions over others, providing procedural information about what to expect and how to go about things). All is not, however, quite so rational and straightforward as this analogy might imply. Self-schemas often exert a distorted influence on what we expect (and thus look for), what we "see" and how we interpret it, and how we go about retrieving certain self-conceptions from memory and applying these in reasoning and decision making. These distortions often take the form of exaggerating our self-importance or the centrality of ourselves in various situations, prompting some to write about the "totalitarian ego" (Greenwald, 1980). Self-schemas are highly conservative in nature; they appear to filter out information that is challenging or contradictory and to predispose the individual to seek out and pay attention to information that is confirmatory and reinforcing (see Goldfried & Robins, 1983; Kihlstrom & Cantor, 1984; and Nurius, 1989, for clinically oriented overviews).

Just as the niche, once established, strives to maintain itself, so too do self-schemas strive for self-preservation. Generally, this serves a positive function by aiding the self-concept to fend off or sidestep threats. Moreover, in addition to this self-consistency drive, the self-concept is typically biased in the direction of self-enhancement (e.g., seeing ourselves as contributing more than others in a team effort, attributing success to skill, and failure to external forces). This bias, too, is important in skewing us toward an optimistic outlook, an optimistic set of expectations, and skewing us toward behavior consistent with these.

Yet these same natural features are double-edged, holding considerable negative potential as well. For example, we see negative effects from the very same processes in the tendency of depressed people to ignore or contradict information inconsistent with their depressed construction of reality; clients who suffer from depression can be seen to anticipate and actively seek out information that reinforces their depressed self-schemas (Segal, 1988). We can begin to see several concrete ways in which the self-system plays a concrete role in the transactions between people and their environments generally, and in people's constructions and maintenance of their niches. For example, in Chapter 2 we discussed our inherent need to not only make sense of the world, but also establish a coherent and stable life story concerning our place within it. Optimally, our life stories are self-enhancing and foster positive growth and development. But here we begin to see ways in which the memory and information-processing systems that undergird self-concept functioning conspire in the direction of conserving what is "known" by the individual, even if this is self-denigrating.

We noted in Chapter 2 the anomic character of situations in terms of picking and choosing the cues that we use to make sense of the situation. This, of course, is not to say that situations contain no physical reality. Nevertheless, when faced with a particular situation, in the process of interpreting others' actions, facial expressions, comments, and voice tone (among other things), we are highly prone to confirming our working hypotheses or theories about the self and the world.

The Working Self-Concept

Traditional formulations have viewed the self-concept as a unitary, trait-like entity: People have a good self-concept or a poor self-concept, which they carry with them into different situations and through time. Yet, viewing self-concept in this trait-like manner has proven to have limited clinical and empirical value. The self-concept has been among one of the most difficult clinical variables to define or study with much precision.

This presents a paradox: We certainly feel like we have a "true self" that is stable, and that describes who we really are. But we also realize that our images or feelings about ourselves can change quite drastically, depending on who we are with and what situation we are in. Recent formulations define the self-concept to allow for both coherence and flexibility, allowing it to remain responsive to the prevailing environment. This fits with the cognitive-ecological model, where our thoughts, feelings, and actions are contextual, interactive with the environment, and multifaceted.

The recent view of the self-concept makes the distinction between an individual's entire repertoire of self-schemas accumulated over a lifetime, and that subset that is activated and actually working for the individual at any given point in time. This subset of self-schemas, activated specifically to allow us to interact with specific situations, has been called the working self-concept (see Nurius, 1986; Nurius & Berlin, 1993; Nurius & Markus, 1990, for background reading).

Certainly all schemas undergo some degree of updating and revision; and the potential for adding new self-conceptions always exists. In fact, the total number and entire range of self-schemas one amasses over time may be quite large. We do not easily drop old schemas, but instead create and shift our emphasis on the subsets that we most consistently draw upon. For example, we may see ourselves as fast runners because we were fast in grade school, even though we have not run a race in 30 years; we may see ourselves as overweight as adults, even though we have not really been overweight since we were preadolescents; we may see ourselves as having poor math skills because we flunked high school algebra, even though we now balance our checkbooks easily and generally manage our money fine. Our accumulation of self-schemas as contrasted with our ability to replace and drop old ones has interesting consequences. We have already mentioned the odd feeling of reliving parts of adolescence during extended family visits. In addition, we tend to maintain a view of our "true" selves that might be quite inconsistent with our daily behaviors. For example, even though we know we manage our money well now, and in every other respect know that we use good basic math skills in our current life, we also "know," deep down, that we just are not good at math. We interpret normal computational mistakes as continued evidence of this fact. This "bad at math" self-schema, even though no longer prominent in daily adult life, continues to reside as a component of our self-concept repertoire.

It is very difficult for us to actually let go of old or outdated self-concepts once they have formed. Furthermore, because we lead our lives within our niche—placing ourselves in similar situations and interacting with similar people on a day-to-day basis—we tend to call up, or activate, a relatively routine set of self-schemas for day-to-day interactions. Both of these reasons—because we accumulate schemas rather than replace them, and because we call up a routine set of them for normal interactions—contribute to our ongoing sense of a stable and coherent identity.

But, consistent with a basic theme of the cognitive-ecological model, we also try hard to activate self-schemas that are responsive to particular situations. Our working self-concept—those self-schemas activated at any given point in time—will be as responsive to and consistent with the circumstances to the extent that the person is able, that is, given the repertoire of self-schemas available and the knowledge structures that exist that help us activate our schemas. We can only draw upon the pool available, and some schemas will be much easier to tap than others at any given moment.

The working self-concept, the self-concept of the moment, is best viewed as a continually shifting configuration of self-schemas that have been activated from memory. Some aspects of self are, of course, more central than others and will therefore be active a great deal of the time. Examples of these may include fundamental features such as gender or race, or attributes either highly valued by the individual (e.g., independence) or those that are centrally self-defining (e.g., being worthless or a failure, for severely depressed individuals).

Different self-schemas are deemed more central, depending also on one's stage of life development. For example, young adults' central concerns and self-concepts focus on achievement and affiliation (see Brower, 1990; Cantor, Norem, Niedenthal, Langston, & Brower, 1987, for reviews). The majority of our self-schemas, however, remain anchored to specific situations. These are activated by stimuli in the environment (such as an old rock 'n' roll tune, a phone call from your second grader's teacher) or by one's internal stimuli (such as when thinking about an upcoming event activates memories of similar events).

Thus, the working self-concept can be highly, even radically, variable at different points in time and under varying circumstances. Consider the changes that the working self-concept undergoes during any given day or week. When we are having breakfast with the kids, making a presentation at work, grumbling about the boss to a co-worker, buying a gift for our sister, working out at the gym, sopping up the red wine we just overturned on our host's white carpet, playing with the new puppy, or having a romantic evening with our partner, we make active and salient an enormous array of quite different self-schemas that provide information about who we are. Stopped at any given point, we would get a different snapshot of the person's total self-concept and his or her life course. In addition, the qualitative nature of that given snapshot, that working self-concept, will greatly influence how the person is feeling, what she is and is not paying attention to, how she is likely to interpret and interact with her environment.

The working self-concept is thus a blend of stable and variable self-conceptions that are tied to the prevailing circumstances. It is important to note that merely because the schemas are drawing upon memory, they need be neither accurate nor particularly rational in order to exist and to have effect. Similarly, highly discrepant self-schemas (retaining the "bad at math" schema while not having any problems now) can reside within the larger self-concept without creating a chronic sense of dissonance or inauthenticity.

THE ARCHITECTURE OF HUMAN MEMORY

The basic architecture of human memory constrains how we interact with the world. We think and remember, interpret and analyze, because of the way our minds store, retrieve, and manipulate information. One major framework in the social psychological literature on the basic architecture of memory is briefly reviewed here. We actually have different types of memory within our memory system, summarized in Figure 3.3 (adapted from Anderson, 1983). These include long-term memory, short-term memory, and the sensory-perceptual system (for clinical-oriented readings on memory and the self-system, see Greenwald & Banaji, 1989; Kihlstrom et al., 1988; Nurius, 1993a, 1993b).

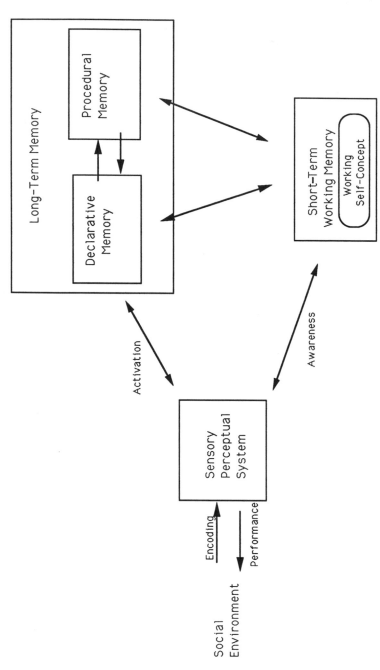

Figure 3.3. Basic Architecture of Human Memory

Long-Term Memory

Long-term memory itself has been distinguished into two major parts: declarative and procedural memory. *Declarative memory* refers to the information-based facts we store in memory. It contains both *semantic* memory based on general knowledge that we acquire about the world and ourselves (e.g., early on we learn what concepts mean, like "friend," "good girl," "dumb," "school"), and *episode-based* memory deriving from our autobiographical experiences (our own encounters in relationships, roles, or events), like being in school and trying out being a friend, as well as others' evaluative feedback to us about who we are and how valued we or our performance is. While our schemas in semantic memory will be somewhat unique, there is generally a great deal of overlap among members of a society in their definitions and understandings of common events, attributes, or phenomena. For example, to sustain a common language, there must be considerable consensus about what different words mean, although the greater the role that subjective experience plays in defining the concept or word, the more variation there will be (contrast individual differences in defining "school" and "good girl"). In contrast, our episodic memory related to our own experiences and introspections will be much more unique to us (for example, our cultural and familial experiences in varied roles and circumstances, with all our introspective thoughts, feelings, and sensations that go with them).

These two forms of declarative memory are highly interactive. We draw upon our semantic memory to give words to and interpret our episodic memory. It is through our experiences that we accumulate information that can be abstracted and stored in semantic memory. Rather than being factually true recordings of observations and experiences, our memory system tends to be highly constructed. Research on eyewitnesses, for example, demonstrates that memories of witnessed events are not only revised, but the observer is often unaware of this revision and is unable to discriminate the revised from the original information (Loftus, 1979). We are capable of creating memories for events that we have not experienced, but instead have been suggested to us (Loftus & Ketcham, 1991).

In contrast to our information-based type of memory, *procedural memory* contains "knowing how" aspects of particular states or activities. Procedural memory thus consists of rules, skills, and strategies for how to do things and act in certain ways. Procedural memory is thought to be stored as "if-then" types of action clauses. For example, the concepts of "competence" or "incompetence" will be stored in declarative memory, but the activities for how to act these ways are stored in procedural memory ("if I stammer and don't look people in the eye, then I will be acting incompetent in that conversation").

Whereas declarative memory is accessible to conscious reflection and articulation; in principle, procedural memory is much less so. We can certainly abstract and describe what we know about how to do things. But, the more we gain skills or habits, the more complex our rules become and the more difficult it is for us to separate out each step, inference, and connection. For example, note how exasperating it is to try to narratively describe how to tie a shoelace; it is far easier to simply show someone how it is done. We have the information firmly encoded in memory, but its form does not readily lend itself to narration or introspection. These differences in accessibility of the various components of our memory have important implications for helping people change behaviors and self-concepts. This will be discussed in subsequent chapters.

Short-Term Memory

Short-term working memory refers to the very limited portion of our total memory that we are actively aware of at any given moment. *Active* awareness refers to our ability to consciously access and use the information we call up. This is an important distinction: We may have a large repertoire of potential information and self-conceptions to make use of, but if we are not able to activate the information and self-conceptions when we need them, they might as well not exist (functionally speaking, that is, since their existence will make a difference if they are to be used in counseling interventions).

Research finds, in fact, that we can only hold seven (plus or minus two) concepts in active memory at any given point in time (Mandler, 1985; Miller, 1956). This means, generally speaking, that we can only make use of a limited amount of the total of what we actually know, at any given time, when we are trying to respond to situations or when we are trying to solve problems in our lives. The self-relevant information active in short-term memory is therefore quite limited, as compared to the broader repertoire of self-concepts stored in long-term memory. Overall, both long- and short-term memory form our knowledge base about ourselves (stored, as we noted earlier, in many different forms of representation). Yet, at any given moment, memory structures in long-term memory can be thought of as our total library or repository of knowledge and experience; our short-term memory can be thought of as the circulating desk, where our memory holdings are exchanged in and out of active use. The practitioner therefore must assess and intervene on the basis of these differences. We will discuss methods and guidelines for assessment and intervention planning, taking these differences into account, in Chapters 6 and 8.

The Sensory-Perceptual System

The sensory-perceptual system in Figure 3.3 refers to our sensory receptors and to the memory and encoding (defining, classifying, storing) capacities these hold. Our sensory receptors require long- and short-term memory to aid them in perceiving or giving meaning to what they are receiving. When we ask the question, "Is that person friendly or threatening?" our classification of the person requires extant knowledge in the form of preexisting categories of "friendly" and "threatening."

The vast majority of our attention and perception is carried out automatically. We rely on our sensory-perceptual system to continuously scan and detect input from the environment that requires purposeful attention. To enable our sensory-perceptual system to function amid a cacophony of inputs, the system must be very selective in what it guides us to notice and to interpret. This ability is often quite remarkable: When we are at a party, talking to someone, we must skillfully filter out the countless conversations and stimuli around us in order to maintain our conversation. But regardless of how intently we are focusing on our conversation, if something highly salient to us is spoken across the room (such as our name, or our native language when the language around us is different), we become immediately alert, and can often pick out the location in the room in which this self-salient reference was spoken.

Part of the selectivity of the sensory-perceptual system has to do with the information already stored in memory that guides its interpretive tasks. That is, the system is designed to search for information that is consistent with what we "know" and what we expect, and to ignore, overlook, or be unable to encode information that either does not exist in memory (e.g., is outside our experience to date) or is contradictory with existing beliefs and expectations. This self-confirmatory bias generally serves us very well, as was discussed in the previous chapter. But it is also easy to imagine the ways in which these normal cognitive processes can pose very difficult barriers when clients "know" things about themselves and their world that are severely distorted or self-injurious.

Links Among Memory Components

These components of memory, long- and short-term memory and the sensory-perceptual system, are highly interactive with one another; in true cognitive-ecological fashion, changes in one require changes in the others as well. For example, when we are working with a client to help her change her self-concept, we strive to effect change in each component. We will work with her to enrich her semantic knowledge, for example, to enrich her conception of what assertiveness is (educating her concerning general attributes of assertiveness: what it looks like in people who have it, and the like). We will work with her to enrich her episodic knowledge of being assertive, enriching her personal assertiveness experiences through guided role plays and by discussing instances when she is assertive with others. We will work with her to broaden her repertoire of how she can be assertive (her procedural knowledge), particularly in situations where real or perceived barriers are encountered, and practice these strategies with feedback to strengthen assertiveness toward becoming a natural-feeling response. We will help her pay closer attention to her environment, to detect cues to guide her response and behave assertively, and to more accurately tune into change-supportive input from others to help her more easily recognize and reinforce herself when she does it. We will work with her to help her more easily activate all these above-noted forms of knowledge into working memory when she desires them and when they will help her in achieving her goals.

Each of these efforts will tend to reinforce each other. For example, it will be in large part through experimentation and practice that the how-to procedural knowledge will be built up. It is through the repeated purposeful invoking of self-schemas related to assertiveness that these knowledge structures become easier to invoke, so that they not only are recruited more automatically, but they can more successfully compete with older self-schemas related to nonassertiveness.

Note how very deliberate, and in that sense, artificial, each of the above steps sounds. Most of our daily life is not spent in this deliberate manner. Instead, as we discussed previously, most of our days are spent in automatic, or mindless, and patterned (routine) interactions within our niche. These deliberate steps can be thought of as the steps of learning that we undergo with any new situation, task, or concept. That is, when encountering something either novel or threatening, we shift from a mindless (automatic) to a more mindful (deliberate) mode of memory and information processing. Ironically, one general goal of counseling is to help clients first shift from a mindless to a mindful mode of functioning relative to dysfunctional self-schemas and interactional routines, and then to help them shift back to a more mindless (i.e., a more natural and less energy-intensive) mode of processing, but only after their new knowledge and memories have become firmly embedded in their routines (Hollon & Garber, 1988).

In creating new schemas and interactional patterns, or in altering existing ones, we shift back and forth between mindless and mindful use of our memory resources. In doing so, we begin to see another relationship between the self-system and the niche. That is, to become a significant, enduring change, the new self-schemas and their presence in working memory (the working self-concept) must be incorporated into the niche. They must go well beyond the counseling session to become part of the interactive routines that constitute the activities of everyday life.

Then, since change in one component of the niche necessitates changes in all other components, enduring change will require that all niche components adjust and accommodate: Situations that used to be resolved in one way will be resolved in other ways, roles taken in one's personal and work life will undergo change, relationships will feel the effects and will react. And all these niche components will need to be addressed, since they will either support or hinder the desired changes. Thus, professional practice requires building up new routines of transaction on two different and interdependent levels: on the micro level of how clients interact with their own self-system and on the more macro level of how clients interact with their social and physical environment.

SUMMARY

In this chapter, the cognitive-ecological concepts of the niche and the self-system were discussed in detail. The niche represents that part of the environment in which individuals live. It is defined by the people and situations with whom a person comes into routine contact; it defines the system of interdependent environmental and cognitive/affective factors that generate the person's day-to-day behaviors.

The self-system represents the aspect of the person that is most central to his or her interactions with the environment. The self-system is defined as being composed of a repertoire of self-schemas, one set of which can become activated at any given time to produce one's working self-concept. Processes of human memory were enumerated that govern how self-schemas develop and become activated.

In the next chapter, we will continue our discussion of the cognitive-ecological model by describing how people strive for life goals.

Chapter 4

GOAL STRIVING, POSSIBLE SELVES, AND POSSIBLE NICHES

Let us now turn to three final features of the cognitive-ecological model. These features have to do with developing a multifaceted life story, and with the role of life goals and goal-striving in daily life. Following these sections, we will conclude this chapter with a discussion of how the cognitive-ecological model can explain common types of problems that clients come in with. This concluding discussion will be used to illustrate how the same "normal" and everyday cognitive and affective processes can both serve us well and create problems for us.

THE ROLE OF LIFE GOALS IN OUR DAILY LIVES

From a cognitive-ecological perspective, daily life is structured by our thoughts, feelings, and actions that are directed toward addressing our life goals and tasks (Cantor & Kihlstrom, 1989). Some personality theorists argue that goal-formation and goal-striving are processes fundamental to our existence (Klinger, 1977, 1989). Goals give our lives meaning, and we use them to define who we are (see Brower, 1992; Brower & Nurius, 1992; Emmons, 1986; Emmons & King, 1989). While some (e.g., Pervin, 1989) see goal development and goal selection as central to any discussion about human intention and free will—since they define the central constructs within the area of motivation and self-expectation—it is essential that we continue to look at goals in terms of people within environments. As we have discussed previously, environments differ according to the consensus of perception of individuals within them, and therefore the environments differentially convey messages about what is or is not appropriate or realistic for different groups and individuals. Environments both constrain and foster access to needed opportunity and supports. Goals and their creation are by no means "all in the head." On the other hand, the individual's perceptions regarding what is or is not possible, what is or is not appropriate, and what is or is not available, stand as powerful personal gatekeepers about what is or is not dreamed and attempted.

At this point, the reader may be aware of an apparent paradox between the notion of goal-directed, future-oriented behavior on the one hand, and our inherent inclination to maintain stability and consistency in our life niches. This has been a criticism of homeostasis models of behavior, as discussed in Chapter 2: While a homeostasis model assumes that a system will always react to neutralize or negate the effects of change (either internal to the individual or external in the environment), evolution and mutation create opportunities for growth and development. From a cognitive-ecological perspective, the individual is both a social product and a social force; changes are viewed as points of decision, where the individual can decide whether one's niche will change in significant ways (i.e., evolve) in response to the change, or will instead become more resilient to it (i.e., maintain the status quo).

While people tend to seek a balance between predictability and curiosity, at different points in our lives we will lean more in one direction than another (such as toward the reassurance of predictability and stability following a particularly challenging or stressful period). Thus, we often exhibit our dual need to maintain the integrity of our niches and sense of personal identity with our need for stimulation and the capacity to learn from and evolve with an ever-changing world. Life goals provide us with ballast, with directional signs and signals that allow us to navigate in a more or less purposeful course through life's changes and surprises. In these ways, understanding one's life goals provides keys to understanding one's life story and life trajectory.

LIFE GOALS AS POSSIBLE SELVES
AND POSSIBLE NICHES

Given that self-schemas represent how various attributes and feelings about ourselves are stored in memory, and given that they exert great influence over how we process information and interact with others, then by analogy, *possible self-schemas* should be the concrete expression of our goals, plans, aspirations, and fears. Both positive and negative possible selves (becoming renowned for one's professional expertise; blossoming into a fantastic athlete; being revealed as uncreative or inept; being rejected or avoided by others) should influence behavior in a manner similar to schemas about present self.

Likewise, *possible niches* should be the concrete expression of our visions of the lives that we may lead, again in positive and negative ways. They can represent our dream house and how it will be furnished, the interesting and attractive people that will surround us when we make it big, the job responsibilities and situations we hope to be in, and so on. They can also represent the vision of what life will be like when we are found out to be the fraud that we fear we are, and how others will shun us. To look at possible selves and niches another way, if a possible self of ours is to be a rich business executive—powerful, decisive, wearing expensive suits—the complementary possible niche might include the expensive car we will drive, the expensive office with its panoramic view, the high-status firm and colleagues with which we are associated, the supportive yet independent partner and (possibly) the creative yet well-behaved children to whom we will come home. Research on the existence and influence of these possible selves and niches has spanned a range of ages and populations (Carson, Madison, & Santrock, 1987; Egan, 1990; Higgins, 1989; Markus & Nurius, 1986; Markus & Ruvolo, 1989; Nurius, 1991).

Possible selves and niches, then, are the concrete forms that our personal goals, aspirations, plans, and fears take in memory. In this way, possible self-schemas and niches give specific form to the selves and lives individuals either would like to have or want to avoid. Even more than present schemas, possible selves and niches need not be particularly realistic nor based on actual experiences and memories in order to be well elaborated in memory. In fact, many possible selves and niches may remain cherished while having little realistic chance of being realized.

Possible selves and possible niches exert influence over behavior, using the same set of factors as those previously discussed for present self- and other-schemas. One of these factors relates to the degree of elaborateness of the schema: How much declarative detail is included? How content or domain-specific is the procedural knowledge stored? How salient and affectively imbued is it (e.g., how vivid are the images from either actual or imagined experiences in episodic memory)? How often is it activated into working memory (i.e., how automatic and dominant has it become in routine information processing)?

Although we mentally try on quite a number of ways of being over our lifetime (particularly in adolescence), forming a well-elaborated possible self and niche requires considerable cognitive work. This involves thinking about them repeatedly; obtaining images, of what the possible self and niche look like and whether they are good or bad, from others' opinions; and storing with them the emotions that become salient when we think about the possible self and niche. Although every passing fancy or fear does not constitute a possible self-schema, we need not have actual experience with it to elaborate upon it. For example, while we may never have been sexually victimized, we can observe the devastation of rape on a close friend or relative and on women we see through the media; we can repeatedly imagine what the experience would be like and would mean for us. We can feel vulnerable to forces of victimization that are beyond our control, and can gain information about the rising incidence rates, and the difficulties to obtain justice. And, thus, we may very well develop a detailed self-schema and niche as a possible sexual assault victim.

We must engage in much cognitive work to develop positive possible selves and niches that we wish to achieve. To make our possible selves and niches realities—that is, to use them like goals to direct our lives— specific procedural knowledge is essential. Procedural knowledge is very difficult to develop without actual experience and practice. This is part of the reason that goals must be framed in active, approach-oriented terms for them to be used effectively in counseling (as will be discussed in Chapter 7). In Chapter 7, we spend a fair amount of time discussing how to help clients turn life goals into treatment or change goals. Imagine the client whose goal is to "not be such a social zero." It is likely that this client has schemas about past, present, and future selves related to being a social zero, and it is likely that this client will not have many self-schemas about having great social skills. Thus, a "not-me" strategy, of trying not to become something, does not effectively point this person in any particular direction. Effective counseling would need to help this client define, elaborate, and incorporate into his niche concrete procedural knowledge on which he can draw to help him reach his goal (such as helping him elaborate on the "outgoing self" by taking the initiative in social contacts, showing interest in others, developing interests of his own to share with others).

The ability to construct, invoke, and sustain possible selves and niches may be one critical determinant of actual goal achievement.

Possible selves and possible niches are an inherent part of the change process; they serve to decrease the perceptual distance between one's current state and a possible future state. Clients are allowed to imagine themselves living the life they hope for, and therefore can practice the procedural knowledge before it actually happens.

Possible selves and possible niches contribute toward galvanizing and organizing behavior relative to a goal. But equally important, they also provide a vehicle for introducing change into the self-concept without directly challenging it. Our clinical experience has found that introducing the notion of possible selves and niches provides a more hopeful way of thinking about potential change, even for clients resistant to change (see also Nurius & Berlin, 1993; Nurius & Majerus, 1988; Nurius, Lovell, & Edgar, 1988, for examples).

Many people, for example, tend to think of themselves in rather fixed ways ("I'm just a shy person," "I've been like this for years; I can't see being able to change now"), yet they find it fun to imagine how their lives could possibly be. Once these possible selves and niches become alive for clients, work can begin on developing procedural knowledge to make them happen. This will be discussed more fully in Chapter 8. Introducing possible selves and possible niches may be the place to start the change process for resistant clients.

When individuals strive to realize a desired future, or to avoid an undesired one, they have likely acquired or fashioned a vision of the new or changed self, living in a new or changed niche. Yet general possible selves and possible niches often do not indicate specific actions or pathways for achieving these end states. General possible selves and niches also do not sufficiently convey the feedback from other people that will help elaborate and shape these possibilities. It is only through exposure to and experience with others that fully developed possible selves and niches evolve; it is only through exposure and experience that procedural knowledge and social evaluations become more thoroughly formed and incorporated into a patterned way of anticipating, interpreting, and responding to the environment. It is through social interaction that possible selves and niches will become more routinely cued into action, will receive feedback, undergo modification, and become a more dominant force in memory and in subsequent action. It follows, then, that possible selves and niches that are never expressed to others, even indirectly, will generally remain too general and non-specific to effectively guide behavior, although they may well impede development of competing possible selves and niches.

Some people, of course, have difficulties even imagining themselves in the future—they cannot see themselves or their actions beyond the immediate next step. Not only do they have an enormous dearth of knowledge about themselves in the future, but their creative capacity to project themselves into the future and to generate possibilities is also seriously impoverished. Strategies for helping people with problems of this type will involve imagining and teaching *means-end* or procedural thinking (see D'Zurilla, 1986; Linville & Clark, 1989; Spivak, Platt, & Shure, 1976; Taylor & Schneider, 1989). This will be discussed more completely in Chapter 8.

Clearly, the self-concept and the niche are both social forces and social products. The self-concept plays a very active role in regulating our efforts to make sense out of and be effective within the world around us, and within our niches in particular. Yet the self-concept is continuously embedded within an equally active niche, itself embedded within the larger social environment. As was discussed, our niche has been fashioned out of the relationship between our needs and desires on one hand, and the resources and opportunities in the environment on the other. Thus, social feedback—from specific others as well as generalized others (such as the media)—influences our self-conceptions, while at the same time our prevailing view of ourselves directs not only our perceptions and actions but also those of others with whom we interact.

Let us now go a step further to illustrate the functioning of the niche and the self-system. In the following section we will describe several ways in which things go wrong. We will not attempt to describe all possible ways in which dysfunction can arise—that would require several books. Rather, we will focus on translating how the model, described in the previous chapter's figures regarding normative human behavior in the social environment, is related to several common forms of problems that practitioners encounter with clients (and, of course, in their own lives). Here we will extend our point that many of the very same social-cognitive factors that are cornerstones of healthy coping and problem solving are also cornerstones of unhealthy patterns, and that aiding the client to substitute healthy for unhealthy patterns will require intervention with these social-cognitive factors.

WHEN THINGS GO WRONG

In this section we will sketch out several categories of dysfunction relative to the variables and processes depicted in Figures 3.1, 3.2, and

3.3 in Chapter 3. We will describe these dysfunctions on two levels—in terms of both the macro-level patterned routines of behaving that characterize important routines of one's niche, and the micro-level processing of the self-system and the memory building blocks that underlie these routines.

If we take seriously the basic premises of the cognitive-ecological model—namely, that all components of a niche are defined by and dependent upon all others, and that a change in any component of the niche threatens the status quo of other components—then it becomes clear why changes in our lives are as disruptive, and potentially stressful, as they often are. The niche that we have negotiated within our environment has required considerable effort to create; it represents the delicate and complex relationships that we have forged within our environment. We depend on our niche as our psychosocial anchor. Under the best of conditions, we work hard to learn the rules and norms necessary to face the ever-changing problems and tasks of daily life, and we have sufficient flexibility, creativity, and optimism to undertake challenge and change with confidence. At worst, when faced with a new situation, we not only lose our perceptual bearings vis-à-vis the particular situation we are in, but we also flounder to make sense of everything in our lives, as if our inability to understand one situation generalizes to others (see Lieberman, Yalom, & Miles, 1973). At times we also develop ways of coping that may have short-term benefits (e.g., immediate relief from strain), but also hold longer-term dangers (e.g., isolating ourselves or fortifying maladaptive behaviors, such as substance abuse). Even happy changes (such as marriage or getting a promotion) are often met with anxiety, irritability, and a period of confusion, disorientation, and unhappiness, since the change must reverberate across one's entire niche.

By describing how people cope with life transitions (leaving home, getting married or divorced, entering school, entering the army, losing a loved one, retiring from one's job), we can view how the niche and self-system work in daily life. When we enter a transition, we take with us elements from our old niche (for example, the life goals and tasks that we hold as important, and the norms for our behaviors and procedural knowledge that establish the means to achieve these goals and tasks). Yet, since the delicate balance that we worked so hard to achieve has changed, these elements do not work, or do not work in the ways that we expect. We are again confronted with the inherent lack of structure in new situations. That is, we must start over again with the deliberate, mindful work of appraising a situation, imbuing situations with meaning, formulating a response, and so forth.

Initially, then, when faced with the task of interpreting meaning in our new situation, we may reach back to our past to make sense of the present. Since we will act according to old patterns that we might have even forgotten we had, we may also experience the feelings that have been stored with these same old patterns of perception and action. We will likely revert to relying on old ways of coping. This will involve general coping styles, such as, "If I am not sure what to do, then I will observe others and gain information." We may also draw upon appraisals of situations we think are similar from our past experiences, and on behaviors that worked for us in the past (whether recent or distant).

A description of the work with a client of one of the authors illustrates this. This client came in because, as she put it, her "life was going nowhere." She was in her late 30s and was working in a clerical job in a small office, a job she had been in for several years. She described her job as "boring and [she felt like she] was treated like a peon." The client was articulate and appeared to be quite intelligent, and did in fact seem underchallenged in her position, but she could not bring herself to quit, nor make any serious attempts to look for something else. This client was also in a relationship that she described as "okay, but not great." The man cared for her, and she expressed feelings for him, but she had neither the ability to express to him some of her dissatisfactions and then work with him to make the relationship better, nor the courage to break off the relationship altogether.

The counselor and client worked for several months together, but for the purpose of this illustration, one insight will be highlighted. The client began to realize that she was allowing others to dictate her decisions for her. She associated this to the way her parents treated her: that she was better than others and destined for great things, but also that she needed constant guidance, lest she should squander her talents. Their mixture of smothering and praise made her feel both that the events in her current life were only a prelude to her "real" life, and that she was afraid to stray too far from them.

What helped the client make this association was realizing how completely she was bringing old ways of viewing herself and the world into her current life and decisions. What was so difficult for her was that it did not feel as if she had been making decisions about her work and love life—she simply was living her life according to how the world worked. This client was truly working under a mindlessness about herself and her life; her old perceptions and ways of interacting were so complete and coherent that she had no clue that all along she had been making decisions about the course of her life. It helped her to realize that the feelings she had about herself and her relationships were utterly familiar to her: She was bringing them forward completely intact from the past to the present.

Upon realizing how she had been making tacit choices about her current life, based on these old scripts and schemas, the client became quite depressed about all the time that she had wasted over the past 20 years. She also became very concerned that she was now behind, and unsure about whether or not she had the capacity to do things differently. Much of the subsequent work with this client focused on helping her develop new possible selves and possible niches—to develop more clarity on how she wanted her life to change—and equally important, on helping her develop and practice the procedural knowledge necessary to actually make the changes she desired.

Most of us do not get quite as stuck as this client. The newness of current situations and our own psychological and developmental status make our old solutions untenable. The real differences between our current state and our previous ones will make the old solutions inadequate. It will be at this point that we will begin to experiment with new solutions in our environment: We will not only begin to see new tasks and problems that become relevant for the goals we wish to achieve, but also begin to test out new behaviors as resolutions to them. Slowly but surely, we will begin to build a new or modified niche for ourselves that is based on the new opportunities and realities of the environment, and on our new skills, plans, and concepts about ourselves and the world, providing relative stability and routine in our lives.

Let us now consider a number of ways in which things can and do go wrong within normative cognitive-ecological systems:

1. Distortions and Impoverishment in Input—Distal and Proximal: In Figure 3.1, we see that distal and proximal person and environmental factors play important input roles. Distortions or deficits in these fueling factors will carry forward into the sequence. Distal and proximal poverty, for example, will likely constrain the scope of opportunities and supports the individual perceives as accessible in his or her life course, impose stressors and barriers (e.g., reduced health, inadequate training), and lack sufficient models to help mold and operationalize certain possibilities (e.g., "No one in my family got through high school, I must be crazy to even dream about graduating from college").

Similarly, consider the individual born with a learning disability, a distal and proximal person variable. In many cases, such distal person deficits become compounded by more proximal deficits, such as in certain academic skills, and self-schemas of oneself as "dumb" or a troublemaker.[1] This person's set of goals and possible selves may then be characterized more by avoiding feared outcomes, which will subsequently handicap effective striving and coping.

2. *Distortions and Impoverishment in Input—Life Course:* As is suggested above, another form of input deficits or distortions contributing to dysfunction have to do with the individual's life course. Here we are referring to one's major goals, priorities, and plans that predispose the individual toward certain situations and undertakings consistent with his or her life course, and that predispose the individual away from others that appear inconsistent.

In such cases, to avoid destabilizing a secure niche, individuals may refuse to put themselves in new situations or positions requiring challenge or change, perhaps never leaving one's hometown, a relationship, or a job, even though these might be dissatisfying. We all strive to sustain our niches, but in the extreme, this individual rigidly rejects change even when change is in his or her own best interest.

A corollary to the lack of positive goals and plans is a life course characterized more by goals of what to avoid and plans for how to avoid them, rather than by goals one actively strives toward. This would apply to the above example of someone with a learning disability, where a youth might learn to avoid and minimize academic involvement to escape ridicule and disappointment. It applies also to the person who feels lonely and bored yet refuses to explore new interests or activities because of fears of social inadequacy. We might describe the person as lacking positive possible selves and possible niches that would help provide the declarative and procedural knowledge for how not to be socially inadequate, or rather, for how to be (look, think, feel, behave, and so on) socially adequate.

3. *Denying or not Understanding Changes:* We noted the ongoing need to modify and recreate niches as changes render former plans and solutions untenable. This rebuilding effort requires a certain amount of energy and risk, depending on the magnitude of change. One form of dysfunction results from foreshortening the niche rebuilding process because of the discomfort and anxiety produced by the anomie of new situations (i.e., the sense of rootlessness, vulnerability, lack of control). In this case, one may simply try to deny that any real changes have taken place at all, and continue to live as before.

This position will become dysfunctional to the extent that the factors that changed in one's niche require real adaptation. Consider, for example, the middle-aged man recovering from open-heart surgery who experiences as threatening the shift from a "vigorous athlete and aggressive workaholic, admired by many" self, to a "weak and dependent heart patient" self. The role of denial of changes is also well recognized in problems of substance use and interpersonal violence.

4. *Maladaptive Perception Patterns in Characteristic Response:* We have detailed how people appraise and evaluate situations in inherently egocentric ways that are biased toward seeing what they want to see. Healthy persons tend to bring an optimistic, self-enhancing, consistency-seeking bias to bear in their routine ways of interpreting situations and themselves (Taylor & Brown, 1988). Ironically, the perceptions of depressed people are sometimes more accurate than the positively skewed perceptions of the non-depressed (Alloy & Abramson, 1979). Thus, part of what can go wrong is the lack or loss of a positive bias in what people expect to encounter, and thus what they search for, find, and act upon.

By looking at Figure 3.3, we can see that we have two sets of filters that we use to shape our thoughts, feelings, and behaviors. One set is contained in the sensory-perceptual system, where the environmental cues that we will attend to are screened and selected. This level of filtering happens quite automatically; it is almost tautological to say that we are not aware of what we do not see. Yet this filtering often becomes glaringly apparent when someone or something points out what we have been missing (think how often one sees the same make of car that one just purchased, almost as if suddenly a whole lot of them have been released onto the streets). The second set of filters acts during the process of drawing schema-based knowledge into working memory, whereby our momentary interpretations and responses will be largely influenced by the set of schematic knowledge that is currently salient and at work.

While we have discussed these filtering processes more fully in previous chapters, it will be important to determine which ones are most critical when working with clients relative to their needs and change goals. For example, if the sensory-perceptual filter is predominant in a client's interpretation and actions in a situation, then we need to help him or her address different environmental cues (using processes similar to cognitive reframing). If, however, our client sees the situation correctly, but calls up schemas that are inappropriate—that is, he picks up the appropriate cues in a situation, but uses them to access inappropriate schematic knowledge—then our efforts will be better spent helping the client develop new schematic knowledge and/or helping him develop new access pathways to other preexisting schemas. These differences in assessment and intervention approach will be discussed more fully in Chapters 6, 7, and 8.

Let us contrast two people's perceptual patterns relative to the same stimulus: an important upcoming social event. This example can illustrate how both sets of filters—sensory-perceptual and working memory—influence one's characteristic situational perception and appraisal habits described in Figure 3.2.

One person will likely bring a set of positive expectations (e.g., she will get to see lots of friends, joke and gossip, dance and flirt). As the event approaches, she runs mental simulations of herself looking good in her new clothes and having a great time. She may well have made arrangements to go to the party with similarly excited people and will arrive bubbling with enthusiasm. She will interpret the situation as an opportunity to realize her envisioned simulations, will interpret others' behavior in that light, and will likely have a working self-concept dominated by well-elaborated self-schemas of herself as fun and friendly, complete with procedural information of how to go about being fun and friendly. Others will help her sustain this working self-concept by responding in a fun and friendly fashion.

In contrast, another person might bring a set of negative expectations to this same social event (e.g., he expects to be filled with anxiety, hug the wall, and look foolish to others). As the event approaches, he runs mental simulations of himself freezing up when others speak to him, and sees himself having a terrible time. He will notice that nobody talks about going with him to the party (although he assumed nobody would want to go with him, so did not initiate any contacts himself). He interprets the situation as a threat, arrives alone and tight with anxiety, notices how everybody else seems to have somebody to talk to, and has a working self-concept dominated by self-schemas of being shy and socially inept. Others will likely help him sustain this working self-concept by interpreting his distant behavior as arrogance or "squirreliness" and either avoid or tease him.

5. *Maladaptive Problem Solving in Characteristic Response:* Here we are extending the sequence of events in Figure 3.2 to focus on characteristic problem-solving reaction patterns. Imagine the woman described above encountering a problem at the party. Perhaps she found that a group of people she was with began talking about computers—the latest types,

their own computers, what they can do with them, and so forth. She knows nothing of computers and, in fact, has always felt rather intimidated by them. She feels herself becoming intimidated in the moment, and her positive working self-concept and self-confidence begin to unravel.

Her problem-solving response is to reflect that she really wants to be seen positively by this group and that her "fun and flirty" self is not well suited to the present situation. In search for another inroad to her goal, she reflects that one general strategy that has worked in the past in meeting new people is to express an interest in what they are talking about. She reasons that showing interest in this unfamiliar topic will make the friends feel good about being able to show off their knowledge, and also that what she learns will help her out in future similar situations. She then implements general interviewing skills, much like she does with teachers and friends of her parents about things that particularly interest her. The friends respond enthusiastically, and even though she is not interested in all the details they tell her about, she is again back on stable ground as a friendly and interested person.

In contrast, when faced with the same interpersonal problem, the second individual's characteristic response is to feel threatened and then to withdraw. He will likely drift apart from the conversation groups. When he does have an interaction with someone, his anxiety and lack of preparation (e.g., simulations about how to approach a group, how to start and continue conversations) will force him to generate novel responses on the spot. Even if he has active self-schemas consistent with the social goal of affiliation (for example, possible selves of being a trusted friend and of being somebody's boyfriend), these may not have sufficient procedural information to effectively guide his behavior, and thus can be overwhelmed by the more affectively powerful social incompetence schemas. Thus, his self-presentation and social behavior (does he smile, make eye contact, hold his body naturally?) are unlikely to be inviting to others, further verifying his pessimistic beliefs and expectations regarding them, himself, and the likelihood of things ever being different.

6. *Environmental Impediments:* We have stressed throughout that both the physical and the social environment are intrinsically involved in the social-cognitive analysis we are offering here. Specifically, the niche and the self-system are products that emerge from individuals' interactions with their environments. Moreover, those environmental contributors can be thought of as taking both objective and subjective form, the latter speaking to the perceived environment from the perspec-

tive of the individual. Clearly, the environment poses impediments and can facilitate individual goals and changes on multiple levels (e.g., cultural, political, economic, relational).

We will speak in more detail about these in Chapter 6. For our present purposes, we want to underscore three particular features about the environment in relation to niche and self-system functioning. The first has to do with the survival point raised earlier about niches. That is, change in one part of a niche holds implications for change in other parts. Thus, an individual working toward significant changes in her life course or problem-solving capability may be posing a change perceived as threatening to others included within her niche. In some cases, this perception of threat is warranted (such as when assisting an individual to leave an abusive relationship). In other cases, the nature of the proposed change does not signal major or troubling changes for the niche. Nonetheless, others in the niche must change (such as when morning routines must change for a family when the mother takes a promotion that requires a longer commute).

A second element of the environment that can impede client change is to work with a niche that has little stability. If, for example, the client's environment is unstable and constantly undergoing significant change, it is very difficult to conceptualize appropriate goals in the niche and self-system, much less to implement intervention plans. This is part of what makes out-of-home placement so difficult for children and youths. As children go from one foster care situation to another, their niche remains in constant flux. On a less extreme scale, frequent changes in the responses of others or in outcomes of events can impede progress (such as inconsistent boundaries and messages in relationships).

Third, a frequently overlooked yet crucial element in the environment is the nature of feedback. Too often, feedback from the environment is too subtle, unclear, or distant to productively influence change efforts. This includes feedback within the context of the counseling relationship. Thus, lack of stability, clarity, and adequate opportunity stand as essential ways in which things can go wrong, with respect to environmental impediments.

SUMMARY

The cognitive-ecological practice model borrows from some cognitive-behavioral forms of treatment in positing that client's thoughts and behaviors are never seen as irrational since they can be seen to be consistent with what the client knows and understands about himself or herself and the environment (see Mahoney, 1991). At the same time, while many cognitive-behavioral treatments take the position that change comes about by helping clients view their problem behaviors as ultimately irrational (as do Ellis's RET, or Beck's models), the cognitive-ecological approach finds more leverage in the helping process by first showing clients how rational they are, given their life course. Only then does the practitioner discuss with clients whether their response is the one that is truly desired, or one that will get them closer to their desired future selves and niches. Assessment and intervention focus on helping clients understand the internal consistency of their behaviors, and on helping clients evaluate them with respect to their goals. Interventions may then take the form, for example, of skill training (to augment skill deficits for better problem solving), cognitive restructuring (to help the client see more behavioral options for himself in a situation), or advocacy work (to help change structural aspects of the environmental field).

In this chapter, we concluded our description of the major components of the cognitive-ecological model with our description of the roles played by possible selves and possible niches in the process of life goal striving.

It was argued that much of our daily behavior is goal-striving (including goals that are represented by our possible selves and possible niches) and directed at solving problems and tasks that arise in our lives. In the concluding section of this chapter, we enumerate several ways in which problems can arise in daily living, based on times when various components and processes of the cognitive-ecological model go wrong.

In the next chapter we will focus on the social context of the helping relationship and ways in which cognitive and ecological processes influence the practitioner in both useful and potentially problematic ways.

NOTE

1. This was true for a client of one of the authors who did not realize he was dyslexic until he was in high school. He had always assumed he was simply "dumb," and was treated as such by his teachers. He reacted to this by being a troublemaker in class.

Chapter 5

SOCIAL PERCEPTION
AND THE PRACTITIONER

We have emphasized in this book that problems brought to the practitioner can almost always be understood as problems in living, as disruptions to clients' niches, and as exaggerations or distortions of many of the same factors that constitute "normal" social functioning. We have discussed ways in which understanding cognitive-ecological variables can inform various components of our work with clients. We now focus our attention on the client-practitioner interaction process and how an understanding of cognitive-ecological factors can enhance practitioner self-awareness and effectiveness.

As with preceding chapters, we will describe normative cognitive-ecological processes in human behavior. The emphasis will be on social perception; on the processes that influence the ways practitioners go about looking for, detecting, interpreting, and responding to information about clients within the context of their role as professional helpers. We will discuss how these processes translate into both assets and biasing liabilities for the practitioner. Specifically, we will first discuss the paradox of bias—as normal and even essential, yet also potentially endangering sound practice. We will then focus on the effects of social perceptual processes on the following common practice tasks:

1. Impression formation and diagnosis
2. Causal explanations and intervention planning
3. The practitioner/client relationship
4. Monitoring, evaluation, and de-biasing aids

THE PARADOX OF BIAS

In everyday language, the term *bias* has a negative, prejudicial, judgmental tone. We tend to associate bias with issues of ignorance, closed-mindedness, and vested interest. Such associations are not only erroneous, they are seriously misleading. They incline the practitioner to confuse normative and necessary sources of bias with inadequacies in one's principles, caring, or clinical skill.

Exasperating as it may sometimes be, bias is simply inherent to human functioning and social interaction. As we have discussed throughout this book, we would be socially paralyzed without our biases. Imagine entering a session with a client with no prior expectations regarding how people should behave, regarding what attributes form meaningful characteristics (e.g., regarding personalities, strengths, or dysfunctions), or regarding the goals or interventions that are likely to be effective. Where would one begin? On what basis could one sort out the information? Particularly in today's practice where time efficiency is so strongly emphasized, how could we possibly manage?

To contend realistically and effectively with the extraordinary panoply of information, we must rely on assumptions, inferences, heuristics, and habits (see Ingram, 1986; Nurius & Gibson, 1991). In fact, clinical judgment is our single most precious tool in practice. Yet it is also this very tool—and its associated observational, inferential, and reasoning processes—that can insidiously and seriously compromise ethical and effective practice.

Let us now look at some specific ways in which core dimensions of practice tend to be susceptible to social perceptual bias. We will first examine this susceptibility in terms of specific practice tasks, and then will identify some general de-biasing aids.

IMPRESSION FORMATION AND ASSESSMENT

We previously made the point about the double-edged effect of expectations; that is, they help us to be on the lookout for needed information, yet by so doing, they direct our attention away from other information that might be more accurate or, in some respects, more useful. We previously discussed how we develop schemas about ourselves. In the process of learning we also come to develop schemas about types of people, situations, and phenomena. For example, we develop schemas for what it means to be "honest," "resourceful," "well-adjusted," "rigid," "depressed," and "manipulative," and we draw upon these schemas for labeling and interpreting others as well as ourselves. Based on these schemas, we develop a host of expectations associated with the attribute in question: which other attributes will be encountered and which will not, why the person or situation is the way it is, how successful or unsuccessful our interactions are likely to be, and so on.

In the same way that we develop and draw upon schemas and scripts regarding the domains and activities of our personal lives, we undertake the same processes with respect to our professional lives. Thus, we use scripts that we have developed when ordering a meal at a restaurant, and also when beginning an intake interview or a mental status exam. We weave together schemas to build implicit personality theories: theories, for example, about how career military people have been trained to be very hierarchical and rules-oriented, which leads to their (assumed) rigidity and authoritarianism. Implicit personality theories, for example, focus us to expect different behavior from accountants, exotic dancers, and radical activists, and to resist inconsistent information, such as "flamboyant accountants," "studious exotic dancers," or "shy radical activists."

The problem vis-à-vis practice judgment is not that we have a priori knowledge structures about different groups of people. It is indeed essential to have aids to help us effectively organize and interpret the deluge of information in practice encounters. In fact, one sign of expertise is having a growing mental library of valid and diagnostically useful schemas and scripts.

The problem lies in the mindless way in which we tend to use these social perceptual resources. As vastly capable as the mind is, normal cognitive processing does have inherent limited capacity—often referred to as "bounded rationality" (Simon, 1979). We noted in our discussion of human memory that we are bounded by how many separate units of information we can handle mentally at any given moment. We are also bounded by our capacity to handle multiple cues in multidimensional analyses, tending instead to rely on simple, linear strategies of information processing and judgment (Wiggins & Hoffman, 1968; Slovic & Lichtenstein, 1971).

For example, when we observe that the majority of adults who physically or sexually abuse children either witnessed or experienced abuse themselves as children, we are extremely inclined to infer a simple, linear cause-effect link: that witnessing or experiencing abuse as a child causes one to then become an abuser. Once established, we seldom question this understanding. Thus, we are unlikely to search for alternative hypotheses, and we do not ask why the majority of people who witness or experience abuse do not go on to become abusers themselves (Straus, Gelles, & Steinmetz, 1980). What are the exacerbating, ameliorating, or buffering factors involved in this interactive set of effects? In short, we are "hard wired" to form impressions very quickly, to search for what we expect, to overlook or misread cues for which we do not have schemas, and to resist challenge or change of our schemas (Nisbett & Ross, 1980).

Within this framework, consider the double-edged effect of task requirements in shaping the form of clinical impressions. For example, by its very definition, task "lenses" of observation and interpretation are oriented toward getting to the heart of the client's presenting problem. After all, that problem, in some form, is what has brought client and practitioner together. Yet, in spite of a value stance toward a balanced, cognitive-ecological orientation, we are often far more focused on interpreting behaviors in terms of deficits and pathology (versus, for example, looking equally vigorously for evidence of normality, strength, and perhaps even a lack of need for professional services). This orientation is typically reflected in the forms we use to record our interpretations and in the structures for how we discuss cases with our colleagues. For example, practitioners who appear to be able to detect greater pathology tend to be accorded higher professional status, the underlying inference being that seeing what others do not see is a sign of professional sophistication (Sarbin, Taft, & Bailey, 1960; Stahler & Rappaport, 1986). You can examine your own assessment forms to determine whether they are constructed in a fashion to help direct your attention in a balanced fashion to factors such as client strengths, lack of dysfunction, or needs beyond the purview of the agency.

Given (a) the inherent limitations of the amount of information we can deal with at any one moment, (b) our inclination to infer linear causal relationships ("if A and B occur sequentially, then A must cause B"), and (c) the typical stresses and pressures of professional work (e.g., time pressures, insufficient case information, forms and procedures that are heavily reliant on categorization approaches to assessment), it is little wonder that the representativeness heuristic exerts such a tremendous influence in our work. Heuristics can be thought of as cognitive shortcuts or guidelines; the *representativeness heuristic* involves judgments of how likely it is that an individual is a member of a particular group (e.g., a diagnostic category) or how likely a given attribute or outcome can be explained by a particular set of prior events (e.g., by interpreting certain patterns in the client's family of origin). In other words, to classify people and events, we match them against images and hypotheses we hold. Therefore, it is difficult for us to see what we do not already have some familiarity with, and we tend to group together factors that seem related, and to resist putting together factors that seem in conflict. (For example, it sounds too much like a bad B-movie plot for a tabletop dancer to be a senior reference librarian by day).

Across the various domains of direct practice, some form of taxonomy or classification system is almost invariably applied, whether referring to a standard one such as the *Diagnostic and Statistical Manual for Mental Disorders* (the DSM III-R, soon to be DSM-IV) or to a homegrown (agency or practitioner-developed) framework. Diagnosis is a prime example of where the representativeness heuristic comes into play, via a similarity or prototype-matching process. This process is one where the client's observed characteristics are compared to those of prototypical examples from a diagnostic category (Genero & Cantor, 1987). For example, to determine whether the client in one's office is manic-depressive, one calls up an image of a prototypical manic-depressive to serve as the standard against which the client's behavior is judged.

Yet, each category is a fuzzy set: The center of the category depicts people who exactly fit, while areas closer to the periphery depict those who still have enough of the defining characteristics to be classified within that category, but are really not quite on center and perhaps could also be placed at the periphery of other categories, such as chronic undifferentiated schizophrenia, in this case (Salovey & Turk, 1990).

One result of a prototype-matching model is that it makes for very heterogeneous groups within the same category, and a considerable degree of subjectivity in deciding where to draw the line, or where to diagnostically place an individual. Then, once a person or event has been classified, the diagnosis hugely influences subsequent information gathering, since we tend to ask questions to confirm our diagnosis rather than ask questions about rival possibilities (Snyder, 1987). This prototype-matching, or schema-driven, model of categorization influences not only the practitioner, but also the client who dutifully responds to cues regarding what is and is not relevant. The client, therefore, reinforces or fulfills the practitioner's hypothesis, regardless of whether it is truly valid for her or him. Parallel processes unfold, relative to use of other prototypes we hold about characteristics of people, situations, and phenomena.

CAUSAL EXPLANATIONS
AND INTERVENTION PLANNING

In this section we will focus on some naturally occurring aspects of social perception that may particularly influence practitioners' causal explanations in the context of assessment and subsequent intervention planning. One very broad-based factor concerns where we first look for information and explanations for what we consider to be atypical or problematic behaviors (e.g., are we more inclined to begin looking toward person attribute factors or at environmental factors?). Research on the fundamental attribution error applies here. The *fundamental attribution error* refers to the marked tendency to first focus on person-centered, dispositional factors in attributing causality for others' behavior, particularly if that behavior is considered abnormal in some way. Ironically, however, we are far more inclined to look toward external explanations for our own "deviant" or problematic behavior. For example, when shy, mild-mannered David Garabedian suddenly stoned to death a woman he barely knew, the immediate attributions were that of personal malice or mental illness. Further investigation uncovered a strong alternative attribution, that of temporary brain poisoning from the intense insecticide chemicals he was exposed to. In a jury trial this alternative explanation was rejected, and David was convicted of first-degree murder (Restak, 1988).

Far less dramatic examples are, of course, plentiful. When we notice someone behaving oddly, we tend to think that there is something odd about him; that is, to explain his deviation from the norm in individual deviance terms. The structure of the DSM is a reflection of this person-centered orientation, since it relies so heavily on factors related to individual health, character, and behavior (Franklin, 1987; Kutchins & Kirk, 1986). Recognition of the contributing role of stressors is an important feature built into the DSM, but normative reliance upon only those sections that characterize mental disorder (axes I and II) renders information about external contributors virtually untapped. In all fairness, the DSM was developed as a classification system of mental disorders, and not as a comprehensive assessment guide to all factors that develop and sustain problems of functioning. What is perhaps more indicative of our tendency to attribute dysfunction to personal characteristics is the lack of tools for assessing environments or situations that have stature and use comparable to tools for assessing personal pathology, such as the DSM (III-R and IV), the MMPI, or the mental status exam. This person-focused orientation is often exacerbated by the skewed and limited amount of information on which clinical judgments must often be made. For example, as practitioners we typically have only small samples of information (e.g., of client behaviors, or of the behavior of significant others) on which to base important judgments and generalizations. We are therefore virtually forced to fill in the blanks with inferences drawn from our own schemas and theories.

The representativeness heuristic influences causal interpretations in addition to influencing initial impressions. This is one mechanism through which preexisting causal theories or theoretical orientations exert influence (Tversky & Kahneman, 1973, 1974). That is, we tend to judge others in terms of how representative they are to a particular prototype or stereotype, and tend to be receptive to causal explanations consistent with these preconceived images and beliefs. It is important to keep in mind that, to a certain degree, reliance upon stereotypes and preconceived beliefs about causal relationships is not only healthy but essential. Again, imagine if we constantly had to enter situations and interactions with absolutely no hunches or notions about how the world worked, and what leads to what.

The problem is not in the tendency per se, but that important distinctions are often overlooked or discounted because of this social perceptual factor. That is, we are inclined to find explanatory factors consistent with our preexisting beliefs, in large part because these are the only factors that we are searching for (thus we overlook competing or incongruent factors) and because we attempt to interpret ambiguous information in ways that make sense to us (i.e., that fit the explanatory model we are using to bring interpretive order of what would otherwise be a jumble of factors).

We noted earlier the example of presuming that history of child abuse is causative of becoming an abuser, which ignores the base rate data that the majority of abuse victims do not become abusers, and that not all abusers have abuse histories. By not paying equal attention to these competing and qualifying factors, we risk premature closure of the inquiry process and we miss important information that would significantly alter our case interpretation and intervention planning. Because social perceptual forces, such as the representativeness heuristic, are part of normal human reasoning, we develop and draw upon preconceived notions about very basic attributes, such as clients' gender, race, and verbal ability. Again, this is not a problem per se, but it is a problem when these preconceptions result in differential diagnosis, problem attribution, therapeutic style, and intervention directions (see Cousins, Fisher, Glisson, & Kameoka, 1985; Franklin, 1985).

Another important social perceptual process, closely related to our searching for intuitively appealing and simplified causal theories, is the influence of personal experiences and epistemology on our understanding of events (Unger, Draper, & Pendergrass, 1986). Our personal histories predispose us to draw upon our own memories and experiences to interpret other people's actions and intentions (Green, 1982); we use ourselves as a referent or barometer for understanding others. It is a normal and understandable tendency that we use what we know best as an anchor in predicting and understanding the world at large. It is also understandable that this tendency is particularly marked if our clients' experiences or attributes are seen as similar to our own; for example, when a recently divorced practitioner believes she knows just what a similar age client initiating a divorce feels and needs, it could be because she's been there.

Our life experiences do provide us with extraordinarily useful tools to augment empathy and understanding. Yet they also incline us to become self-centered versus client-centered when parallels lead us to assume that we are a valid referent for others' experiences. It takes a concerted, mindful effort to override this blurring of self-centeredness versus client-centeredness, a task we will discuss more fully at the end of this chapter. We also take this up again in our discussion of "normality" in the following chapter.

Thus far we have focused on several social perceptual factors as they influence some of the earliest points of contact with clients through initial observations and assessments. Let us now consider intervention planning and some of the social perceptual factors that influence it.

Although a host of factors influence intervention planning, two warrant particular attention: anchoring effects and the availability heuristic. *Anchoring* refers to excessive weighing of early information that subsequently serves as a template against which further information is judged. For example, if we discover early in an interview that our low-energy client is sleeping 12 hours a night and has lost several pounds unintentionally over the past month, we might tend to hear subsequent information within an inference that this client is depressed.

These impressions tend to be generated very early, often within the first several minutes of contact. This inclination reflects in part our inherent need to reduce uncertainty and to have some theory with which to proceed in figuring out the situation before us. Rather than tentative hunches or theories, however, these early impressions often feel like factual observations and have proven resistant to change in the presence of new, contradictory information, and in the absence of clear behavioral manifestations after the initial impression was formed (Ross, Lepper, & Hubbard, 1975).

The *availability heuristic* refers to how easily information is brought to mind, how easily activated it is from memory, and how easily it is constructed in imagination. Client information that is particularly distinctive, vivid, or personally significant to the observer tends to be most accessible. This is not surprising: Information that stands out tends to be more memorable. Ironically, this suggests that information that is actually most typical or representative, or that is not particularly interesting to the observer, tends to pale by comparison and to recede in memory and awareness (Tversky & Kahneman, 1974). Thus, our most atypical and nonnormative, yet most vivid and distinctive, memories are likely to be easier to recall, and to recall with greater detail and feeling due to the availability heuristic.

An additional factor that increases availability is the recentness with which we have been exposed to something. We are more susceptible, for example, to see in our clients the problems or patterns that we recently heard about while attending a stimulating workshop, or because we just saw a dramatic case covered by the media, or through a case presentation in our work setting. In the same way that we see everywhere the same model of car that we have just purchased, we tend to see the wounded child within our clients after attending a "healing the wounded child" workshop, particularly if this holds special appeal to us or was marked by salient examples or experiences. Thus, to the extent that availability of information from past experiences influences our thinking about present clients, the availability heuristic will shape—in both positive and negative ways—what we use to anchor and guide our perceptions, interpretations, and final judgments both about what interventions are needed and about what outcomes to anticipate.

Consequences of anchoring and availability, therefore, are to incline the practitioner to remember and rely on client information that is obtained early and that is exceptional. One risk for intervention planning is to orient the practitioner to problems, goals, and intervention plans that may be poorly representative of the client's actual needs. A second risk is to incline the practitioner toward areas of life and thinking that may misrepresent the client (e.g., if we start down a path based on a premature impression, we run the risk of missing information more fully representative of the client's primary needs).

To be sure, there are also many useful features and consequences of the factors described in this section. Our causal theories and personal experiences, for example, provide a richness to our understanding and compassion for our clients' experiences. Our causal theories and personal experiences help us zero in on the most relevant factors and contribute to our practice wisdom and expertise. These information-processing heuristics both serve us well and provide potential pitfalls. Indeed, this contributes to what makes the professional practice role so difficult. It requires detecting and mindfully managing the processes that not only serve us well but also introduce risk.

PRACTITIONER/CLIENT RELATIONSHIP

A fundamental factor that each of us brings to the professional relationship, as both client and practitioner, is our *model of helping.* There are few, if any, direct parallels between the professional therapeutic relationship and other relationships in people's lives. Yet, because we are "hard-wired" as humans to call up existing schemas to help us make sense of new situations, we will act and react in the professional relationship in ways consistent with how we act and react in various other interpersonal situations. There are many points of overlap between the professional relationship and other types of relationships, such as with one's minister, teacher, physician, boss, members of one's family, friends, co-workers, and even media models of professional helping (such as those portrayed in the movie *Ordinary People,* the old "Bob Newhart Show," and talk show psychotherapists).

Transference and countertransference phenomena can be explained in this way (although a psychoanalytic interpretation differs as to presumed causes of these phenomena). That is, clients may act toward us as a child does to a parent because the parent-child relationship is one available model (schema) that allows them to make sense of and respond to certain cues in the professional relationship (such as the power dynamics, the self-disclosure encouraged, and the client's need for approval so common in the professional relationship). Similarly, we may act toward a male client, for example, as if he is a younger brother because something in the interaction triggers related memories, and, knowingly or not, we draw upon our set of "younger brother" schemas to help us make sense of the cues we are receiving. Our relationship and experiences from many domains of our lives form the basis of our operating models regarding who is what kind of person and what is supposed to happen in certain situations and relationships. Moreover, rather than the helping or therapeutic relationship, there are actually numerous forms that will unfold, depending on the nature of the setting, on the type of problem, and on the responsibilities and constraints of the situation.

As will be described in Chapter 8, the degree of discrepancy between the practitioner's and the client's models of helping can be a powerful factor in the type of alliance they are able to build together (Brickman, Rabinowitz, Karuza, Coates, Cohn, & Kidder, 1982). Many practitioners, for example, operate from a principle of client empowerment, of helping clients obtain a broader perspective and become more effective in managing their own lives. Yet an empowerment perspective places considerable responsibility on the individual client for solutions. If clients hold a different view—for example, drawing upon experiences with authoritative medical and legal helping professionals who provide clear directives about what to do—the risks are high for misunderstanding and frustrated expectations.

The professional relationship is also influenced by the amount of interpersonal attraction, based on perceived similarities, between client and practitioner. For example, similarities in learning or thinking styles (e.g., Kolb, 1985) and in personality dispositions and preferences (e.g., Myers & McCaulley, 1985) have been indicated as influencing perceived empathy, helpfulness, and relationship satisfaction.

It is ironic that potential problems can stem from our inclination to view similarities in others as attractive. The first is that similarities between practitioners and clients may make the task of learning new approaches to problem solving and reframing situations more difficult than when practitioners and clients bring different approaches to the relationship (Kruzich, van Soest, & Sullivan, 1990). In our supervisory relationships, for example, it will feel comfortable and affirming to work with someone who sees things very similarly to the way we do. Yet, this very similarity reduces the opportunity for exposure to differing schemas, styles, models, and habits, and may incline us toward groupthink and assumption that a particular approach is the only right way.

A second potential problem with perceiving similarities between practitioners and clients is the inadvertent inclination of practitioners to shape clients in their own image. This involves a tendency to view success in terms of how closely clients come to look like us, to share (or at least express) our values, perspectives, and goals. Evidence from early clinical research has demonstrated, for example, that treatment goals were often defined as the conversion of the client's value and belief systems to that of the practitioner (Bandura, Lipsher, & Miller, 1960; Rosenthal, 1955; Welkowitz, Cohen, & Ortmeyer, 1967), with clients reporting and sometimes constructing dream material that was consistent with the practitioner's orientation (Whitman, Kramer, & Baldridge, 1963, as cited in Salovey & Turk, 1990).

In this vein, Snyder and Thompsen (1988) note several inherent structural and motivation factors that may serve to set the stage for practitioners shaping clients in their own image. Examples of these factors include the following.

1. Clients have typically entered into a relationship with the practitioner to receive help with a problem, making them susceptible to accept hypotheses, prognoses, and prescriptions generated by the practitioner as legitimate.

2. There is typically a large differential between client and practitioner in their relative power and expertise, inclining the client to seek the approval of the practitioner.

3. Due to the above factors and the high subjectivity of the phenomena under discussion in clinical work, there is a built-in tendency for the client to begin filtering information she will report in a fashion that appears consistent with what the practitioner expects, finds important, and reacts to in a reinforcing manner.

A final set of factors we will address concerns the effects of mood on practitioner memory, judgments, and responsiveness. Discussions of the effects of emotion on the professional relationship have involved book-length treatments. Here, we will limit our discussion to the effects of mood on practitioners' information-processing within the context of clinical, practice-related judgment. For a more thorough discussion, the interested reader is referred to Singer (1988) and Isen (1984).

The effects of mood on clinical information-processing is similar to its effects on other types of human information-processing, although perhaps amplified by the affective intensity that often characterizes clinical material and interactions. One effect is the tendency for practitioners to notice and respond to information that is consistent with their own mood state (Bower, Gilligan, & Montiero, 1981; Natale & Hantas, 1982; Salovey & Rodin, 1985). Salovey and Turk (1990), for example, tell the tale of "Dr. Doakes," a psychotherapist in private practice, whose mood and subsequent practice-related memories, interpretations, and decisions closely matched his fluctuating moods in response to personal life events (winning a local lottery, paying his child's orthodontic bill, and receiving his income tax return). It is hardly noteworthy that mood affects thinking and can thus serve as a double-edged sword for practitioners. What may be less evident is the tendency of mood to cause a shift in the focus of one's attention to oneself. Thus, the practitioner inadvertently becomes more self-centered versus client-centered as a function of mood, and different types of mood affect practitioners' motivation to help in different ways. For example, individuals feeling joyful are inclined to offer help to others when the joy is self-focused, but resist or withhold helping when the joy stems from empathizing with the other's happiness (Rosenbaum, Salovey, & Hargis, 1981; Salovey, 1986). The reverse tends to be true for sadness: Helping is not very likely when the sadness comes from the practitioner's own experience, whereas empathic sorrow does motivate a helping response (Thompson, Cowan, & Rosenbaum, 1980, as cited in Salovey & Turk, 1988).

As quickly as it becomes evident, the self-system plays an extremely powerful role in the inference, reasoning, and response processes of professional practice. Again, this is generally well known, as reflected in our "effective use of self." What is less well understood is how much and how subtly our a priori beliefs, expectations, organizing frameworks, personal needs, and current mood influence these processes. As we have indicated throughout this chapter, this double edge of social perception—in this case of the "intrusiveness of the self"—holds both very positive and very negative consequences. In the following section, we will consider some aids to help tip the balance toward supporting its positive effects while managing and avoiding those that are negative.

MONITORING, EVALUATION, AND DE-BIASING AIDS

In several respects, the potential sources of error and bias related to ongoing client monitoring and outcome evaluations are a function of many of the factors described earlier in this chapter. In other words, later observations, inferences, and judgments flow from those established in early stages of the helping process. And, as we have repeatedly stressed, these tendencies are generally extensions of normative tendencies that can serve as both resources and risks in the context of professional helping. Let us briefly revisit examples of what this includes.

1. We have a tendency to search for information consistent with diagnostic impressions and to overlook or discount contradictory material. For example, note the powerful influence of diagnoses, such as histrionic personality, or labels, such as ACOA, on the questions we pose to clients, and on how we discuss the client in supervision.

2. We tend to interpret information in a fashion that confirms a priori beliefs and theoretical orientations. For example, if we approach a case from a family systems perspective, we are highly prone to search for information to support that perspective, and reluctant to actively search for information that suggests different interpretations.

3. We are at risk of creating a behavioral confirmation of our expectations by actively eliciting and reinforcing preferred or at least expected speech and behaviors. For example, clients may unwittingly contribute to our self-fulfilling prophecies by answering the questions posed to them, by volunteering information on closely related themes, and by responding to our verbal and nonverbal signals regarding what we deem significant. The human service helping role may amplify normal tendencies for clients to follow the lead of the practitioner by relying more heavily on the practitioner's judgment than might be the case in other types of relationships.

4. Both collectively and individually, we are inclined to judge outcomes as successful when the client has made a significant conversion toward the practitioner's values, outlook, and style of living. For example, practitioners are trained to develop perspectives regarding what constitutes normality, healthy choices, and ethical ways of behaving in the world, and to help clients with problems in living or with distorted perceptions by shaping them toward thoughts and actions more consistent with these images (see Meichenbaum, 1977).

In this section we will discuss general guidelines for how to better manage and direct the inherent biasing factors we have described. We will discuss the need for:

1. an efficacious perspective
2. use of disconfirmatory query and inference strategies
3. de-automatizing decision making

4. decreasing reliance on memory
5. triangulation and evaluating evidence

Efficacious Perspective

Evidence to date indicates that practitioner bias is not significantly reduced by simple awareness of the risk of bias, by admonitions to not be biased, or by good intentions to not function in a biased manner (Bransford, Sherwood, Vye, & Reiser, 1986). Like most things, goal achievement in this arena requires a concerted effort toward revising skills, habits, and the supports that we rely on. In the ongoing process of revising some of our natural social perception tendencies in the context of our professional helping role, we will repeatedly entertain two key questions: (a) To what extent do we see any given guideline or tool as being effective towards minimizing bias and error? and (b) To what extent do we see ourselves as being capable of effectively implementing the guideline or tool?

These distinctions reflect what Bandura (1977) calls *outcome-efficacy expectations* and *self-efficacy expectations*. These expectations are useful in helping us determine whether personal barriers to efficacy are information-related (e.g., "What are the tools and guidelines I need?") or skill- and attitude-related (e.g., "How can I become more accomplished or comfortable with using these tools?").

An additional efficacy dimension relates to the client's participation, particularly in the more vulnerable points within the helping process described here (e.g., assessment, goal selection, and intervention planning). One way that information-processing errors become real problems is by keeping the client outside the loop. It is imperative to find ways for clients to have significant input into decisions about their own work, and to create opportunities to equalize the practitioner-client relationship—by using a participatory model of helping, and by using explicit power and information equalizers, such as contracts (see Egan, 1990, for a broader discussion of helping as a social influence process). We discuss the use of contracts more completely in Chapter 7.

In short, an efficacious perspective is one where practitioners (a) recognize cues or risk conditions for error or negative bias, (b) are informed about aids they judge to be effective in reducing these risks, (c) see themselves as capable of effectively incorporating these aids into their practice, and (d) then actively do so. We would expand this perspective to include deliberate efforts to include clients in these considerations and efforts. Part of this reasoning stems from our value base and part from pragmatism. Pragmatically speaking, the more that the covert processes of inference, theorizing, reasoning, judgment, and decision making are made explicit and overt by discussions with the client and/or appropriate others, the better the chances that gaps, presumptions, and problems can be detected and corrected. Moreover, because the processes of bias and error are inherently human, this collaborative stance can provide important modeling for how clients can anticipate, detect, and correct similar processes in their own lives and change efforts.

We will discuss models of helping more fully in Chapter 8. We briefly encapsulate this work here by saying that while responsibility for the cause of bias may not rest with the practitioner per se (since it is inherent to all human reasoning), responsibility for the solutions does rest with the individual practitioner, although we also believe that change is needed at multiple levels in social agencies—such as how supervision is conducted and how agency forms and procedures are constructed and used. Managing bias requires that declarative knowledge about the problems and remedies for bias must be transformed into procedural knowledge about how to implement preventative and remedial aids. Furthermore, these aids must be so well practiced that they become part of the practitioner's professional habits and patterns (see Chapter 3). The prescriptions we offer are designed to help build these skills.

Disconfirmatory Strategies

Perhaps the single most prevalent theme we have discussed here is the many ways in which we all seek to confirm our sense of reality—our schemas—about ourselves, others, and how the world operates. Therefore, the importance of explicitly generating and evaluating alternative hypotheses of reality becomes critically important. By making explicit what our hypotheses are about a given client or presenting problem, we are alerted to our social perception anchors and assumptions and are in a better position to anticipate our subsequent steps, such as which schemas are more likely to be activated. As noted above, this insight is a necessary but not entirely sufficient step.

Purposefully pursuing and evaluating competing hypotheses is a critical next step. From a cognitive-ecological perspective, seldom is any single cause adequate to explain the effects that we see in the form of a client's problem in living. Therefore, competing hypotheses really should be seen as contributing hypotheses. When we observe a woman staying in an abusive relationship, we may be inclined to attribute her actions to a self-defeating personality. Competing and contributing hypotheses may be that she is protecting loved ones who will be threatened if she leaves, that she has not had the input necessary to define her experience in terms of abuse, or that she is impoverished with respect to economic and interpersonal supports and feels trapped in her situation. Again, we must train ourselves to look for the set of factors in clients' niches that contributes to the presenting problem. As we will discuss in Chapter 6, the presenting problem must be understood within the context of the niche, as both its product and its contributor.

Given an inherent tendency to attribute atypical or deviant behavior to the person rather than to the situation (through the fundamental attribution error), our initial hypotheses or theories will often be heavily slanted toward attributing causation to the person. This has even been found true among those adhering to ecological perspectives (see Davis, 1984). Thus, the competing and contributing hypotheses that we generate should explicitly include situational factors to embed the problem in the client's niche.

This is a place where colleagues can serve as useful de-biasing supports. Most practice settings have built-in opportunities and requirements for contact with others regarding the management of cases—supervision and group case consultation being common examples. These should be structured to provide practitioners with opportunities to generate and consider rival and contributing hypotheses concerning clinical and other aspects of helping behavior. Since an individual may draw upon some of the same biasing aspects of social perception even in self-interrogation, the use of others, particularly others who think somewhat differently, may be the best way to provide challenging and corrective information.

De-automatizing Decision Making

Closely related to the above is slowing down and de-automatizing reasoning and decision-making processes. We discussed this earlier, using the framework of increasing mindfulness (Langer & Piper, 1987). The challenge is not one of de-automatizing now and then, but of developing habits of de-automatization. This may sound like a contradiction in terms—that is, once something becomes a habit, will it not necessarily become automatic? Concretely, what it means is building tools and techniques of self-interrogation into one's everyday methods of practice. This becomes a self-vigilance that stems not so much from depending on one's good character or intentions as an open and reflective practitioner, but from purposefully building mindfulness tools and techniques into the foundation of our reasoning and decision-making patterns.

One example of these tools and techniques involves the routine use of strategies to disconfirm our hypotheses. Questions to ask oneself to this end include, "If I were wrong about my hunch, how would I know?" "If I were to look at this from 'X' point of view, what additional information would I need to know?" "I'm feeling quite invested in my thinking about this case; why is that and how might that be limiting my assessment and intervention planning?" "I'm feeling defensive (or angry) in reaction to reasonable questions about how I've interpreted this case; am I seeing questions about my interpretive framework as threats to my professional worth?"

Observing self-interrogation in others is important as are frequent opportunities to try out these skills oneself. This might include asking supervisors or colleagues to think aloud about their formulations and predictions about a case. It could include routinely incorporating disconfirmatory strategies into supervision and case conferences (such as, "You've got some leads here consistent with the direction you're taking, but I also notice some pieces that don't seem to fit so well with that interpretation. Could you tell us more about them?"). Building prompts for self-interrogation into intake forms and case-recording norms is another effective strategy to gather more comprehensive or balanced information. As an exercise, take a look at the forms routinely used in one's work with clients and consider ways they could be revised to help enhance self-vigilance and promote balanced information and judgments.

Decreasing Reliance on Memory

Take a look at a typical case file. Depending on the service setting, it is likely to be fairly thick, containing a multitude of forms, inventories, notes, and communiques from various sources. It is really quite remarkable how much information practitioners must gather, sort through, weigh and synthesize, summarize and report. This chapter has illustrated that we draw upon a multitude of heuristics to deal with this extraordinary task.

This chapter has also illustrated that the more we rely solely on our memories, the more at risk for bias and error we become. For example, Arkes and his associates (Arkes, Dawes, & Christensen, 1986; Arkes & Harkness, 1980) found that symptoms consistent with a diagnosis, but which were not exhibited by a client, tend to be remembered later as having actually been exhibited, and that inferences based on theoretical perspectives tend to worsen rather than strengthen clinical prediction relative to the use of external sources of information. Thus, one very good, yet often overlooked, de-biasing aid involves greater reliance on the information already gathered through the myriad of forms, tests, and narratives contained in client files. For example, aids such as paper-and-pencil instruments and the organizational capabilities of computers can help us greatly with what we humans are not strong at, such as reliable recall from vast stores of information, and visual displays of patterns of clinically relevant events and interrelationships (Brower & Mutschler, 1985; Brower & Nurius, 1985; Nurius, 1992).

Pragmatically, what might such memory aids look like? Again, look over the forms routinely used in your professional practice activities. How balanced are these with respect to the type of information gathered? How much do they include the client's perspective? How easily do they relate to other case information to help verify inferred patterns or hypotheses? Paperwork can be made more relevant for interventions by explicitly linking it to specific clinical decisions we routinely make: building in prompts to help us not overlook important assessment factors; using rating scales to minimize dichotomizing people and to better differentiate degrees of functioning; incorporating graphic aids to help motivate and empower clients as they oversee and learn from their progress (Nurius & Hudson, 1993).

This also suggests that our client files should contain only information that is relevant and useful for clinical decision making. It is more often the case that material is collected because "it's always been done that way," or in order to satisfy a stakeholder, such as a third-party funding source. It might be more efficient to actually have two files on each client, or to have separate sections or modules of case information: one specifically for the clinical process and for clinical decisions, and another that might more accurately be called an administrative file, containing materials necessary for the administration of the practice setting. In reality, information related to these two arenas is neither independent of nor irrelevant to one another. What we are focusing on here are practical factors in how to manage case information in ways that meet all needs of the service setting with as little cost and intrusion to direct service needs as possible.

Other examples of the use of clinical records to de-bias decision making include use of audio and videotapes (as well as videodisks, database management, and decision support software) to help monitor and record the client-practitioner interactions. Videodisks combine videotaped sequences (simulated or real) with interactive input from the viewer. For example, a training videodisk can present a family interaction sequence, which can be stopped at a point to ask viewers how they would respond to the situation. Depending on the response typed in at a keyboard, the video sequence could continue along one of several lines, querying and responding to viewers' input as the sequence progresses (see Reinoehl & Shapiro, 1986). Database management software aids in pulling together information. This could involve pulling separate pieces of information from one case into a single report, or pulling together the same information (e.g., diagnoses, post-treatment functioning, case dispositions) across different clients to examine trends in a particular setting (see McCullough, Farrell, & Longabaugh, 1986).

Triangulation and Evaluating Evidence

We are using the term *triangulation* to mean the synthesis of multiple sources of information to form a clinical picture. When multiple sources are used, one can then ask whether high consistency and coherence exist, or whether there are apparent discrepancies which raise questions. Part of triangulation involves simply making explicit the information that is already collected by the practitioner (e.g., observations of client's affect and nonverbal cues, or judgments regarding the stage of development of the client-practitioner relationship). Triangulation also involves systematically pursuing multiple perspectives and indicators, and knowing how to weigh and interpret them once they are collected.

A number of books describe how to obtain data from multiple sources (see Barlow, Hayes, & Nelson, 1984; Cormier & Cormier, 1991). The discussion of what to do with the information has been discussed less frequently. How do we weigh contradictory evidence, for example? Or, given the inherent tendencies discussed earlier to actively search for, elicit, and interpret information consistent with our schemas, what are some conceptual tools we might use to help us more accurately evaluate the evidence we have available?

One tool comes from using our training in one domain and applying it to another. This is, in fact, part of why we have written this book. In every problem area, there are theory and knowledge specific to that area that are important to guiding practice reasoning. Yet, there is also information related to normative social functioning that needs to be incorporated into this practice reasoning, and we have articulated some of that functioning in a cognitive-ecological framework. There are other theory and knowledge bases that would similarly need to be synthesized, such as that regarding life span development and biology.

Another tool that helps us handle evidence obtained from various sources is to explicitly synthesize into practice knowledge the methods used in research and evaluation. Suppose that you are working with parents who are clearly exasperated with their youngster; they see him as being "all over the place" and as "really just trying to get us mad." As one looks at all the factors, is this a case of poor parenting and boundary setting, of attention deficit disorder, of child neglect and possibly abuse, of a combination of factors? Only a broad-based assessment strategy that taps the child's cognitive and emotional functioning, his conduct at school, parental perceptions and behavior, and family interaction patterns within the natural environment, combined with practitioner observations and theories, will help to confirm or disconfirm these hypotheses.

A third tool to help us evaluate evidence from multiple sources can come from our training in statistical principles (Fong, Krantz, & Nisbett, 1986). For example, understanding probability theory and base rate information increases the accuracy of risk assessment, whereas understanding correlations can reduce the common error of inferring a causal relation when only co-occurrence exists (important since these erroneous causal inferences prematurely terminate the search for true underlying causal and/or mediating factors).

Consider, for example, the important professional practice skill of risk assessment. Accurate assessments of risk entail knowing what information to gather and how to weigh this information. As if one needed a reminder of our generally poor abilities to reason statistically, try answering the question below (from Schwartz, Gorry, Kassirer, & Essig, 1973, as reported in Arkes, 1981):

> Assume that a test for cancer was available that has the following characteristics: (1) the test is positive in 95 of 100 patients with cancer, and (2) the test is negative in 95 of 100 patients without cancer. Assume also that an average of 5 people in a population of 1,000 have previously undetected cancer. The problem is posed as follows: If the test described is

given to a randomly selected patient from the population, who has not previously been diagnosed with cancer, and the test is positive, what is the probability that the patient actually has cancer? (1973, p. 467)

The great majority of people who were asked this question (in this study, physicians and medical students) said either 50% probability or greater. The correct answer is 10%.[1] Other studies of calculating risk assessments (e.g., on aggression against others, and of suicide) have found similar degrees of error—sometimes overestimating, sometimes underestimating actual occurrences. The potential dangers associated with being chronically poor risk assessors quickly become clear.

In short, understanding basic statistical and probability principles helps round out the total picture and helps the practitioner more effectively sort through, weigh, and interpret the various kinds of evidence that are part and parcel to professional practice (see Arkes, 1981; Arnoult & Anderson, 1988; Faust, 1986, for further discussions).

SUMMARY

In this chapter, we have reviewed how social perceptual factors both serve us well in the practice setting, and can create bias and error in our practice-related reasoning and decision making. We identified several heuristics that can foster problematic forms of bias (the fundamental attribution error, and the representativeness and availability heuristics), and identified several tools to help practitioners remain mindful and deliberate in their use of schemas and their cognitive processes.

In closing, we should make explicit a set of biases that are always of concern to the practitioner. This concerns the YAVIS bias (viewing Young, Attractive, Verbal, Intelligent, and Successful clients in a positive light, and negatively viewing non-YAVIS clients) and the prejudicial effects of sexism, racism, classism, ageism, and heterosexism. As we have discussed previously, we are all products of our cultures and, more specifically, our niches. The attitudes and beliefs of the dominant culture are almost certainly part of our early socialization, even if we later make distinctions differing from a dominant view.

Exercises such as values clarification and sensitization are important to helping us become more aware of cultural influences on our perceptions and inferential processes. Yet, in and of themselves they are insufficient to combat the deleterious effects in practice of normal human bias in social perception. As illustrated, we are all products of our social environments. But according to cognitive-ecological principles, we also are all forces of change for ourselves and our social environments. The vulnerabilities to bias we have examined in this chapter are part of our human nature. Yet combating them is also part of our professional responsibility. This underscores the need to not only acquire application experience with the tools we have described here, but to also set up a structure that helps us do this repeatedly and routinely—until it becomes second nature. We have argued that de-biasing aids and bias-monitoring strategies should become an integral part of the functioning of professional practice settings—through the forms required, through supervision and case consultation procedures, and through the reinforcement of clear and specific clinical reasoning and planning.

The quality of the knowledge base brought to bear in professional practice is of utmost importance. Ironically, the most highly touted expert may be the most at risk for error and doing harm, that is, if the underlying conceptual framework and knowledge base drawn upon are incorrect. Expert status makes one's judgment less likely to be questioned. We have noted that with increased expertise comes increased mindlessness in information-processing, rendering more experienced practitioners more vulnerable to bias and error than novices, who may be more self-vigilant in their examination of their clinical inferences and decisions.

As has been shown for all aspects of the person-environment interaction, constructions of reality regarding professional practice tend to resist challenge and change. It is taxing and uncomfortable to constantly question and revise our important and deeply held realities. Yet, this is an essential skill for the responsible and effective practitioner.

This chapter is the last to outline general principles and processes. The remaining chapters will apply these principles and practices directly to the basic phases of professional practice.

NOTE

1. One factor that is very often overlooked in estimating odds is that the likelihood of the hypothesis being true (e.g., that someone will have cancer), must be considered in relation to the likelihood of the hypothesis not being true. Thus, any hypothesis must be analyzed in light of its true/not true probability ratio in order to understand it accurately.

The true/not true ratio produces a risk likelihood estimate that the hypothesis is true divided by the probability that the hypothesis is not true.

In the cancer example, this would look like the following:

probability true = 5/995 (meaning that 5 out of 1,000 will have undetected cancer)

probability not true = 5/95 (meaning that 5 out of 100 will score positive even when they do not have cancer)

Thus,

$$\frac{\text{probability true}}{\text{probability not true}} = \frac{\dfrac{5}{995}}{\dfrac{5}{95}} = \frac{5}{995} \times \frac{95}{5} = \frac{475}{4975} = 9.54\%, \text{ or about } 10\%.$$

Chapter 6

ASSESSMENT

In previous chapters we outlined a number of key concepts and themes that are the foundation for the practice processes to follow. Among these are the four themes that pervade this book: First, that both adaptive and maladaptive patterns often stem from the same normative processes, implying that presenting problems must be understood within the context of the client's niche and everyday social functioning. Second, that we use the idea of social constructionism to understand ourselves and our world, that we constantly construct meaning out of our lives by picking and choosing the cues to see and respond to, and that we create a sense of coherence in our lives through our construction of our life stories. Third, that human behaviors, even those behaviors that are problematic for us, are most productively viewed as our best efforts to solve everyday problems and tasks, and to strive for life goals (i.e., possible selves and possible niches). Fourth, that life changes and growth come about by enhancing mindfulness and intentionality in ourselves and our clients, mindfulness that builds informed choice into our patterns and routines as a way to enhance self-determination and empowerment in the face of the strong inertia to live our lives solely within our schema-driven perceptual worlds.

In previous chapters we also identified a number of concepts that we use in the cognitive-ecological model: the niche and self-system as target elements for the person-environment interaction; schemas, the working self, and possible selves and possible niches as key elements that regulate behavior and social interaction; and the elements of cognitive and affective functioning in human memory—procedural and declarative memory, and the perceptual-sensory system—that provide important building blocks toward desired individual change.

Chapters 1 through 4 identified and discussed features of the cognitive-ecological model and how they describe human behavior and social interactions in daily life. Chapter 5 discussed how to enhance our own mindfulness to counteract clinical bias. The remainder of this book describes how a cognitive-ecological model can direct practice efforts. We have chosen to devote each remaining chapter to a major phase of the counseling process. This chapter will discuss the assessment processes and present steps for completing a cognitive-ecological assessment. Chapter 7 will describe goal setting and contracting; Chapter 8 will cover processes involved in intervention planning and implementation; and Chapter 9 will focus on maintaining positive client change and helping clients transfer and sustain their learning and change efforts from the professional practice setting to their ongoing lives.

In this chapter we first consider the assessment experience or process itself and how that influences the picture that we obtain and build regarding the client. We will then look at the referents, or standards of normality, that we use when evaluating whether someone has a problem and how great that problem is. The remainder of the chapter will be devoted to discussion of specific steps and focal points in assessment.

THE ASSESSMENT PROCESS

To make an assessment of our clients is to take a fragmented pool of idiosyncratic and varied information and create a coherent picture of the client, her current life, and the reason she is seeking help. From a cognitive-ecological perspective, more specifically, the counselor aims to develop a picture of the client within her niche, and to understand the presenting problem as arising from her niche.

Assessment begins with one's first contact with or about the client (for example, when we read a client's chart, or get input from others about the client or her situation). Data typically comes from the intake forms the agency uses, from an initial phone call and/or a referral from another agency, and from one's face-to-face interactions with the client. The counselor's job is to take this often disparate information and make sense of it. How is it that the referring agency describes this client as closed and defiant when he's been very forthcoming with me? Why does this client look like she sees her life as hopeless and joyless even though she's able to list a number of good things happening to her at home and at work? Why was this client so talkative over the telephone when I have called him to schedule our appointments—in fact, I've had a hard time getting him to hang up—but he's so quiet when he comes in to see me? What are the client's beliefs and expectations regarding her problem; regarding me and what our relationship will be like; regarding what needs changing, whose role it is to make desired changes, and how that will come about?

One overriding goal of assessment, then, is to make sense of all the information that we know about our clients—to create a coherent picture of their life by understanding them within their niche and by understanding their presenting problems as making sense, given their niche. In simpler terms (though not simple to achieve), the goal of assessment is to synthesize information about human functioning in social environments (i.e., theory and research) with the specific observations about this client's functioning (i.e., individual experience), in order to understand how the client's life and problems must look and feel to him.

The Social Context of Assessment

As we have discussed in previous chapters, we are quite adept at making sense of information, of piecing together the puzzle of our clients' lives in order to understand them. We are "hard-wired" to makes sense of information we receive. Yet we have also raised the caution in the previous chapter that our perceptual biases make us see what we expect or want to see in our clients. That is, our adeptness and propensity to search for patterns and assign meanings do not necessarily mean we do so objectively or accurately. Biases in our perceptual and cognitive systems are especially problematic in the assessment phase, as we are very often forced to rely on our intuitions and speculations to form judgments about the meaning of our clients' behaviors. Two points need to be kept in mind to help us keep our biases in check.

First, the information that we receive about our clients has to be understood as coming from a particular context; that is, it arises from a particular set of environmental factors. Part of this has to do with the life context of the client's presenting problem and part with the immediate assessment context. When we obtain information about a client through a face-to-face interview, for example, we are only seeing a view of the person as he or she reacts to an interview situation. No matter how skillful the interviewer, the situation itself contains behavioral expectations and power differentials that the client reacts to. Interviews rely on verbal interactions, and linear, logical question-response formats. For clients who are at ease and perform well under these conditions, the interview can provide information that is a reasonable representation of their logical and verbal abilities (though not necessarily a representation of their other interpersonal abilities). For clients for whom this situation is foreign or in whom these verbal and logical abilities are not well developed, we are likely to understand the person as having serious problems or deficits. This is easy to imagine when we interview children. With a moment's thought we can understand why a standard interview format does not work with a 5-year-old boy. When we ask what we consider to be straightforward questions of this boy, whom we are requiring to sit still for an hour-long interview, we should not be surprised to see him answer vaguely and tangentially and have a very difficult time sitting still. If we use the same standards to judge his behavior as we do for a 25-year-old man, we would probably assess the boy as having serious attention deficits and thought disorders.

It is easy, with this example, to understand that we must adjust our interpretation of the information we receive to the context of the situation (in this case, the fact that it is an interview situation) and to the realities of the person (in this case, the fact that the boy is 5 years old). But this point must be kept in mind for all clients, and in situations far less obvious. Consider, for example, the contrast between the withdrawn 12-year-old boy in the counseling office of a small rural town and the same child who, during a walk around the neighborhood, offers details about the area, the people, and ultimately about his problems in school. It was the context change—and more precisely, the expectations implied in the context—that made a big difference for this client.

When we obtain information about clients through particular mediums (from interviews, from standardized test instruments, from third-party reports, and so on), therefore, we must keep in mind that the information is understood as a product of the person-in-situation. It does not, even under the best of conditions, represent a total picture of the person. Generally, interviews do not help us understand such things as how clients typically behave with their children, how they behave when among friends or on vacation, or even how they behave in other types of interviews (such as job interviews). We must observe the client (or as close an approximation as possible) in these other situations to know how he or she will really act within them.

We can, and very often do, make interpretations about how the client's behavior in the interview might translate to the other situations. But these should be treated as no more than our tentative best guess or hypothesis about how the client acts. Therefore, the second point to bear in mind is that our minds work to integrate new information into our already existing knowledge bases. In other words, we understand new information (information from our clients) by connecting it with information that we already know (about how we might act in the situation, about how previous clients have acted, about how the literature says individuals should or typically do act). We must be alert to our perceptual biases that cause us to see things that confirm what we know, and to not see or to ignore things that are foreign or discrepant to us.

Chapter 5 identified a number of exercises that we can do to help ourselves remain honest in our judgments of our clients throughout the assessment process. Bear in mind, however, that despite our best intentions, simply being aware of the pitfalls has proven virtually useless as a sole preventative or corrective strategy (Arkes, 1981). As with any interventions, inclusion of change and objective feedback aides are needed to produce and sustain the durable change we seek. Moreover, as we will discuss later in more detail, these issues and remedies apply to the larger environment (e.g., norms of supervision and agency functioning) as well as to individual practitioners.

STANDARDS OF NORMALITY USED
IN THE ASSESSMENT PROCESS

Before we turn to a more detailed discussion about the various components of a cognitive-ecological assessment, we must raise an issue that underlies the assessment process, that of the standards that we use to evaluate client behaviors. One core theme in this book has been that practitioners should evaluate clients' behaviors in light of normative cognitive and affective processes of human behavior and social interaction, part of which have been presented in previous chapters. This would imply that client assessment should be based on something of a "standard-free," or "self-as-standard" identification of the processes common to both normal daily life and the problems in living that clients present. Moreover, we have argued that clients determine for themselves whether they have a problem, and hoped-for changes in behavior are based on the goals that they have for their lives. For example, when a client comes in because he is feeling anxious and depressed, we use his own vision of feeling less anxious and depressed as the basis for developing intervention goals. This value of client-centered and goal- or solution-oriented practice is evident in many standard counseling texts (see Corey, 1991; Cormier & Cormier, 1991; Hepworth & Larsen, 1990).

Yet a standard-free or self-as-standard assessment is seldom, if ever, achieved. Instead, as a context to evaluate our clients' behaviors, we often draw upon implicit or explicit standards of normality. Even when we use our clients' own standards as guides for goals, progress, and change, we implicitly or explicitly evaluate whether the clients' stand- ards or goals themselves are reasonable, valid, and likely to result in healthy, desired outcomes (i.e., think about evaluating whether our eating disorder client's goal to lose 15 pounds is valid). Through social comparison, clients will very often base their goals and feelings on idiosyncratic or skewed standards of normality. Moreover, when we experience discomfort we are all inclined to frame our goals in terms of getting rid of that which is aversive, rather than exploring what can be added, strengthened, or better managed. Thus, it is responsible practice to place clients' goals and standards into a larger social context. If the client's perceptions of health are distorted or unrealistic, we might instead help her redefine how she looks at challenges and the lows in life. Or, if the client is depressed and anxious, due to external factors such as poor housing or work conditions, we might instead help her more fruitfully channel her feelings into community action.

We contend that the use of standards of normality is not wrong in and of itself. Instead, it is the use of standards implicitly or mindlessly that can be harmful and/or ineffective in our work with clients. Longres (1990) identifies three definitions of normality (first identified by Offer & Sabshin, 1984) that are commonly used by practitioners: normality as statistical average, normality as health, and normality as utopia. Reviewing these definitions can help make our use of them more mindful and deliberate in various assessment settings. Our discussion focuses on the problems and benefits of each of these definitions of normality.

Normality as Average. Many standards of normality are based on a statistical average (be it the mean, median, or mode) and standard deviation for whatever behavior is being evaluated. For example, when we assess the age-appropriateness of a child's behavior—such as the infant's reaction to strangers, the second-grader's ability to concentrate in class, or the teenager's propensity to argue with parents—we are evaluating it against how most children act at that age. When we assess a client's paranoid thoughts, we do so against a standard of how we believe most people might react under the same situation or conditions. While the normality-as-average definition does serve as a relatively objective standard against which we can evaluate our growth and development, it is the "basis for social norms under which diversity is scorned and neutrality or conformity is championed" (Longres, 1990, p. 350). Thus, people who are not typical relative to the majority run the risk of their difference being viewed in abnormal terms. We may find such a definition acceptable with respect to certain aspects of social functioning (such as adult-child sexual activity) but not with other aspects (such as concepts of what is gender-appropriate behavior).

Normality as Health. Normality can also be defined as the absence of pathology or illness, as the state in which we are not suffering from serious problems and/or are not hurting anyone else. For example, the *Diagnostic and Statistical Manual* published by the American Psychiatric Association uses such a definition in that its implicit definition of a healthy client is someone who does not meet any of the diagnostic criteria.

Central to a health-anchored definition of what constitutes a normal state of being is the question of who determines the presence or absence of problems or illness. Many mental health practitioners maintain a pragmatic stance that "if it ain't broke, don't fix it," where we take the client's definition of problems and goals for change at face value. For example, if clients are not troubled by their own compulsive behavior, and it poses no serious or imminent threat, one could argue it is not our place to make this a focus for change. We would want clients to be making informed judgments in this regard (e.g., to be aware of the consequences of their behavior and of their options). Yet, here the criteria centers on the adequacy of the individual's social, psychological, and physical functioning, and in the absence of problems, and less on how common or typical certain behaviors or phenomena are.

Along with some benefits, this pragmatic approach does pose some problems and risks. Criteria defining pathology, or conversely, health, may be relatively clear for medical or biological problems, but much more difficult to define in relation to mental health and social functioning, where any number of psychological, interpersonal, and cultural issues must be taken into consideration. Even when we start with our clients' own definition of their health or illness, we still have to determine whether these definitions are appropriate and constructive. We would not, as was mentioned above, be prepared to proceed without question to help a teenage girl lose "just 15 more pounds" if she already weighed a normal amount. It is, in fact, part of our professional responsibility to provide input in the direction of health-promoting options, and not the responsibility of the client to know in advance what is and is not health promoting.

A final point to consider is that normality-as-health largely defines health as a matter of survival or coping. While it is certainly true that simple survival in our modern life is difficult enough, an exclusive focus on survival and coping implies that we only take a reactive stance to the myriad of forces and challenges that confront us on a daily basis. Such a definition leaves little room for a proactive stance or growth, or our desires to change the forces around us. As we saw in preceding chapters, human beings are by nature highly active: intrinsically motivated to learn, understand, experiment, and achieve a sense of mastery. Being proactive is essential to being able later to either avoid or grapple with problems in living that would otherwise erode health.

Normality as Utopia. In contrast to definition based either on what is common or typical, or on the absence of problems, a normality-as-utopia definition takes the view that normality is an ideal state toward which to strive. It defines an ideal psychological and social state of human functioning. Clients will often come in to treatment because they wish to attain an almost utopian state: "My marriage (work, child, life) now is okay, I guess, but it lacks spark, passion, excitement . . . " In previous chapters, we saw how people tend to draw upon a positive possible self or niche as an image of the future toward which to strive. Some of these positive possibilities will be ideal or utopian in nature ("I'll be a kind and patient mother, a sexy wife, a rising star in my work, dedicated to a healthy life-style, a conscientious volunteer in my community . . . . ").

While the normality-as-utopia definition presents several benefits, such as images to strive for, it also has several problems. Its visions are often vague and imprecise, even to those expressing them. Its definition is subject to forces that may represent the interests of particular ideologies, theorists, and cultures over those of people living within them (again, think of the normal-weight teenager who wants to lose more weight). Yet the normality-as-utopia approach does "reject the status quo of reality and encourage striving for the best possible world and the best possible place in it" (Longres, p. 357). In that respect, it may serve as a kind of utopia toward which practitioners and clients can strive in their work together.

We do not wish to advocate for the consistent advantages of one of these definitions of normality over any of the others, nor to argue that this is an exhaustive array of how normality is defined. Rather, our goal is to urge practitioners to make explicit what is typically implicit: What images, literally, do we bring to our work concerning what is normal or deviant, what is healthy or pathological, what is appropriate or not? Again, we are not arguing that the goal is to purge ourselves of such values, standards, or images. As we discussed in Chapters 3, 4, and 5, it is essential that we make use of schemas and information-processing knowledge lest we become paralyzed by the enormity of what must be considered at any given moment. It is, however, a practitioner's mindful and discriminating use of such knowledge of normal person and environment behavior that will contribute to thoughtful and productive assessment and intervention.

GOALS OF ASSESSMENT

The assessment phase of treatment can be organized around three central goals (Cormier & Cormier, 1991; Gambrill, 1983; Guidano & Liotti, 1983; Meichenbaum, 1977). The *first goal* is to gather information about the client and the presenting problem in such a way as to suggest treatment goals and a course of action. This is the most commonly understood requirement of assessment. It is important to have both a wide and deep understanding of clients' presenting problems, meaning that the counselor must often ask questions about a number of domains of life. It is also important, however, to understand that being a counselor does not give one the right to intrude on all aspects of the client's life. One must always ask questions only if they have a direct and justifiable connection to the presenting problem. This should, of course, include questions that follow up hunches or hypotheses concerning the antecedents and consequences of clients' behaviors.

In choosing areas to assess, the guideline discussed in Chapter 1 applies: In one's role as practitioner, every act must be for the client's benefit. Specific areas of the client's life that are likely targets for questions will be discussed below.

Whereas the first goal can be thought of as informational, a *second goal* is more educational in nature and has to do with laying the groundwork for how treatment will proceed, thus providing an initial map of the norms, roles, and rules through which the phenomenon of professional practice and change will take place. It is during the assessment phase that the practitioner begins to describe, model, and elicit client input regarding the norms for what clients can expect from the practitioner and from themselves (see Chapter 8 for a discussion of the different models of helping counselors and client hold). Together, the client and practitioner begin to establish ground rules concerning the scope of the work together, the limits of the relationship, the model of helping that each has in mind, and expectations for appropriate actions. Part of what this entails is identifying the structure of a problem-solving process. While this takes place in the context of a formal helping relationship, many of the norms, roles, and activities are transferable to other life situations. One concrete form in which these parameters get specified is in the form of a treatment contract. However, this is not instantaneous, and throughout the remainder of treatment, these norms, roles, and rules form the basis for the relationship and the work that the client and practitioner undertake together, as the practitioner both articulates and models how to express emotions, how to ask questions, how to listen to answers, how to practice new skills, and so forth.

Connected to the educational mission of practice initiated in assessment, a *third goal* is one of instilling motivation. Through the process of assessment (i.e., posing questions, asking for elaboration, verifying one's assumptions and interpretations, and building a progressively more complete picture), the practitioner has an opportunity to reveal how she or he is getting from here to there, to understand the client and envision their work. Assessment is largely a learned and learnable skill. We are not posing questions at random. As we saw in Chapter 3, we are drawing upon both declarative and procedural knowledge—declarative knowledge of our theories of human behavior in the social environment, and of specific problem etiologies, as well as procedural knowledge about how to seek out information from others, how to explore possibilities that confirm our early hunches as well as alternative explanations, how to get unstuck when one feels lost, and so forth. This knowledge can, to varying degrees, be shared with clients to not only demystify the process but also assist them in gaining tools for their continued self-help.

Many, if not most, professional practice models state that the counselor must "start where the client is"—that we should use language that matches our clients' language, that we need to empathize with their problems and be guided by their concerns, that we must respect their goals and values. Using the assumptions of the cognitive-ecological approach posited earlier in this book, this basic counseling tenet can be further specified to create the assessment goal of learning how the client feels and experiences his or her life. This is a restatement of "starting where the client is," but focuses specifically on the client's perceptions, emotions, and experiences to highlight the perceptual, cognitive, and affective processes that the client uses to shape and experience life. The counselor must have the empathy and imagination to experience the client's daily life, to feel what he or she feels, to understand his or her daily routines, to understand his or her goals, dreams, and fears. Through this work, the counselor is assessing clients' sensory-perceptual systems, their procedural and declarative memory, their self- and other-schemas, their possible selves and niches, and how these components fit together to understand the niche they have created for themselves.

STEPS IN THE ASSESSMENT PROCESS

Part of what makes assessment challenging to discuss is the wide range of settings in which practitioners work. Practitioners in a child and family agency or a community mental health center will naturally emphasize different factors relative to counselors in drug rehabilitation centers, hospital emergency rooms, or employee assistance programs. Our aim here will be to focus on dimensions of clients' problems in living and contexts that tend to be universally important, and about which a cognitive-ecological perspective can enrich our understanding. The following steps are not meant to be followed in a lock-step sequence with clients. Nor do they produce information that is necessarily mutually exclusive. Instead, think of these steps as touchstones, or areas for information gathering:

1. Identify presenting problem(s).
2. Identify situations in which problem(s) do and do not exist.
3. Identify client's characteristic reaction and problem-solving patterns related to presenting problems.
4. Identify client's distal environment, proximal environment, and distal and proximal person factors (i.e., the environmental and individual realities of the niche) related to these problems and situations.
5. Identify the client's daily routines, life tasks, and possible selves and niches related to presenting problems.

6. Determine how the client's presenting problems are best understood given the niche. What is the presenting problem a solution to within the niche?

Assessment is not, ultimately, something that is initiated and then completed once and for all. It continues throughout treatment as new information becomes available and relevant. The practitioner tries to integrate the new information into what is known about the client's life up to that point, so that the resultant understanding of the client's life and the presenting problem's place within it becomes more complete. One of the authors worked with a client for several months before the client revealed that he was bulimic. While the work that was done up to that point had relevance to the client (work on self-esteem and assertiveness issues, particularly in relationship to authority figures in his life), the earlier presenting problems had not felt as acutely self-threatening as did disclosure of his eating disorder. It is often the case that additional problems will emerge in later sessions, due to ongoing changes in the client's life, new goals or greater awareness of factors the client realizes could be changed, or, as in the present case, increased trust in the relationship with the practitioner.

At the same time, certain outcomes must be obtained by the end of the initial assessment phase, namely a valid and reasonably comprehensive understanding of the presenting problem and how it fits into the client's niche. These outcomes are necessary to set up the work of establishing goals, to begin developing an image of preferred scenarios and the indicators that would signal progress or lack of progress, to guide choices about what kinds of interventions are best suited, and to establish the necessary relationship conditions that will facilitate change. At this point, let us discuss in more detail aspects of assessment related to each of the steps identified above.

Steps for a Cognitive-Ecological Assessment

1. Identifying Presenting Problem(s)

Clients seek professional help because of some problem or set of problems in their lives. They may not be able to fully articulate the problem when they enter, but their view of their life situation nevertheless becomes the place to start the assessment. Following efforts to make the client feel comfortable, an initial question is often one such as "What brings you in today?" or more fully, "I have reviewed the material I have on you (from intake forms and the like), but I would like to start with your view: What brings you in today?" Note that two ground rules are implicitly laid out right from the start: first that the counselor will respect the client's view. Information will come from a variety of sources, such as from standardized intake forms and contact with others related to the client or the case, but that these do not take precedence over the information and view provided by the client in her or his own words. The counselor is saying, "I am here to focus on what you need. I'm interested in what you have to say, what you think and feel." Second, the counselor is establishing that part of what is important to talk about are feelings and personal perceptions related to present daily life. By asking the client about her current life, the implicit message is that what really matters is what is happening now. Later in assessment and in subsequent stages, some of the practitioner's underlying reasoning will be more explicitly shared with the client as a means of teaching or strengthening problem solving (identifying problems, goals, impediments, alternatives, strategies).

It is important to leave initial questions open-ended, to give the client as much freedom as possible to answer in any way she sees fit. There is plenty of time to ask specific questions later as the client's outlook is better understood and as more specific information is needed.

After identifying the presenting problem or set of problems, it is important to then ask questions to define it further: How often does it occur? With what intensity? How long does it last? What are others' reactions to it? Through these questions, one can place the presenting problem into an A-B-C sequence:

What are its *antecedents*? That is, what are the factors that appear to trigger or set the stage for the presenting problems? This does not meaningfully include everything or anything that precedes the problematic situations or events. Rather, antecedents are those factors that appear functionally related; for example, that set key processes into motion related to the presenting problem. Some of these antecedents will be relatively distant and others will be proximal. For a person with acute social anxiety, distal antecedents may include messages from one's childhood that one was dumb, unattractive, or inadequate. Proximal antecedents would be more immediate triggers of anxiety, such as an invitation to a social event, thinking about upcoming events, and entering the event itself.

Of course, we also want to know more about the core *behaviors* that make up the presenting problem. Behaviors include thoughts, feelings, and actions of the client as well as others. For the socially anxious individual, this may include negative self-statements (that are either verbalized or not), feeling tense and awkward, and behaving in a tentative manner (hanging back, doing little to contribute to conversations, backing away from stating an opinion). Perhaps there is a family member or friend present who says things that embarrass the individual or who puts pressure on him or her to be more like the others.

Finally, what *consequences* are involved? As with antecedents, consequences are those factors that are functionally related to the presenting problems, not just any factors that follow certain behaviors. Generally, consequences can be thought of as maintaining factors, those that help sustain or reinforce cycles involving the presenting problem. Again, for the socially anxious person, behaviors of others that convey discomfort or rejection will likely tend to reinforce the person's self-schemas of being awkward, shy, and on the outside of friendship circles, and to augment feelings of anxiety and the desire to escape the distressing situation. On the part of the client, avoidance or early retreat from social situations has the payoff of relief from immediate distress. Yet it also eliminates opportunities to create new self-schemas (declarative knowledge about alternative selves): It reduces the chances to practice more socially skillful selves and it reinforces existing beliefs ("I can't do this") stored in memory.

Although the above illustrates negative ABC cycles, we should note that it is not the phenomena of triggers and maintaining forces per se that is problematic. These same phenomena are part of what keeps well-functioning people functioning well. The tenacity of the self-system, for example, in seeking out expected and belief-consistent information, is an asset as long as those expectations and beliefs are balanced and positively adaptive. Thus, part of assessment involves looking at processes and interactions that may presently produce negative results, but which may also hold the potential to be redirected more positively.

Another important component in this initial data-gathering phase of assessment is to evaluate how serious the problem is (i.e., whether the client is at risk for suicide or homicide), as well as whether any medical problems or illnesses exist that need to be treated, and whether aggression or violence is present as well as drug or alcohol abuse. After checking into these areas directly, a survey of functioning across major areas of life: family, work (or school), leisure, friendships, and meeting one's own basic living needs (eating, sleeping, shelter) is often appropriate.

Remember that one core theme in the cognitive-ecological model concerns the reconstructive nature of human memory: Rather than literal recordings that are stored and replayed much like videotapes, our memory is very dynamic and undergoes change over time. Guidano and Liotti (1983) note that assessment will be strongly influenced by this reconstructive nature. That is, when we ask questions of our clients, and when clients supply answers, our questions and their answers elicit a much more logical and sequential set of information than what actually occurs. When we ask clients how their kids came to behave so poorly at mealtimes, we are implicitly asking them to create a hypothesis of their children's behavior, and then to support their hypothesis with data. Clients understand this implicit message and supply information after filtering it both through their current understandings (accurate or not) and through their guesses as to what seems most pertinent to the presenting problem.

Thus, when we obtain information from our clients, even information we might consider very factual, we are gathering an edited reconstruction of the past as well as information about how the client thinks. This would include, as discussed in a later step, what reaction and problem-solving patterns are characteristic; what cognitive, perceptual, and affective processes are frequently used. Are there patterns that can be identified in how the client reasons and attempts to cope (or to strive)? Are certain self- and other-schemas activated frequently and others infrequently? Likewise, does the client show propensities to use certain types of knowledge over others? Remember that one goal of assessment is to understand what life is like from the client's perspective. The way clients construct the world (past, present, and future) provides important clues for this perspective.

2. Identifying Situations in Which Problem(s) Do and Do Not Exist

In the cognitive-ecological model, all behaviors must be viewed as a product of the person-situation interaction. The presenting problem exists because of a unique combination of factors in the person and in particular situations. Thus, in the next step of assessment, it is important to discover the situations in which the problem exists and those in which it does not. This is related to, but not the same as, discovering the conditions under which the problem exists. Here we mainly wish to demonstrate the utility of one core theme: that both adaptive and maladaptive behaviors can stem from the same normative processes, depending on the particular situation that the person is in.

It is explicitly recognized that people might have certain traits, such as a need to control situations, or a need to feel loved and comforted. Yet, in order to survive and thrive in one's niche, these traits must be functional for the person under certain conditions. The person with strong control needs may function very well at work, where she is a supervisor. The problems that clients come in with, therefore, are only problematic within certain situations or contexts.

Consider these two examples. Clients very often seek treatment because of worry or anxiety. A cognitive-ecological perspective would hypothesize that their anxiety is functional under some situations and not others, or was functional under prior conditions but not current ones. Thus, it is important to sort out which situations are the difficult ones for the client. One client experienced severe panic attacks only when she went grocery shopping, and interestingly, not when she went shopping for other household items or for clothing. Furthermore, she only experienced these attacks when she was alone. When she went grocery shopping with her husband, the attacks did not occur. She did not know why these attacks started (and the counselor could not find a clear precipitating event), but the client was particularly worried since they were beginning to occur more frequently and under a wider set of circumstances. She was beginning to feel some panic symptoms (rapid heartbeat, slight dizziness) in anticipation of going out, and was beginning to feel phobic about leaving her home alone.

A second client came in for treatment, also because of anxiety, but his primary symptom was excessive hand and foot sweating. When asked when this problem was most severe, he remarked that it was in anticipation of meeting people and having to shake hands with them. The counselor asked if this were true for all people, for example, if he met peers in social situations. He said that it did happen then, but it was most severe when he had to meet prospective clients (he was a salesman). He almost became obsessional in his worry that he would give the wrong impression to the clients, and would ruminate about his hands literally for hours prior to the meeting. This of course had the effect of magnifying his hand sweating, and so he found himself in a vicious cycle that he could not control.

Many of the questions to ask here are straightforward. When does the problem occur? Are there times when it doesn't happen? Tell me all the times it has happened in the past week (2 weeks, month, and so on). Are there certain kinds of situations that are particularly bad for you? Do you know what makes them bad? What are your guesses? In contrast, are there times you feel particularly free of the problem, or times when the situation turns out differently? If so, describe those to me.

Note that these questions direct the client to think of herself *in situation.* This serves to reinforce the basic treatment approach that behaviors are products of unique person and situation combinations, which helps clients lay less blame on themselves and others. These questions also serve the function of reinforcing another aspect of the cognitive-ecological approach—that we generally are very sensitive to the cues in our surroundings, picking and choosing those cues to respond to, and responding in ways that make sense to us.

Straightforward as these questions may seem, it is often difficult for clients to respond in detail or be able to see variables outside their operating theories about what happens and why. This is part of the reason that aids such as logs or diaries can be extremely useful. They help the client pay greater attention to the details and data of the situation, slowing down their own cognitive, affective, and behavioral patterns enough to capture more descriptive detail and less inferential assumption. Such tools help to more fully bring the situation into the counseling session, and are widely used in differing forms. There are a number of factors to weigh in what kinds of aids to use toward what purpose. For example, the very act of helping clients more fully see and assess their target situations will tend to influence their subsequent behavior. This reactivity is typically therapeutically advantageous. For a broader discussion of tools and issues, see readings such as Bloom and Fischer (1982), Gambrill (1983), and Hepworth and Larsen (1990).

3. Identifying Client's Characteristic Reaction and Problem-Solving Patterns Related to Presenting Problems

Above, we can see that identifying the presenting problem(s) and exploring the situations they exist in overlap considerably in the development of a functional analysis of target behaviors. Rarely are problems explainable within a social or environmental vacuum. Many problems feel like they are contained within one's thinking or personality (e.g., shyness, depression, worry), and some problems are experienced as deriving nearly completely outside oneself (e.g., "If we didn't have this rotten kid, our marriage would be just fine." "I wouldn't lose my temper if she didn't do things to get me so mad."). As alluded to above, part of the educational function of assessment is undertaken through directing the client to think of herself or himself in situation. This serves to reinforce the basic conceptual approach that behaviors are products of unique person and situation combinations, which helps clients think in less blame-oriented ways and provides a framework for future situational analysis. We begin to lay the groundwork for helping clients see their own characteristic reaction patterns vis-à-vis particular issues in their lives.

Figure 3.2 outlined factors that significantly bear upon how people perceive, interpret, react to, and attempt to solve problems. The steps in this figure can be used in the assessment phase to identify and understand how clients both view situations and work to solve problems in those situations most related to their problems and goals. Through this examination, assessments can be made concerning clients' cognitive-ecological components—their memory processes, self- and other-schemas, possible selves and possible niches.

By leading clients sequentially through the steps in Figure 3.2, much information can be obtained about clients' perceptual, cognitive, and affective processes, and particularly how these processes affect their presenting problems. And while it is rare that we naturally distinguish the problem-solving steps we take when we confront problems and tasks in our lives, for the purposes of assessment, it is helpful to explore each step separately.

For example, with a depressed client reporting increasing anger and marital tension, the practitioner asked her to describe the most recent incident in which she became more angry with her husband than she felt was warranted. In that incident, the client became angry with her husband for being excited about an upcoming weekend trip, and (in her words) "badgering" the client to "hurry up and get ready" on the Saturday morning on which they were to leave. This description provided a beginning point for how the client construed and experienced the event.

The practitioner then asked a number of questions about the specifics of that morning: What time did they wake up and what time were they to leave; what packing or other arrangements needed to be made; what had each said to the other and what had she thought and felt at different points? In this way, the practitioner and client were able to recreate a picture of the situation, some of which was highly salient for the client and some of which had gone largely unrecognized in the moment. By asking questions about what images and expectations she had about the upcoming event, what she thought and felt in the moment, and what she thought her husband felt and meant, the practitioner could begin to assess the client's working self-concept and the schemas she brought to bear in the moment.

The client reported that the situation felt like a sweep of events; that one thing led to another, and before she knew it, they were fighting. This was particularly confusing to her because she did want to take this trip, and had previously felt excited and had enjoyed her husband's enthusiasm. When asked to think about and reflect on the individual steps of that morning, however, she realized that she had begun the day feeling vaguely anxious, and felt rushed and pushed by her husband. She believed that her anger and yelling were due to her feeling uninteresting—"like a slug"—and her fears that she was going to become a drag on the trip and spoil her husband's time.

These negative conceptions represented a negative possible self (i.e., the uninteresting slug of a spouse) to avoid or move away from. It was linked to an associative network that directed her thoughts, emotions, and actions in predominantly negative ways. Even though she had positive schemas stored in memory regarding herself, her husband, and their times together, these were part of different associate networks that were difficult to access in the moment. Thus, the salience of these negative schemas combined with a relative inaccessibility of competing schemas, with the result being that she responded defensively and pushed back, saying that her husband had pushed her into the weekend and that she did not really want to go.

Her husband's reaction to her counterattack, of claiming she was being forced into the weekend, was to back off from his enthusiastic expressions of excitement. So her behavior worked to give her some breathing room: He felt frustrated and hurt by her remarks, and became quiet and withdrawn. However, for him, the images of this special time together were still quite salient, and he tried an alternative approach. After finishing packing the car with their things, he said, "I am looking forward to going away with you, you know." The client was better able to hear this statement, as opposed to witnessing his excitement. It provided a different type of trigger, more consistent with her positive associative network, and more easily construed as a message of affection than one of threat. Despite the fact that both the client and her husband were now feeling somewhat bruised by their fight, the client's own enthusiasm for the trip began to return as she was able to draw upon different schemas, scripts, and skills.

By going through these steps in Figure 3.2, the practitioner and client were able to get a better picture of the cues that were important to the client in this situation, of how these were processed to make sense of a situation, of how she drew upon current resources and perceived options, and of how she acted and evaluated her actions. She saw how her concerns about "being a slug" inclined her to interpret her husband's excitement as demands to be interesting and excited when she feared she could not be, how her anger was an attempt at self-protection, and how his later, modified statement reaffirming his desires to be with her cued a different set of emotions, self-schemas, and possible niches, which allowed her to respond more proactively and less defensively.

In addition to some of the details of a problematic pattern of reaction and problem-solving, this example illustrates the client's quick ability to work with her cognitive and affective material, in terms of both her ability to recreate transactions in some detail, and her ability to gain perspective in the midst of troubling interactions with her husband and begin a significantly different chain of reactions. Certainly, all assessments do not go as smoothly, nor do problem scenarios so clearly illustrate client strengths and resources. The point here is the value of slowing down and closely examining the steps in a cognitively oriented problem-solving sequence that elicit how perceptual, cognitive, and affective processes affect and interact with social and environmental factors. Furthermore, by going through these problem-solving steps for a number of situations, the client and practitioner are able to begin to see patterns and themes in the client's niche—that is, which cognitive, perceptual, and affective processes are likely to become activated under which situations, and which self-schemas and other-schemas are likely to become salient. Collectively, this information can provide important details about phenomena that, in the moment, feel overwhelming, defeating, and barely, if at all, under her control. As a function of elaborating the picture of what is happening and how the client is experiencing the transaction, we can better see leverage points and resources for desired change.

When assessing how clients proceed through the steps of problem solving, it is first important to use open-ended probes to get their actions, feelings, and interpretations as fully and realistically as possible. However, it is often helpful to present alternative actions, feelings, and interpretations along the way. Often we have not articulated our thinking or feeling in situations, and particularly in those that are confusing or upsetting. Thus, presenting alternatives helps determine whether the client is aware of other ways of perceiving a situation or responses to it, and helps assess what ease or difficulty the client appears to have in trying on new possibilities. In previous and subsequent chapters, we discuss more fully the importance of creativity; in this case, this refers to the clients' ability to generate a variety of possibilities (e.g., interpretations, feelings, actions) if initial success is blocked. In the assessment phase, it is useful to explore how flexible or rigid the client's cognitive and affective processes are; both how open she or he is to alternatives and what capacities she or he appears to have to envision and entertain alternatives.

When a practitioner generates alternatives at each step of problem solving and makes evaluations of clients, this is done by comparing the client against some sort of referent. This may include comparisons to how an average or healthy person would perceive the situation, or how one ideally might perceive the situation (referring back to our discussion of normality). There are typically a number of differing ways a situation might reasonably be construed and responded to, and rarely is there a single correct standard. However, as previously noted, we generally do enter into assessments with preexisting notions of what is preferred or more functional. Thus, one challenge the practitioner shares with the client is to be aware of alternatives, to be flexible in considering options, and to mindfully select a standard based on its appropriateness for the case and for the particular client.

In addition to exploring how clients' perceive situations and solve problems, the information obtained through one's cognitive-ecological assessment can also generate information about relative imbalances in a client's cognitive and affective processing. For example, as was discussed in previous chapters, a relative balance will exist for most people between their general or abstract declarative (knowing about) memory and their more experience- and practice-based procedural (knowing how to) memory. That is, through various sources (friends, family, media, schools and groups, formal helping) we encounter ideas and models about what things mean, how one is supposed to behave, and so forth. Over time, we may be able to talk in some depth about what we should be doing, while not being able to act on our thoughts and plans. That is, we often have more declarative knowledge than procedural knowledge.

People, particularly adults, are inclined to believe that once declarative knowledge exists, they should then be able to "just do it"; that is, once they have declarative knowledge, the capacity to enact or actualize that attribute or action should flow naturally. Ironically, we often look at tasks that are predominantly motoric, such as skiing or playing an instrument, as obviously requiring repeated practice, but are prone to look at more emotionally and interpersonally complex tasks, such as initiating conversation with new people, communicating personal boundaries, or remaining calm in the face of objects of our childhood fears, as something that should simply come with being grown-up. We recognize the component parts as behaviors we have undertaken many times, so it should be straightforward to simply do what we now see as being needed. Part of what we have here, however, is a problem of imbalance: too little procedural knowledge of desired responses and too much declarative knowledge, which serves to confuse us. As we noted in previous chapters, the more accomplished our procedural knowledge of an activity becomes—whether it be an emotional reaction, a cognitive interpretation, or a motoric behavior—the more automatic and less conscious it becomes for us. Thus, we may well find ourselves not really able to articulate how we do certain things, or how we know or feel certain things that are highly familiar to us, even if we know that we were more articulate when these things were new to us.

A goal of counseling is not necessarily to simply augment for clients one or the other type of knowledge to bring them into balance. If a client's characteristic reaction pattern is functioning satisfactorily, it may be unnecessary to ask her to describe what she does and how she does it, and it may not be necessary for the client to acquire highly developed skills for all objectives. Instead, this point of assessing relative balance, or better stated, assessing clients' propensities toward some cognitive processes over others, is useful in understanding clients' presenting problems, in planning interventions, and in communicating with the clients toward establishing rapport and a good working relationship.

Likewise, by taking clients through the problem-solving steps, one is afforded an opportunity to explore the workings of clients' possible selves and niches. Given the motivational and structural importance of these future-oriented images of ourselves and our surroundings, we must understand how they are both working for and against our clients under differing circumstances. Do our clients have difficulty visualizing themselves and their surroundings in new or different ways? If so, is this due to deficiencies in ability, supports, or hope? Or, can our clients easily imagine themselves in the future, but are unable to see how they can get there from here (which may also indicate deficits in procedural knowledge)? In the first case, one might describe the client as anchored too much in the present, on a treadmill where she moves from crisis to crisis, or living an existence within which she feels trapped and unable to envision some big picture of where it all will lead. In the latter case, one might describe the client as focusing too much in the future, not seeing how his actions connect (or do not connect) to his dreams, or neglecting or discounting present situations because they are not as interesting or compelling as his dreams. In both cases, by understanding how our clients' possible selves and niches operate, we are in a better position to make use of them in our intervention planning and relationship building.

4. Identifying the Distal and Proximal Environment, and the Distal and Proximal Person Factors Related to Presenting Problems and Situations

In addition to defining the presenting problem and the situations in which it occurs, it is important to understand the context for the person's life by assessing their distal and proximal environments and their own distal and proximal personal characteristics. As described in Chapter 3, and in Figure 3.1, the distal environment contains things such as the client's economic condition, relevant political and social attitudes, and the economic climate as it bears upon the individual. It includes those things that are relevant to the person that emanate from the larger society. Proximal environment includes such things as characteristics of the client's neighborhood, characteristics of their family and friends, their particular housing and meals, and their work or school setting—those things that are important to the client in his immediate environment. Distal person factors are those personality traits or physical characteristics that serve as a backdrop to the presenting problem. These will include such things as the client's demographics (age, sex, and race) and health, as well as dispositional characteristics and early learning and experiences. Finally, proximal person factors include the client's recent or current skills and abilities, her current developmental stage, and her self-perceptions and attitudes about the world. Some distal factors have been sustained over time and continue as proximal factors, but many no longer have direct effects, or current effects are different from earlier ones.

It is important to assess these four sets of factors since they create context for the current niche. They create a boundary around it and serve as biopsychosocial realities that the person works within. The client described earlier who complained of sweaty hands is understood differently if he is a young, single, white man who worked in the stock market during the mid-1980s; versus if he is a recent Cambodian refugee, in his early forties, who is trying to keep his family out of poverty; versus if he was an unemployed African-American, in his late fifties, during the height of the Civil Rights Movement, who recently moved to a northern city to find work. As a practitioner, one would understand the pressures on each of these men differently, would understand their problems in relation to different life contexts, and would (hopefully) be sensitive enough to their life situations and niches to work differently with each of them. Problem symptoms in and of themselves do not accurately guide intervention selections; the context is needed to gauge which combination of person and environmental changes is optimal and feasible.

In assessing these four classes of factors, some of the information will come from one's own experiences and knowledge (such as the political and economic climate of the day). Yet it remains important not to assume that the practitioner's experience of these social factors, and the culture from which the practitioner comes, are the same as those of the client. One must ask directly: What is it like for you (your family, your kids) in your neighborhood? How are you doing with paying your bills? Are you in much debt? Do you have much contact with your (extended) family? Do they live close by? What are these relationships like? Do you have close friends? How long have you known them? What things do you like to do when you have free time? Do you have free time? What subjects are (were) you good at in school or work?

Again, the idea is to begin to develop the big picture of the client's niche: Where he lives and what it feels like to be that person. As we have previously emphasized, the nature of the information needed will vary by setting. We are describing an objective to gain an understanding of the everyday life experience of the client, to assess suspected problems, while still maintaining a direct connection to the presenting problem.

5. Identifying the Client's Daily Routines, Life Tasks, and Possible Selves and Niches Related to Presenting Problems

At this point in the assessment, both the client and the practitioner have a clearer picture of the presenting problems, the situations that they arise in, and the parameters of the client's niche that appear to bear significantly on the problems and/or potential solutions. In our attempt to understand the client's life, we have likely begun to gain an image of what the client does in a day-to-day sense. From a cognitive-ecological perspective, we will want to now focus more specifically on this: How does she spend her time? What motivates her during the day? What is she striving for? Again, the goal is to understand how the client's daily life is related to her presenting problems.

In this step, straightforward questions are again most appropriate; for example, When do you get up? What is your morning routine like? What do you do on a typical day? What time do you get home (assuming the client works or goes to school)? How is dinner prepared? When do you go to bed and fall asleep?

Of course, the particular questions asked will depend on the problems and situations most central to the client's niche. A number of interesting issues arise when these questions are asked. For example, getting a family up, having breakfast, and starting the day is often a very stressful time for families. How are the roles divided? Who wakes whom? Who takes showers first? Who prepares breakfast and cleans up? Likewise, dinner preparations are also another stressful time: When do parents arrive home? What are the kids doing while dinner is being prepared? Are roles distributed throughout the family, or concentrated on one member?

Even in nonclinical families, mealtime routines reflect family functioning. Haley (1976) describes mealtime rituals as providing a window into how families function. Is there a routine at all? Is it "everyone for themselves" or does the family sit down to dinner together? Do the parents talk among themselves, or is one of them drawn into breaking up sibling arguments while the other reads the paper or "zones out"? Do the parents and older children share dinner preparation duties, or are family roles played out during dinner preparation as well as other family gatherings?

Unstructured time, such as weekends or after-dinner times, can also be stressful for families and individuals. Often families function well when they can stick to known routines; during unstructured times it can sometimes appear as if the members do not know what to do with themselves or each other, or that they have objectives that are at cross-purposes. Conflict can arise as a function of this lack of norms or communication.

Knowing daily routines in clients' lives leads naturally to questions about what they strive for and what motivates them. We have found that this information can be obtained efficiently and in meaningful ways by asking about clients' life tasks, possible selves, and possible niches.

Life tasks represent those daily tasks or projects that one works on and devotes energy to solving in the normal course of the day—they often are what our daily routines are most specifically directed toward. They need not be monumental tasks, such as those of self-improvement; they may be as mundane as getting the kids out the door on time for school after a decent breakfast. Possible selves and niches motivate us by serving as concrete representations of life goals. They represent the discrepancies that exist between our current state and our desired and feared images of our lives.

There are different levels of specificity to consider when assessing life tasks, possible selves and possible niches. Some questions will address clients' overall outlook, and others will address the very specific selves and tasks that are salient in any given moment (e.g., moments that are particularly distressing or problematic, as contrasted with those that are more satisfying). Asking directly about this information works well: How do you see yourself 5 years from now (in general or with respect to particular life domains)? Or, what things are you trying to get done today? As we learn about these aspects of our clients' lives, of their routines, life tasks, and possible selves, we can help them more fully piece their life story together. We begin to understand what motivates them, how they came to be where they are today, what the etiologies of their thoughts and feelings are, and what it feels like to go through a day in their lives.

We can then use this information to begin asking more probing assessment questions about specific situations that appear most related to the target problems or goals. Simultaneously, enough rapport begins to develop between practitioner and client to allow the practitioner to speculate about the life tasks and possible selves and niches implied by certain routines: "When you're trying to get dinner ready and the kids are whining because they're hungry, and you shove them in front of the TV, do you worry that you're becoming your mother?" This question was asked of a single mother of two pre-teens who had gone back to school to complete her college degree. She had come in because she felt like she needed better ways to control her kids who "always needed something" from her and felt terribly guilty that she could not do enough for them. As the practitioner and client further examined her daily routines, information about her life tasks could be inferred through statements such as, "You know, you do so much during the day for so many others, it sounds like what you really want is to be left alone for a while."

It quickly becomes apparent that assessment of factors related to problems is intimately related to exploration of goals, of intervention strategies likely to yield desired outcomes, and of indicators of incremental realization of these goals. We will discuss some of these connections more fully in subsequent chapters, but the process of assessment clearly provides a foundation that helps guide these later steps.

6. Determining How the Client's Presenting Problems Are Best Understood Given the Niche
What Is the Presenting Problem a Solution to Within the Niche?

The practitioner and client now have many of the pieces to understand the client's niche relative to the presenting problem. At this step, the task is to put the pieces together in such a way so that the presenting problem is understood to be a functional part of the niche. This idea is similar to the notion of "secondary gain" (as it has been called in psychoanalysis; see Freud, 1965), common to many theories. That is, what gains does the client receive through his or her symptoms? Or, what are the needs being met, however costly or maladaptively, through patterns that have become problems in themselves? From this point of view, behavior that may appear neurotic or irrational can be understood to contain functional elements.

The practitioner and client, therefore, are striving to answer such questions as: What factors in the client's environment elicit and/or support the problem behavior? What other problems are addressed or solved when the client or others engage in the presenting problems? What are the schemas, scripts, and information-processing patterns that help explain the client's experiential reality in problem situations, regardless of how others might understand the same situation? What are the deficiencies and impediments, as well as resources and capacities, regarding alternative problem-solving patterns?

In the cognitive-ecological approach, one assessment goal is to understand what the client's life is like, what it feels like to be her, what the niche is that she lives in. Thus, the functional analysis of the presenting problem (that is, it having a function within the niche) extends to describe how the various pieces of information obtained through the assessment fit together to create an understandable and coherent worldview. As Guidano & Liotti (1983) state, it is not important that this worldview is right in an objective sense, as long as it conveys the understandings, feelings, and experiences of the client. It is right (that it, it is face valid) from her point of view. The description of the niche reflects how the client experiences the world. It contains recurring themes and challenges, similarities and patterns, routines of behavior. It reflects goals, dreams, and consistent self-images in response to the realities of her environment. It reflects the client's struggle to create a life for herself—where she has been and where she wishes to go.

SUMMARY

Assessment is the process by which we work to understand our clients and the problems they bring to us. It begins the moment we first make contact with the client, and includes piecing together into a coherent picture information from often disparate sources. It is important to keep in mind that the assessment information that we gather must be viewed in context: Interview data is information about how clients react under interview conditions, and standardized assessment instruments provide data on how clients react to standardized instruments. It is the practitioner's job to help the client put these different pieces together to develop a picture of the client's life and how the presenting problems fit within it. It is also important to remember that we are susceptible to our own inherent perceptual biases, which will lead us to look for information that confirms what we believe we know already, and which blinds us to alternatives. Furthermore, simply being cognizant of our biases will typically not alleviate them.

The goals of assessment are (a) informational, (b) educational, and (c) motivational as we work collaboratively with clients to gather information, to establish norms, roles, and rules for how change will take place, and to demystify this initial stage of the helping process as a resource for later self-help efforts by the client. Ultimately, as professional practitioners, we should strive to understand what our clients' lives feel like to them, and to handle each phase of intervention to provide as much educational and motivational benefit as possible for the client.

The basic steps to a cognitive-ecological assessment identified and discussed are:

1. Identify presenting problem(s).
2. Identify situations in which problem(s) do and do not exist.

3. Identify client's characteristic reaction and problem-solving patterns related to presenting problems.

4. Identify client's distal environment, proximal environment, and the distal and proximal person factors (i.e., the environmental and individual realities of the niche) related to the problems and situations.

5. Identify the client's daily routines, life tasks, and possible selves and niches related to presenting problems.

6. Determine how the client's presenting problems are best understood given the niche. What is the presenting problem a solution to within the niche?

Assessment begins the process whereby the client realizes he is an active collaborator in the work. From a cognitive-ecological perspective, since ultimately one wants to understand what the client's life feels like, it is absolutely critical that the client and the practitioner strive together to identify the key elements that make up his life story and that guide subsequent meaning making and problem solving. In addition, by making the process and skills of assessment transparent, the client is able to learn how to repeat these activities in the future.

This collaborative process of reconstructing one's life story demonstrates to clients that they make choices as to how they respond, and what they respond to. This is meant to initiate an empowerment process, whereby the client begins to realize that she can take more active control over many aspects of life, and that she can rely less on automatic and mindless (Langer, 1989) reactions to life events. Assessment initiates this process since it is within the assessment phase that we initiate our genuine relationship with our client, that which will serve as the basis for the positive work in which the practitioner and client will engage (Bordin, 1975).

In the next chapter, we will describe how to take our assessment of the client and develop change and maintenance goals.

Chapter 7

GOAL-SETTING
AND CONTRACTING

The previous chapter on assessment described how assessment interviews initiate the helping process and the collaborative relationship between the client and the practitioner. We discussed how one should use the assessment process to learn how clients feel and experience their lives. Information is collected to help practitioners and clients make sense of presenting problems and learn how they fit into clients' niches, with particular attention to the cognitive, affective, and social patterns that characterize their efforts to cope and solve problems in daily life.

In this chapter, the information obtained from the assessment is used to develop goals for treatment, which are laid down in a treatment contract. As discussed in previous chapters, goals—and the idea of life goals in particular—have a special place in the cognitive-ecological model of practice. We use life goals to coordinate all activity in our lives; they are the organizing images that give our unfolding lives shape and meaning. We will continue our discussion of life goals in this chapter, and particularly how they can be developed into the type of goals that can be used to help clients seeking change. After this general discussion, we will describe the purpose and characteristics of intervention or service goals, and then how to establish them with clients. Finally, we will discuss how to establish contracts with clients. Contracts aid the practitioner and client in remaining on track: They specify what the client can expect from the intervention and from the practitioner, as well as what their own responsibilities will be. Contracts are another tool to help demystify professional practice, to foster mindfulness, and to establish a collaborative relationship between the practitioner and client.

WHAT ARE GOALS?

Goals define end states for the changes we are committing energy and resources toward. We generally think of goals as signs that provide information about whether intervention assistance is headed in the right direction, and when it has reached its destination (i.e., whether the client has accomplished what she wishes to or has made changes to a sufficient degree to shift change efforts outside of formal helping). Goldfried (1982) writes that goals provide structure and benchmarks for intervention, regardless of the practitioner's theoretical orientation. Whether from a psychodynamic or a behavioral perspective, goals are used to help structure intervention decisions and monitor progress. They serve as one concrete mechanism for the client and practitioner to communicate about the helping process.

From a cognitive-ecological perspective, *life goals* are given center stage in the understanding of how human beings process information, interact with others, and lead their lives. We use life goals (or more precisely, possible selves and possible niches) to set the course for our current life decisions and actions. Our decisions and actions are based, in part, on our ongoing monitoring of the discrepancies between our current state and our possible states (using processes described by the thermostat analogy discussed earlier): how we can either decrease distance between our current state and our desired possible selves and niches, or how we can increase distance between our current state and our feared or negative possible selves and niches. We can chart our life trajectory on the path between our past life story, our current niche, and our future possible selves and possible niches.

From a cognitive-ecological perspective, our daily life is structured by the thoughts, feelings, and actions directed toward addressing our life goals and tasks (Cantor & Kihlstrom, 1989). Some personality theorists argue that goal-formation and goal-striving are processes fundamental to our existence (Klinger, 1977, 1989). Goals give our lives meaning, and we use them to define who we are (see Brower, 1992; Emmons, 1986; Emmons & King, 1989; Pervin, 1989).

Goal-Striving and Niche Stability

At this point, the reader may be aware of an apparent paradox between the notion of goal-directed, future-oriented behavior on the one hand, and our inherent inclination on the other to maintain stability and consistency in our life niches. This has been a criticism of homeostasis models of behavior, as discussed in Chapter 2: While a homeostasis model assumes that a system will always react to neutralize or negate the effects of change (either internal to the individual or external in the environment), evolution and mutation create opportunities for growth and development. From a cognitive-ecological perspective, changes are viewed as points of decision, where the individual can decide whether his niche will change in significant ways (i.e., evolve) in response to the change, or will instead become more resilient to it (i.e., maintain the status quo). This choice related to one of our core themes, of enhancing mindfulness versus responding to change in mindless, automatic ways.

While people tend to seek a balance between predictability and curiosity, at different points in our lives we will lean more in one direction than the other (such as toward the reassurance of predictability and stability following a particularly challenging or stressful period). Thus, we often exhibit our dual need to maintain the integrity of our niches and sense of personal identity, coupled with our need for stimulation and the capacity to learn from and evolve with an ever-changing world. Goals provide us with ballast, with directional signs and signals that allow us to navigate in a more or less purposeful course through life's changes and surprises. In these ways, understanding clients' life goals provides keys to understanding their life story and life trajectory.

THE RELATIONSHIP BETWEEN LIFE GOALS AND TREATMENT GOALS

Life goals and intervention goals, while by no means independent, are two different things. *Life goals* (possible selves and niches) are what we use to structure meaning and direction in our current and future actions. *Intervention goals* are what are used in the practice setting to structure intervention decisions and actions. Life goals and treatment goals are connected in that intervention goals will be shaped by and formed in the service of life goals. However, they are not identical, and much work must happen between the practitioner and the client before life goals can be translated into goals effective for planned change efforts. In this chapter, we will discuss how to develop intervention goals from clients' life goals and change goals. As will be discussed below, we often use life goals in mindless ways: They are often vague, unarticulated, and even unrecognized in our daily conscious thoughts (such as when we are surprised to notice our obsequiousness in the workplace as our way to get in with the boss). Even when life goals are rather clearly defined, the ways of operating that we often build up become so automatic that we sometimes lose sight of the original goals, becoming invested in the modus operandi that we set in motion.

　　Life goals are motivating to the extent that they are both personally salient and clear (Bandura, 1986; Blai, 1987; Markus & Nurius, 1986). Furthermore, our self-esteem is directly related to where we see ourselves in relation to our life goals and to what we most value (Dweck, 1986). To be most effective, intervention goals must be precise, time-defined, and explicitly agreed upon by the practitioner and client. Therefore, the process of translating life goals to intervention goals consists of helping clients develop the declarative knowledge necessary to make their possible selves and niches more clear, and the procedural knowledge necessary to make their possible selves and niches more attainable. It often feels as though the practitioner and client uncover the life goals by articulating them in the assessment process. Intervention goals are then explicitly developed in discussions between them.

　　We have found that goals can be developed with clients most easily and effectively when they initiate from a prior discussion of life goals. As discussed in previous chapters, the discussions with clients of possible selves and possible niches are lively and very often can be quite fun. Clients can be imbued with the excitement of possibility, and through the process to develop treatment goals from life goals, are assisted to envision the steps necessary to go from their current state to their goal states. Possible selves and niches are enlivened when clients are helped to imagine specifics about how they will feel, who they will be with, what they will see, smell, and hear, what they will be wearing, and what they will be doing. The more that clients use their enlivened possible selves and possible niches in their life-course decision making, the less likely they are to be distracted by short-term setbacks, and the more likely they are to make positive steps toward realizing their goal states.

　　It is important to keep in mind that different people will vary in the extent to which they rely on goals to structure daily life. A dimension of individual difference exists in terms of how various people lead their lives according to goals. On one extreme are those who define very concrete and explicit goals to structure their every decision and behavior. We might view these people as compulsive, extremely driven, or Type A in their planning style. A very different person would be one who has a number of personal goals but relates to them in an impulsive manner, being stimulated by the strongest current of the moment and jumping from one to another. Goals for these individuals may not have an ordering in terms of priority, or a coherence in terms of how they collectively add up to a life story and general life plan. As a function of this, their goals are likely to be vaguely articulated, lacking the salience and procedural information to help sustain and direct their energy. Some individuals are not drawn to thinking of their lives as particularly goal-oriented, and others have goals that are articulated primarily in terms of what they want to avoid.

Knowing how goals function for different people matters in professional practice for two reasons. First it is the job of the counselor to match interventions to suit the style and preferences of the client. If a client does not think of his or her life in terms of explicit goals, then one needs to take a soft line in their use: adjusting the language used to match that of the client, or helping the client develop images of what he would like his life to look like (i.e., helping to develop a clearer picture of possible selves and possible niches). On the other hand, if the concept of goals is compatible with how the client thinks, then building upon this orientation will be a more natural bridge between life goals and intervention goals.

Second, while clients will differ in their reliance on explicit goals in their lives, one tenet of the cognitive-ecological approach to practice is to educate clients to understand the goal-directed nature of their own behavior. Clearly and reasonably defined goals have been found to be one of the primary predictors of positive change in practice (see Cormier & Cormier, 1991). Part of the effectiveness of a cognitive-ecological approach is to help clients understand that their own behaviors are rational and reasonable—that is, goal-directed and problem-solving— given the niche from which they come. Part of the process that leads to successful outcomes in a cognitive-ecological intervention is making more explicit the implicit goal-directedness of clients' behaviors. This process begins in assessment when the practitioner helps clients understand their behaviors and presenting problems as springing from their niches, and continues in the goal-setting phase as life goals and intervention goals are made more explicit and concrete.

Goals sometimes flow naturally from the problems identified—such as when an assessment uncovers an unwanted alcohol addiction, and the goal becomes helping the client reach and sustain sobriety. Achieving these goals then becomes the focus at subsequent steps of intervention planning. At other times, the assessment identifies problems that can be addressed through any number of reasonable goals—such as when problems exist between neighbors living in the same housing complex, and appropriate goals may range from setting up rules for noise and privacy, to finding new housing. In some instances, clients seem to bypass identifying their problems altogether. They will tell us their solution ("my family should all be together for dinner," or "Johnny needs to stop hanging out with those trouble-making friends of his") before telling us the problem ("we seem to be drifting apart as a family," or "Johnny is getting into more and more serious trouble with the law").

In all cases, it is the task of the practitioner to work with the client to develop goals that are clear and specific, functional and feasible, motivating and attractive, that are positively phrased and are likely to be accomplished, and that are acceptable to the client's values and culture. These are some of the features of intervention goals, discussed below, that are universally important toward both attaining an outcome that the client views as successful and providing the client an opportunity to practice a component of effective problem solving. Developing treatment goals along all of these criteria is difficult. It is a true professional skill on which one improves with practice and experience.

The idea of using goals to structure practice is sometimes disconcerting to practitioners. For some, the fear is that these make professional practice too mechanical, not leaving room for genuine and spontaneous feelings. It is again important to observe that we all use goals in our daily lives. They can be very concrete and narrow—such as "initiating conversations with at least three new people before next week" for a person interested in developing her social skills and trying out some of the ideas she is learning in counseling. They can also be as vague and broad as "surviving the coming 2-week vacation when my preschoolers aren't in day care," a goal of a single mother who was the client of one of the authors. We all use a combination of well-defined and ill-defined goals in our daily lives.

Goals, by themselves, are not dehumanizing; it is instead their method of use that can become formulaic and lock-step. In fact, as described in Chapter 4, goals are a critical first step in the process of constructing visions of alternatives for oneself and one's niche, of acquiring procedural knowledge for how to actualize these, and of developing the positive expectancies and motivational momentum needed to sustain the hard work of significant life change. As a practitioner, it is important to help make clients' use of goals as functional for them as possible. This may mean helping some clients develop more concrete, explicit, and realistic goals. It may also mean helping other clients relax their rigid reliance on goals, standards, and schedules to become more flexible in their abilities to handle daily life events and pressures. And, of course, we must also guard against becoming either too rigidly reliant or too lax in our purposeful use of goals in our work with clients.

THE PURPOSE OF GOALS IN TREATMENT

Cormier and Cormier (1991, pp. 217-218) list six purposes for defining goals in direct practice. They are discussed below in terms of the cognitive-ecological model:

1. Goals provide a direction and structure for professional practice; they provide guides and expectations to the practitioner and client for what can and cannot be accomplished. By developing goals specifically with the client, the counselor increases the chances that the intervention or service will in fact address the client's concerns.

Even when counselors work hard to develop goals with clients, it is not always the case that clients can articulate those goals that are most important to them In the previous chapter, we saw an example in which initial goals needed to be reviewed after the client, who worked for several months on issues related to self-esteem and assertiveness, spoke of his severe bulimia and desire for help with this. In some cases, clients are keenly aware of their distress and desire for relief, but cannot always articulate their concerns or goals At different points in life, we sometimes just do not know what to think, or what we can do, or how things can become better. This was discussed in the previous chapter in terms of assessment functioning as an ongoing process rather than a phase that is completed early on and never revisited. The same must be said for goal-setting: Practitioners need to be flexible enough to adjust goals or create them anew when new information becomes available in later sessions, and yet also balance flexibility with helping the client learn how to maintain focus in the midst of potentially overwhelming feelings and events and to persevere in a change process that itself often feels frightening and foreign.

2. Goals permit practitioners to determine whether they have the skills, competencies, and interest to work with a particular client toward a particular outcome. Goals, in other words, provide a clearer picture of what the client desires and needs from the practice relationship and from professional service. Practitioners can then determine whether they can meet the client's needs.

One element that can come into play here is our inclination to identify problems and goals that we have resources to handle. While this is understandable and perhaps even necessary, it prevents us from determining whether the identified problems and goals are most central or likely to provide the kind of change most needed by the client. Thus, a pragmatic balance is needed between parsimony in the nearly endless array of potential problem areas we could explore and openness to clues about needs for which we must refer the client elsewhere.

3. Goals serve the purpose of facilitating successful outcomes by contributing to our ability to cognitively enrich and rehearse problem solving and performances, and by directing our attention to the resources in our environment that are most likely to facilitate solutions. The following chapter discusses processes that we can engage in to assist our clients to link their treatment goals to their current life state.

Goals provide another clue into understanding how our clients think about themselves and their problems. How clients perceive solutions to the problems in their lives provides information about how they see their own power in the situation, what factors are most important in the situation, and what strategies and solutions have been preferred and/or practiced.

4. Goals serve as a basis for selecting and using particular practice strategies and services: Changes desired by the client will in part determine the kinds of interventions that will lead to successful outcomes. Without goals to help define what clients seek from their work with the practitioner, it is almost impossible to explain and defend one's intervention decisions.

Furthermore, the link between goals and the determination of strategies for change is important to model for the client. Many people have identified their problems and have a good idea of what they would like to achieve. And, understandably, they feel that if they knew what to do next they would not need to come in for professional help. Thus, techniques such as breaking global goals into more specific and incremental subgoals, and evaluating interventions as being effective toward attaining these goals, represent concrete means to further clients' abilities to carry forward their problem-solving work.

5. Goals provide standards against which progress can be measured. As such, they serve as one yardstick for indicating how much clients have already accomplished, what services have been obtained, what undesired consequences have been prevented, and what is left to be done. Again, how goals are defined will affect their utility in this regard. Goals stated as relatively abstract and distant states (such as improved self-esteem) are not terribly helpful in determining where a client is at any given point relative to where the client is hoping to end up.

With the "illusory glow" that clients often feel due to the unburdening that takes place in initial sessions (Mann, 1973; Serban, 1982), it is easy to overestimate early client progress. Moreover, when subsequent change does not keep pace with the initial changes made in expressiveness and relationship building, it is equally as easy to underestimate the actual progress that has taken place. Goals provide a means by which the client and practitioner can keep themselves accurately anchored in the reference points of the client's life (e.g., where they were when they started out, and what they initially saw as reasonable or desirable to accomplish). Initial goals may well undergo revision; for example, people often raise or otherwise change their expectations when they are feeling better and have experienced some success. Goals also provide a means for the client and practitioner to stay focused on a limited set of priority objectives and to reduce the risk of getting distracted and fragmented. Again, early goals may well need to be revised, but that should be done explicitly and carefully.

6. As briefly noted above, the process of defining goals and using them to plan interventions, like the assessment process before it, has therapeutic and educational benefits in and of itself. Clients will very often gain considerable insight, clarity, or a sense of direction and purpose as a result of the goal-setting process. Clarifying and prioritizing goals helps all of us develop a more functional view of our problems, and helps place problems and goals within a more manageable context. Clients' levels of hope and motivation for the work of change often increase when goals are clearly defined and steps to achieve them are determined (Locke, 1984).

By way of a summary, remember that from a cognitive-ecological perspective, clients are understood to have problems in daily living when their niches are disrupted, for a variety of reasons (for example, losing one's job, changing schools, getting married or divorced, experiencing harassment, or any number of psychological, emotional, or environmental changes). The basic intervention strategy, therefore (discussed more fully in the following chapter), is to help clients reestablish the smooth working of their niche through some combination of person, environment, and social transaction change. And while this does not necessarily mean reestablishing niches to their former states, clients are helped to reestablish their niches in ways that functionally adapt to the internal and external changes that created the disruption in the first place.

In assessment, the main tasks are to understand clients' presenting problems within the context of their niche. During the goal-setting and contracting phase of the helping process, the main tasks are to identify the ways and means to achieve the reestablishment of the niche, or rather to identify priority aspects of this reestablishment process. This points to an often overlooked distinction in types of goals (Rosen & Proctor, 1981). *Ultimate* goals are those that define an ultimate aim or endpoint ("obtaining a stable full-time job in my field of training" following an injury that prevents current employment options). *Interim* goals are those that define steps that are necessary along the way to accomplishing ultimate goals ("establishing what the potential job pool includes"; "strengthening job readiness skills"; "getting an interview with the XYZ Company"). Finally, *instrumental* goals, or *objectives,* are those that define skills necessary to attain interim or ultimate goals ("completing the Department of Vocational Training's night class on seeking and keeping a job"; "successfully completing job interview role plays until I feel fairly comfortable with it"; "filling out applications with the companies identified as appropriate for my skills").

Too often, discussion related to client goals does not progress beyond identifying ultimate goals. It is important to determine the interim steps and instrumental skills required in order to define the pathways toward achieving these ultimate goals. As discussed in the prior chapters, one objective in the change process is to assist clients to expand their problem-solving repertoire and to transfer use of this repertoire into daily life and routine patterns. By working with clients to determine their interim steps (i.e., helping them concretize their possible selves and niches and their problem-solving sequences) and instrumental skills (i.e., gaining semantic and procedural knowledge to undertake change efforts), we are helping them develop their repertoire of schemas for themselves, others, and preferred situations. We are therefore working to develop a wider range of responses to situations that they can apply in more mindful ways.

CHARACTERISTICS OF
EFFECTIVE INTERVENTION GOALS

For goals to be effective in practice, they must possess several characteristics.

Specific and Clear, Verifiable and Measurable

First, they must be *behaviorally specific and clear*, making them *verifiable and measurable*. A goal of "being less stressed out" is not as clear and specific as "being able to sleep well, regularly spend time with friends, and maintain my anxiety at a low to occasionally moderate level." Goals must also be verifiable and measurable. Helping someone "improve my self-esteem," while quite common as a goal, is not verifiable or measurable in and of itself. One must first carefully operationalize what self-esteem means for the particular client, and how self-esteem is manifested in daily life. From this follows the ability to document how to know when the client's self-esteem is improved and how much improvement is needed to be satisfactory. One common method is to use standardized instruments to measure goal progress. Temporal changes in scores on the instrument then become an explicit part of the goal definition. Thus, one way to explicitly anchor "improving my self-esteem" would be to reword it in terms of "getting my score on the Hudson Index of Self-Esteem down below 50 and then keeping it stable at a score of 35 or less."

But the point is not that we must always use standardized instruments to operationalize goal progress. It is important to determine with clients how to best define and operationalize progress. While we advocate the use of behavior-specific and repeatable measures in practice, we also realize that different practice settings will lend themselves to certain kinds of measurement strategies over others. For some clients, it may be possible to use paper-and-pencil instruments; for others, one must rely on more unobtrusive observations (e.g., by the practitioner, other staff members, family members, or teachers). Some practice settings are structured to facilitate observation by third parties; in others, one is lucky to find a relatively quiet corner in which to talk. The following chapters will explore how various measurement strategies can be used effectively under various conditions.

When standardized scales are used to measure progress, it is often the case that a pre-post strategy is used, generally at the point of intake or early in the service period, and again at the point of termination or case closure. Increasingly, practitioners are drawing upon brief, focused assessment tools on a periodic basis (e.g., every 2 or 3 weeks). In terms of ongoing, frequent indicators of progress, one must make explicit the criteria for evaluating progress. One might ask: "With this client, how will the client and I know when her self-esteem is improved? Will she appear emotionally 'brighter' and more energetic? Or will she initiate conversations and topics more?" Very often, we intuitively think we know when our clients are getting better, but we do not ask ourselves explicitly to identify the types of changes we expect, or to document these characteristics, or, consequently, to share this reasoning and observation with our clients.

Let us consider some of the ways that working toward being more explicit in this facet of our clinical reasoning might be important. One has to do with the incremental nature of change. Virtually anyone can detect significant, marked changes in individuals; however, lasting change of long-standing problems is rarely as easy. More typically, it is two steps forward, one step back; sometimes small steps are taken, with often uneven rates of change (e.g., acquiring new skills before feeling comfortable with them, or before seeing oneself as authentic in changed aspects of life-style or relationships). We need aids to help us and our clients detect and keep track of the more subtle or unexpected aspects of change, given the often fragmented reality of modern life and the pressures of time-limited counseling. In some cases this may mean becoming more aware of factors that were previously underattended, such as learning to identify early stages of one's emotional responses that previously were overlooked. Moreover, being explicit about our implicit hunches or expectations helps guard against the inherent inclinations we all have to "see what we believe." It is simply too easy to see change when none exists, or to discount or overlook changes that we are not expecting to see.

The suggestion for this characteristic of establishing goals, therefore, is to be explicit in one's observations about clients' improvement. If improving self-esteem involves a client's feeling better about herself, then one component in better defining the goal may be to observe significantly more self-acknowledgments and affirmations and fewer self-denigrating and discounting statements. Often certain circumstances in a client's life are more challenging for clients than others, and pose challenges that intervention sessions do not. Thus, goals may be specifically framed in terms of the most relevant conditions in the client's social niche (for a fuller discussion of this process, see Brower & Mutschler, 1985; Brower & Nurius, 1985).

Functional Result States

Second, for goals to be effective, they should describe a behavioral, cognitive, or affective resultant state that is functional for the client, rather than describing a process. A goal stated as a process is one like "to lose weight." This goal can be more effectively stated as "to lose 15 pounds." The goal must also be functional; it would not be healthy, for example, to specify that these 15 pounds should be lost in a month's time.

By stating goals as functional result states, the client is helped to enliven the possible self or niche that is being developed. "To lose weight" does not help one envision oneself as thinner. It tells one what to do, but not how one will look. "To lose 15 pounds" (or better yet, "to lose enough weight to fit into my 32-waist pants") creates a clear future self-image toward which one can strive.

Mutually Agreed Upon,
Related to Presenting Problems

Third, goals must be mutually agreed upon and explicitly related to clients' presenting problems. This sounds like an obvious point to make, but can be difficult to accomplish. Working with involuntary clients poses unique problems when trying to agree on goals. It often takes quite a long time, for example, before a spouse abuser will agree to work on anger control. His beginning view of goals to be achieved may involve stopping his wife and family from making him angry—she never attends to his needs, the kids need discipline, and so on. In this case, it can be quite difficult to develop goals that are mutually agreed upon. In such cases, the initial set of goals may well not reflect the practitioner's judgment about the ultimate goals needed, but will provide a beginning point for building later agreements (e.g., the ultimate goal being significant changes in his beliefs and attitudes regarding aggression and responsibility for his own behavior, yet beginning with an initial goal of ceasing violence to keep from being jailed and losing his parental rights).

The circumstances that render a case involuntary generally also influence beginning points of negotiation for the professional relationship. For example, the court system is increasingly mandating counseling as a condition to avoiding or reducing jail sentences. Similarly, clients deemed as being at imminent risk to themselves (or others) may be required to receive services before freedom can be regained. The practitioner then needs to work on at least two goal levels: one to satisfy the externally perceived risk (e.g., toward reducing aggressive behavior and/or risk to others) and one that more explicitly reflects the client's greatest concerns (e.g., power hassles and better rapport with family; feeling less threatened and more in control).

Garvin and Seabury (1984) suggest that this approach can mediate clients' resistance to engage in professional practice since clients can be encouraged to make use of the opportunity to address their own concerns. The practitioner will need to make sure these two sets of goals are complementary, of course—that the client's goals are not working at cross-purposes to the mandated treatment. Taking this approach explicitly with involuntary clients provides an inroad for client self-determination and for the development of collaboration and trust, both important for intervention goals to be achieved and maintained.

But even with voluntary clients, it still takes considerable skill for the practitioner to develop goals that are agreed upon and that relate to presenting problems. It will often be the case that the practitioner will gain an understanding of clients and their problems that is not immediately clear or obvious to the clients. For example, a client came in after a recent breakup with a girlfriend, hoping to gain control over his suicidal feelings and depression. Through the assessment, the practitioner realized that the client was sexually abused as a child, that current intimacy problems and self-denigration appeared related to this trauma, and that the current problems posed risks for future relationships and continued suicidal feelings. The question becomes how to build the practitioner's assessment into goals that the client sees and wants. In this example, the practitioner was able to use the client's desire to gain control over his feelings as a pivotal point around which a series of goals was identified, to first address the client's immediate feelings and then leading to better understanding and coping with the trauma factors that put him at future risk.

In other cases, clients may be less open to broadening or revising how they frame their goals. The practitioner must then decide how to best meet clients' immediate needs without reinforcing dysfunctional coping strategies. The practitioner is not always correct, of course, in these perceptions about what will lead ultimately to more functional or satisfying behavior. In almost all cases, practitioners will need to reconcile their understanding of their clients, the presenting problems, and the clients' niches with the clients' own views. In fact, it will be only in those cases where clients are a danger to themselves or others (and in some involuntary settings) that the practitioner's perceptions will overrule those of the client.

Adequate to the Problem

Fourth, goals must be adequate to the problem they address. When the goal is accomplished, the problem situation should be significantly improved. With a suicidal client, it is not enough to help the client feel better or be less depressed. Instead, it is necessary to establish goals that more clearly and adequately attend to the client's safety in both environmental terms (e.g., no immediately available means of suicide, or having an adequately protective environment) and in person terms (e.g., no longer feeling suicidal or being imminently at risk). Chapter 9 will discuss guidelines for determining how to set adequate levels of improvement: how to develop clinically significant cut-off points based on baseline assessments, how to identify minimum levels of health and safety, and so forth.

Positively Stated, Providing Motivation

Fifth, goals should be positively stated and provide positive motivation for the client. Goals framed as positive states to achieve are more attractive and motivating than those framed as negative states to avoid (Bandura, 1986). "I will talk to one new person this week" is a more positively stated, and therefore more motivating goal than "I will feel less self-conscious at the next party I go to." Or, instead of "I won't blow up at my kids as often," this goal can be redefined as, "When I begin to feel fed up with my kids, I will leave the room before yelling at them, and then count to ten. If I still feel angry, I will call my sister to come over to watch the kids, and then leave the house for an hour." Note, too, that this redefinition describes result states rather than processes (as suggested above). It also describes several strategies for how the client will accomplish her goals, providing a head start in the development of interventions and the monitoring of successful change.

Realistic, Given the Niche

Sixth, goals should be realistic in terms of proximal and distal environment and person. In other words, goals need to fit within clients' abilities or capacities and be supportable within their niche. It makes little sense to state a goal of "achieving straight As" for a student who generally gets Cs and Ds. Similarly, although understandable, the goal of "be able to give my kids everything they need" is unlikely to be realistic for a single mother who struggles to make ends meet each month. This is not to argue that aspects of goals such as these are not realistic, or that, ultimately, they may not be achievable (such as assisting the working mother to gradually enhance her life circumstances and earning potential). This issue of realism is very often linked to distinguishing ultimate goals from interim goals. It also is linked to the translation of vague or incompletely visualized possible selves and possible niches into those that are more clearly developed and defined. It is not always the case, of course, that more clear goals will be more realistic. However, it is the case that unclear goals cannot be realistic, if for no other reason than they will not present a sufficiently clear picture toward which to strive.

Have a High Chance for Success

Seventh, goals should be feasible. They should have a good chance of being accomplished. Heus and Pincus (1986) define *feasibility* as the state in which resources for change are greater than the barriers. Formal helping provides the opportunity for clients to feel a sense of accomplishment and change in their lives. Whenever possible, goals need to be developed strategically to facilitate accomplishment, reinforce positive change. We will discuss how to do this below in our discussion of prioritizing goals based on their ripple effect.

Determining feasibility also includes evaluating possible advantages and disadvantages to accomplishing the goal. From a cognitive-ecological perspective, any change in the client's niche, including positive changes engendered by goal attainment, affects other components of the niche to a lesser or greater extent. For example, it is sometimes the case that when women who are abused decide to take steps to stop their spouse's abuse, they place themselves at greater risk for abuse, and are forced to relocate themselves and their families. This is not to say that further difficulties arising from positive changes should prevent the changes from taking place. Rather, it is incumbent upon the practitioner to help the client anticipate these difficulties or complications in order to carefully weigh the costs and benefits, the impediments and resources, and to be prepared to contend with feasibility complications as they arise.

Consistent With Clients' Values and Culture

Finally, in order for goals to make sense to clients and to maximize their ability to create lasting change in clients' niches, goals should be consistent and congruent with clients' values and cultural system. Goals that are inconsistent with clients' values have little chance of being attractive and motivating. Those inconsistent with clients' cultural background likewise have little chance of being supported by others in their niche. The work to bring goals in line with clients' values and culture will be greatly facilitated by the work that was initiated during assessment to understand as much as possible what the client feels and experiences in her life. Having this knowledge of the client's life makes it much easier to shape goals to fit within it.

ESTABLISHING TREATMENT GOALS

The process to develop goals, to set a goal-based intervention agenda, can be quite difficult. It is difficult to select and define goals that are neither trivially simple nor too vague and global, that are neither totally foreign to clients' ways of thinking nor reinforcing the dysfunctional processes that have led to the problems presented. The cognitive-ecological model provides some help in this regard, having encouraged the practitioner to understand the client's niche and see the world as the client sees it. In this section, we will continue developing the theme of translating clients' life goals (i.e., possible selves and possible niches) into concrete treatment goals.

It is the authors' experience that the key is to work with clients to see how their problems are a reasonable and understandable product of their niche (as discussed in previous chapters). Engaging with the client in this process, above all else, creates the larger context from which clients can begin to understand how a range of goals can relate to the presenting problems, and how presenting problems can be addressed through a variety of venues.

1. Develop a Niche Summary

To begin the process of establishing treatment goals, it is helpful to first summarize what is known about the client, her niche, and her presenting problem: "From what you've told me, it sounds like the main problems have to do with figuring out ways to discipline your kids, particularly to keep them from fighting with each other so much when you're trying to do your homework. It sounds like you're now on an emotional roller coaster of getting uncontrollably angry and then feeling guilty and getting really down on yourself as a parent. How does this sound to you?" Note two things in this example. First, the summary statement connects explicitly to the client's feelings and experiences, and not just to her thoughts or to the situation. For example, this statement could have been stated without reference to the client's roller coaster feelings at all, or could have only made reference to the client's self-perceptions of being a "bad mother." By making summary comments that are explicitly tied to clients' feelings and experiences, the summary is given more impact and immediate relevance: It becomes a "live" comment that has real meaning for the client, rather than a model for how to overintellectualize problems.

Second, note that the practitioner specifically checks out the validity of the summary with the client. By being asked whether the summary makes sense and is complete enough, the client is given the chance to modify or reject entirely the practitioner's summary. It is reinforcing the fact that the client is the expert in her own life, and a true collaborator in the process of understanding the problem and formulating goals and interventions.

2. Develop a List of Treatment Goals

After agreeing on a summary statement of the problem and what it feels like to be inside that problem, a list of desired ultimate, interim, and instrumental goals can be generated. This process begins by starting with clients' life goals (i.e., their possible selves and possible niches), and then working backwards through the interim and instrumental goals that will be required to accomplish the life goals.

Thinking about the client example above, one life goal was to become a "good mother" who did not feel so frustrated by her kids. We would start then by developing the possible self and niche based on this life goal. The client would be asked to imagine what she would look like as a good mother, what she would be doing, what her kids would be doing, how they would spend their days, and so on. She would be asked to cognitively and affectively complete her picture of "good mother," including her imagined interactions with her kids.

Once this picture is more clear, the client is aided in imagining the instrumental and interim goals that will help her reach her ideal state.

Each aspect of the possible self and niche should be examined: how she would act on her own, versus how she would act with the kids, versus how the kids would act among themselves, and so on. Ideally, goals should be initiated by the client: "So you want better ways to keep your kids from fighting. How would you like to see them behave?" The practitioner might have to prompt to help the client envision and articulate what desired changes would look like: "How would you like them to settle their disputes?" or "What would it be like after dinner if your kids didn't fight?" The idea is to get the client to imagine a good outcome, see the picture of the solved situation in her mind. The idea is to help the client visualize possible selves and niches as the embodiment of desired goal state.

3. Develop a Priority List

After developing a summary and a list of goals, the third step is to prioritize them. This will be discussed in terms of intervention sequencing in the next chapter. To initiate this discussion in terms of prioritizing treatment goals, a few guidelines can be described here. Priorities should first be based on safety issues or medical needs (stopping abuse in a home before teaching parenting skills; assessing suicide risks and providing a protective environment before addressing underlying depression; getting medications adjusted for a schizophrenic client before helping him find a job; stabilizing electrolytes before addressing self-esteem for an anorexic client). After that, goals can be prioritized according to their attractiveness and/or importance to the client. Goals can also be prioritized according to the barriers that exist that might prevent a goal's attainment. Goals may be prioritized, in other words, according to their ease of being accomplished.

If all things are equal, goals should be prioritized according to their leverage in the niche, their ability to create change in other aspects of the niche and in other systems related to the niche. For example, if improving the above client's assertiveness skills will have a large positive ripple effect on her ability to parent, on her self-esteem, and on her ability to maintain the household schedule, then this goal should be addressed before others. Some goals can be ultimate goals by themselves and serve as instrumental goals in relation to others. Teaching a client how to use relaxation techniques may directly address his goal of "taking time out of my day for myself." It may also serve as instrumental to his other goal of "feeling more confident and competent when I have to do public speaking." Again, goals can be prioritized according to their relative leverage in the client's niche, their ability to facilitate accomplishing other goals and/or their ability to precipitate positive changes throughout the niche.

4. Develop a Timeline

After the goal list has been prioritized, a timeline should be established to specify when ultimate, interim, and instrumental goals will be accomplished. It is important to determine that "I will help the kids negotiate their own problems before our Christmas break." Determining a time frame, by itself, provides additional motivation for goal attainment since most people work to complete tasks according to deadlines (Mann, 1981). This is not always the case, however, and in all cases, it is important that the timeline is seen as the client's own rather than one set by the practitioner. If clients perceive that the practitioner is setting deadlines for them, it becomes too easy to fall into the situation where the practitioner is more invested in the change than the client, or worse, where clients begin to resist or work against goal attainment as a response to the feeling that the practitioner is pushing them into actions about which they feel ambivalent. Not only involuntary clients and those prone to passive-aggressive interactions are vulnerable to this.

The principal point of a timeline is to provide markers to help clients gauge their progress. Timelines help greatly in determining when to make adjustment in an intervention that does not seem to be working very well. They help the client and practitioner become clearer with one another about what does or does not seem realistic, and timelines are part of the process of forming a contract. Obviously, the timelines are rarely, if ever, absolute and can be renegotiated as advances, setbacks, and complications arise. We should note, however, that insufficient resources are forcing agencies and insurance companies to increasingly set limits on services (Pardes & Pincus, 1981). In short, factors external to the individual case will at times play a role in planning.

5. Develop Necessary Resources

The fifth step in establishing goals is to identify resources that will be required to accomplish the goals. These resources may take the form of help from others who have skills not available to the practitioner (such as an activities counselor who can help plan after-school activities for the kids, or a colleague who has done a lot of assertiveness training and can recommend books and other instructional materials). Resources may also take the form of other systems that need to become involved for the success of the interventions. These may include such things as talking to classroom teachers to gain their cooperation in a social skills training program to be used with the client's fourth-grader, or marshaling support from the client's social network.

6. Develop a Plan for Review and Evaluation

Finally, plans should be made to routinely review the progress made toward attaining the goals established. These plans should be based not only on the time frame determined above, but also on an understanding of how progress will be measured. Will the client practice role-plays in the office to document her increased parenting skills, or will evaluation be based on self-report? Will school teachers be contacted to provide information about a child's aggressiveness, or will this information be obtained from the parents? In order to monitor change, will the clients systematically reassess themselves—by way of a standardized measure (such as the Beck Depression Inventory), a self-rating measure (such as a 1-7 anger scale), or an observational measure (such as the number of times per day one compliments or acknowledges the efforts of their estranged adolescent child)?

The thermostat analogy described earlier is useful in terms of evaluating progress. Practitioners and clients can evaluate the discrepancy between clients' present state and their goal state. When this discrepancy is evaluated, a number of decisions can be made: (a) continuing to follow the interventions previously specified, when the progress made is determined to be due to the effects of the interventions; (b) deciding to adjust or change intervention strategies, when it is determined that the effects of the previous interventions have run their course and the distance to the goal state can now be achieved through other means; or (c) deciding to adjust the goal itself, when it is determined that the client's present state is more satisfactory (or has deteriorated) than was previously thought, or that the previous goal is no longer desirable. The point is that monitoring clients' present states in relation to their goal states allows both the client and practitioner to better evaluate their present condition within the context of where they want to be.

Again, to reinforce the fact that the practitioner is working with the client, and to maximize the demystification of the treatment process, these decisions about how and when progress will be evaluated should be made an explicit part of the goal-setting procedure.

Cournoyer (1991, p. 236) provides a good illustration of how a practitioner works with a client to define and establish a treatment goal:

Practitioner: Now that we have a pretty clear list of the problems, let's try to establish specific goals for each one. The first problem we've identified is that your fourteen-year-old son skips school two or three days each week. Now, let's imagine that it is some point in the future and the problem has been resolved. How will you know that it is no longer a problem?

Client: Well, I guess I'll know when Johnny goes to school every day and his grades are better.

Practitioner (reflecting goal; seeking feedback): When Johnny goes to school daily and improves his grades, you will feel that it's no longer a problem. Is that right?

Client: Yes.

Practitioner (seeking specificity; feedback): Okay, now let's try to be even more specific. I assume that when you say "Johnny will go to school every day" you also mean that he will attend all his classes and that you don't expect him to attend school when he's sick, is that accurate?

Client: Yes.

Practitioner (seeking specificity): What do you think would be a reasonable time frame for accomplishing this goal?

Client: Well, I don't know. I'd like him to start now.

Practitioner (sharing opinion; seeking feedback): That would be great progress. But I wonder if that might be expecting a bit too much. Let's see, it's now one month into the school year. As I understand it, Johnny skipped school some last year too and this year he is skipping even more. What do you think about a two-month time frame for accomplishing the goal?

Client: That sounds really good.

Practitioner (establishing goal): Okay, let's establish this as our first goal: "Within two months from today's date, Johnny will attend school every day except when he's sick enough to go to a doctor." Let me take a moment to write that down for us. . . . Now, about the grades. As I understand it, he is currently failing most of his courses. How will you know when that is no longer a problem?

Note that in this example, the worker is quite active in helping establish a goal that is clear and specific, contains a timeline, is feasible and verifiable, and is consistent with the client's values and presenting problem. Note, too, that the practitioner began to process by asking the client to imagine the possible niche where the problem is resolved, and then they worked backwards from there. Since this example is taken out of context, it is unclear what criteria were used in selecting this goal in priority over others. Based on the first statement made by the worker, it sounds like this problem was selected because it was first on their list; it is hoped that it was also selected because of its urgency, its central importance to the client, and its leverage in the client's niche.

In some ways, this illustration presents an easy case of goal establishment: The problem identified (skipping school) is fairly concrete and defined in and of itself. Other problems, particularly those involving dealing with powerful emotions, belief systems, and idiosyncratic styles of inferring meaning, are not as clear. Cournoyer (1991, p. 237) provides another case example that illustrates goal-setting with this type of problem:

Client: Yes. It does feel like I've lost everything I had hoped for. I guess it's normal to feel sad when a marriage fails.

Practitioner (reflecting content; sharing educated opinion): Your dreams for the future of your marriage have been shattered. As I see it, it's a sign of health to feel a sense of loss and sadness when a marriage ends. Wouldn't it be awful to feel nothing?

Client: Yes, that would be worse. Like it all meant nothing. My marriage meant a lot to me.

Practitioner (seeking a final goal): I wonder if it might be possible for us to establish a specific goal in relation to these feelings of sadness and depression. When it's no longer a problem, what will be the indications? (Note, again, the value of starting by helping the client to develop his possible self and niche concerning "feeling less sad.")

Client: Well, I don't know exactly. I guess when I'm finally over her I'll feel a lot better.

Practitioner (reflecting content; seeking goal specificity): So, it will be a positive sign when you begin to feel better. And what will be the indications that you're feeling better?

Client: I guess once I'm over this, I'll be able to sleep and eat again and not think about her so much, and I might even be dating someone else.

Practitioner (reflecting content; establishing goal; seeking feedback): So, when you begin to eat and sleep better, and you think about her less, we'll know that things have taken a positive turn. Let's make the goals even more specific so that we will know when you have completely achieved them. How about this: "Within six months from this date I will be (1) sleeping six or more hours per night at least five nights per week, (2) regaining the weight that I have lost, (3) thinking at least seventy-five percent of the time about things other than my wife or the marriage, and (4) going out on a least one date." How does that sound to you?

Client: Real good. Right now I probably think about her ninety-five percent of the time, and the idea of going on a date sounds just awful. If I were thinking about other things, doing other things, and dating someone else, I'd know that I was over her.

Practitioner (establishing goal): Good. Let me jot that down so we can remember it.

In this example, note that the practitioner works hard to make the goal of "feeling better and being over his wife" specific and clear, based on the behavioral, affective, and cognitive signals provided by the client. Readers can judge for themselves whether the timeline and objectives set in this example are overly optimistic. Nevertheless, the process remains a good illustration of how one can take the feelings expressed and translate them into something that both the client and the practitioner can verify and evaluate.

SETTING SERVICE
AND INTERVENTION CONTRACTS

When the practitioner establishes goals with the client, a tacit contract will have been created. Goals will have defined what the intervention will focus on, how long it will take to complete, and what steps will be required to achieve them. What is now required is to formalize this tacit contract with the creation of a formal working agreement or contract.

The *intervention contract,* as described by Garvin and Seabury (1984), is often thought of as both a product and a process. It is literally the verbal or written agreement between the practitioner and client that specifies the work to be done. It also, however, describes the ongoing decision-making process that the practitioner and client undergo to negotiate and renegotiate the contract. Garvin and Seabury suggest that contracts should contain a *purpose* statement (i.e., why the treatment is needed in the first place), a description of *target problems, goals,* and *objectives,* as generated through the assessment and goal-setting processes described above, and a description of *specific actions, activities,* and *responsibilities* to be taken by the practitioner and client.

Thus, the contract specifies the goals and objectives for intervention and also specifies the logistics: meeting dates, times of meetings, how to contact the practitioner if the client needs to cancel or reschedule, fees and expectations for payment (if any). The contract is the opportunity to further the demystification of the helping process, to reinforce the notion that social service practice is a business relationship (albeit "humanely businesslike," as Reid [1987] describes it), convened for the express purpose of helping the client with her or his presenting problems. The contract provides a mechanism for the practitioner and client to identify their expectations and agreed-upon commitments, discuss and negotiate discrepancies, and help stay on track in the consensual purpose of working together.

Therapeutically, a contract also provides a backdrop of reality against which to discuss subsequent thoughts and feelings that arise as a function of working together. By demystifying the helping process through the specification of client and practitioner expectations, clients are given license to ask questions and make statements about the process, and practitioners remain more clear about the changes and reactions to intervention that can be expected from clients. These efforts let both parties present themselves straightforwardly and honestly, allowing the expression of genuine feeling, and allowing the development of a genuine relationship that is appropriate to the context.

Transference and countertransference feelings and perceptions are more easily seen against this backdrop of clear expectations. For example, clients with patterns of testing limits in their relationships—who will then inevitably test limits in the practice setting—can be reminded about the ground rules they agreed to. Rather than becoming a point of contention between the client and practitioner, their testing of limits can then be more easily discussed in terms of how well it is or is not serving them, and how it relates to their niche and self- and other schemas. The parallel is true for practitioners: For example, when entertained and distracted by their clients' extraneous material, it is easier to realize that their alterations to the contract may indicate their own feelings of transference, rather than their efforts to work most effectively on their clients' behalf.

The authors have found that a very good way to formulate the initial contract with clients is to deliver some version of the following about two-thirds of the way through the session in which the contract is to be specified. It will, of course, be important to not say this as a monologue, but to seek the client's reactions, and to encourage the client to fill in the specifics with you.

> Okay, we've now got a much clearer picture of the problems that concern you the most and the specific ways you would like to see those changed for the better. We've talked some about the possible obstacles and assets in working toward these changes, and of what seems realistic. At this point, I'd like to pull all of this together into a working agreement or contract. This can be a blueprint for us of what we're aiming to build and what practical considerations we need to keep in mind.

> Let's initially plan to meet once per week for 8 weeks, at this same time, for an hour. We'll focus on X, Y, and Z goals as we've been discussing them. We discussed fees and method of payment earlier, and that seems okay. At the end of the eighth week (give exact date), we can see where we are and decide whether we need to continue and, if so, if changes are needed. We will also be using a couple of things over these 8 weeks to help us keep track of your progress.

When the practitioner and the client finalize these details, it is generally a good idea to write this down, and to have a form or format available for this purpose. Some intervention approaches advocate providing a copy of the contract for the client to keep (see Reid, 1978; Reid & Epstein, 1972, on the task-centered approach). It is our belief that the decision to make a copy of the contract for clients is most sensible on a case-by-case basis, with the option generally left to the client. Some clients will value or benefit from having a copy; whereas for others, it is sufficient to keep it in their file. Nevertheless, if a copy is not given to the client, it is recommended that the practitioner write a version of the contract down in his or her case notes to be used as an aid to intervention planning, monitoring progress, modifying services, and in determining an appropriate point of termination.

Contracts Make Treatment More Palatable

One general guideline is to break the service or intervention period into discrete segments by making contracts for no more than eight sessions at a time. Contracts can be made for shorter time periods, of course, depending on the circumstances of the practice setting and of the case. Similarly, the practitioner and client can renegotiate the contract for additional 8-week segments, as circumstances permit. This 8-week (or shorter) contract provides a "digestible" package for clients. They then know what to expect from you and what is expected of them, and generally find it easier to commit to a known time frame than an open-ended one.

The explicit time frame facilitates built-in mechanisms for monitoring and evaluating progress. It provides built-in discussion frameworks for clients who are dissatisfied with the course of intervention and who may otherwise be reluctant to discuss their concerns. The structure and operating agreements that make up a contract are important for minimizing the anxiety that goes with uncertainty—reducing anxiety about the emotional, time, and financial costs that may be expected; enhancing the client's sense of control; and reinforcing the attitude of partnership and collaboration necessary as a basis for good practice.

Contracts Help Practitioners Remain "Humanely Businesslike"

It would be easy to handle contracting in a manner that trivializes its potential. This occurs when it is treated as a tedious aspect of paperwork, or when attention is focused only on factors such as the meeting hour, place, and time period. The process of contracting invites the practitioner to discuss what intervention will likely be used and why. What will the practitioner and client be doing together, and what is the practitioner drawing upon in this strategizing about client goal attainment? In the next chapter, we will discuss in detail various beliefs about helping that people hold, and the importance of establishing compatible expectations between practitioner and client about what is to take place. Thus, although intervention specifics must initially be tentative, identification of the intervention to be employed and the roles of all participants is an essential element of a contract (Hepworth & Larsen, 1990).

The reader may have noted that one theme throughout this book describes the treatment or intervention relationship in businesslike terms (as introduced in Chapter 1). Reid (1978) describes the helping relationship as proceeding best when it does so in a "humanely businesslike" manner. By this, he means that the professional practice relationship is a business relationship. It is the job of the practitioner to help the client with her presenting problems, to provide the needed resources, treatment, controls, or training, depending on the charge of the practice setting and goals of the client. This is not to say that intense feelings will not develop between client and practitioner, or that the content of the discussions and interventions will not be of a personal and highly emotional nature. Yet, the sole purpose of the relationship is to benefit the client for the purposes identified by him.

The emphasis, as was stated in previous chapters, is that every single act of the practitioner should be for the client's benefit. The practitioner is not the client's friend, family, or lover. And while many people are attracted to the helping professions because they have often taken the part of listener or counselor with family and friends, the role of professional practice in our clients' lives must be kept distinct from these other interpersonal roles. Practitioners do not serve the clients' best interests by stepping out of role to assuage anxieties or otherwise take care of a client, or to actualize the practitioner's own power or caretaker needs. Nor do practitioners serve the clients' best interests if they expect emotional bonding to take place.

Again, this is not to say that a genuine relationship does not develop between practitioners and clients, or that these feelings are not a part of effecting a lasting impact on clients' lives (Bordin, 1975). But it is always important to understand, and to demonstrate through our actions, that this relationship is a professional one, based on the business contract of the client seeking and purchasing help from the agency or practitioner for psychological, interpersonal, emotional, or other problems appropriate to the practice setting.

SOME FINAL GUIDELINES
FOR SETTING GOALS AND CONTRACTS

As has been stressed previously, setting goals and establishing contracts that are effective for professional practice is a difficult task that requires much skill and experience. When attempting to do so, it is worth keeping a few guidelines in mind.

First, goals and problems can seldom be completely specified at the outset of the practice processes. The practitioner and client are making their best guess—based on their work together and on the practitioner's ability to translate into practice knowledge of a practice theory and theories of human behavior—as to what the problems and the most appropriate solutions are. It is important to remain open to additional information about clients and their situations, which will be learned only as the relationship and course of work develop, and as the client undergoes change as a function of initial intervention and life changes. There is a balance to be struck between helping the client stay focused on the hard work of significant change and being flexible about shifting focus as new dynamics develop and become apparent.

Second, while it is true that we cannot treat our goal statements as being set in stone, it is also true that we do not serve our clients well by not specifying initial goals to direct the initial sessions. Reid (1978) suggests that we specify something by the end of the first session, if nothing else, just to lay out a next step in continued exploration and assessment. For complicated and multiproblem cases, it makes sense to end the first session by saying something like:

> I'm beginning to have a better understanding about what brought you in for help, and you do seem calmer now and better able to describe what is troubling you and what you'd like to see happen here. We talked about the immediate problem today, as well as some of the background, but we didn't get a chance to talk much at all about your home life or your work. My suggestion is that we meet again next week in order to figure out more clearly what we can do to help you. How does that sound to you?

> I'd like to suggest two things for the week before we meet again. First, I'd encourage you to lean on your sister for support more, like you said helped when you did it the other day. Second, I need a little more information about how certain aspects of your problem play out. I have a note-taking journal I'd like to show you for recording times when these problems come up. If something does come up and you can't wait to talk until next week, call me and I'll see if we can meet any earlier. Hopefully, we can avoid your having to feel like you're at the end of your rope again. Do you have any questions or concerns at this point? Okay, let me tell you more about this journal.

Note that a number of interventions were made in this quasi-contract. It reinforced that the client already appeared to be making progress and provided observable referents for the client to self-observe. The suggestion was made to continue using the coping resources that worked recently (leaning on the sister), and it was explicitly stated that the client now has access to the practitioner as a backstop if things get too overwhelming before the next session. It was also made clear that more information was necessary before the practitioner could determine how to best help the client; that no "magic cure" could be administered. Finally, the client's input and acceptance were solicited, and an image of collaborative work in further sessions was emphasized.

Third, the process of goal-setting is a part of the overall effort to promote clients' problem-solving capacity. Thus, modeling is implicitly and explicitly occurring as the practitioner demonstrates the steps of moving from problem identification and prioritization in initial assessment to setting interim, ultimate, and instrumental goals and objectives. It is important to model how to resist the urge to take action prematurely. People are naturally inclined to doing something to relieve their distress (or to help others relieve their distress). Yet this too often results in superficial relief and a compounding of the problem (taking emergencies into account, of course). Assessment information is rarely as complete or accurate as we would like, and thus goal-setting must be an iterative process (e.g., making use of early-stage contracts, as illustrated above, and adjusting interim and instrumental goals based on feedback). In brief, both practitioner and client need to slow down the impulse to take premature actions, and to follow as thoughtful and information-directed a course of goal-setting and intervention planning as is reasonably possible.

Finally, it is important to be straightforward and honest about one's understanding of clients' problems and lives. One should err on the side of assuming one knows very little rather than on the opposite. As we have discussed in previous chapters, we are inclined to treat our unverified presumptions as facts if they fit our inferences, schemas, and scripts about types of people, problems, and situations. Moreover, cursory approaches to verifying our understanding of clients signal an attitude that clients' problems are so routine or mundane as to be predictable. They limit the practitioner's opportunities to build rapport by demonstrating rather than asserting understanding of clients' perspectives and experiences. The practitioner should strive to maintain the "humanely businesslike" role with clients, demystifying the relationship and intervention processes and equalizing the power differential that inherently exists between practitioner and the client. One wants to engender trust and a sense of collaboration from clients. This is accomplished by treating them like the experts that they are in their own lives.

One last point should be made about the use of goals in treatment. It is important to keep in mind that structuring intervention around goal attainment should not be confused with assuming that success is necessarily the point at which clients' problems are solved. Certainly, there are some needs that can be met in a fairly definitive and therefore solvable way—such as securing needed housing, training, child care, or medical supplies. But with the complex problems in living typically brought to the professional practitioner, it is rare that a client will literally solve a problem, at least not in the same definitive sense that taking aspirin makes a headache go away. Solving one problem often creates others within the niche, and very often there are causal and contributing factors present that seem intractable.

This is not meant to argue that one must always look deeply at clients' problems in order to address real change—a charge typically posed by "anti-behaviorists" who talk about "symptom substitution" and the trivialization of professional practice promulgated by the behaviorists. Nor is this only meant to echo the standard ecological view that one cannot solve individual problems in a vacuum.

Instead, this example is raised to make the point that our lives are seldom so uncomplicated that we can address one problem in a singular and absolute way, solving it once and for all, and in a way that makes our lives completely better.

Life is normally filled with ups and downs. Rather than attempting to eradicate these downs, professional practice more accurately can be thought of as helping to better manage current problems and to better avoid, minimize, or grapple with future problems. This is not to trivialize the real suffering that comes with the downs of life, nor to suggest that solutions can never be attained. Professional intervention in its many forms is meant to address those times when one's niche has been disrupted, for any number of reasons: when extra help is needed to get through particularly bad life changes or experiences (loss of a job, loss of a loved one, dealing with traumas, coping with psychosocial developmental changes, and so on); when clients need extra help making difficult life decisions (marriage, divorce, job changes, and such); when serious illnesses strike (both physical and mental illnesses); and when one's life problems become so great as to be unbearable. Therefore, intervention goals should conceptually be aimed at helping clients reestablish their niche—not necessarily putting it back the way it was, but rather helping clients develop routines, life tasks, self-system changes, and social supports that allow them to incorporate the changes or stressors in functional ways.

It is true, as stated in ecological theory, that one cannot look at one problem without looking at the client's niche from which it sprang.

Social learning theory has amply demonstrated that the environmental factors surrounding one's life must support individual change goals for these changes to be achieved and maintained. Particularly in times of considerable pain and stress, what we most yearn for is to be free of that suffering and distress: to feel happy, hopeful, and unfettered. To varying and incremental degrees, professional practice works toward such goals. But the image—fostered by both practitioners and clients—that the practitioner will provide ultimate answers and solutions, or that practice has the power to turn one's life around to truly eradicate what feels so burdensome, reflects understandable but ultimately counterproductive wishes. In many cases, gains can indeed be remarkable. But, they are born of hard, focused, collaborative work toward a viable and sustainable future. As practitioners, we strive to impart hope into our clients' lives, providing them with the skills and resources that will allow them to navigate life's trials and tribulations while remaining on their life course. Goal-setting is a crucial step in that process. In the next chapter, we discuss models of coping with daily life that incorporate this notion that life is complex, and that a good and normal life is filled with ups and downs.

SUMMARY

This chapter described the processes of goal-setting and contracting. We discussed the importance of life goals, how they differ from intervention goals, and how one helps clients translate life goals into intervention goals. Goals and contracts help structure intervention by providing standards for evaluation, criteria for determining resources and skills needed by the practitioner and client for successful incremental outcome, and a context for determining which interventions will be employed.

In this chapter we emphasized the theme of joining with clients by demonstrating that their presenting problems are understandable and reasonable products of their niches, and that goals directed at addressing these problems can come from a range of venues and can be directed at a range of targets in their system. This approach reinforces the themes of enhancing mindfulness and of life story construction emphasized in a cognitive-ecological model of practice. The authors have found that this approach also serves to automatically lessen client resistance. From a cognitive-ecological perspective, resistance reflects an understandable ambivalence and difficulty in making significant life change—of having to give up their schemas and patterned ways of interacting—in the face of changes in their niche or within themselves. The desire to maintain the status quo is a direct result of the frightening feeling of not being able to make sense of one's surroundings when one lets go of self- and other-schemas. Thus, the more a practitioner pushes clients to reject what they know about themselves and the world, without first providing a safe environment and directions for viable alternatives, the more resistance will be observed. It is more advantageous to start from the position that clients' knowledge is functional and appropriate, given what they know to be true; and they are seeking help because of changes that are new or that they no longer can ignore. Therefore, the practitioner can help clients make changes in their worldview, if that is one intervention objective, by first joining with the clients' worldview and then developing alternative understandings and responses together.

Goals should contain the following characteristics:

1. They should be specific and clear, verifiable and measurable.
2. They should define functional result states rather then processes.
3. They should be mutually agreed upon and related to the client's presenting problems.
4. They should be adequate to the problems they address.
5. They should be positively stated and motivating for the client.
6. They should be realistic given the client's niche and her skills and abilities.
7. They should be feasible, or there should be a good chance they will be accomplished.
8. They should be consistent with the client's values and culture.

Establishing effective and workable goals is a difficult process, one that is ongoing throughout the formal helping relationship. Steps for establishing effective intervention goals are:

1. Summarize the assessment—the client's niche and presenting problems within it.
2. Starting with clients' possible selves and possible niches, list key ultimate, interim, and instrumental goals necessary to address the identified problems.
3. Prioritize goals based on urgency, safety, ease of accomplishment, and their leverage or relative impact on the niche.

4. Develop timelines for when the goals will be accomplished.
5. Identify key internal and external resources needed to accomplish the goals.
6. Make plans to review the progress made by the client.

Contracts formalize the goals and structure of the work between client and practitioner. They provide a mechanism for both the client and practitioner to remain focused on the agreed-upon tasks. Contracts break up long-term interventions and services into "digestible" pieces, allowing clients to voice their concerns and questions. Their use engenders trust and cooperation between the client and practitioner by demystifying the helping processes and by explicating expectations for both parties.

In the next chapters, the processes of intervention selection, and monitoring and maintaining positive changes, will be discussed.

Chapter 8

INTERVENTION PLANNING
AND IMPLEMENTATION

As we have discussed throughout this book, as human reasoners we are prone to search for and use what we know best, and to interpret environmental information in ways that confirm our construction of reality. This same interpretive bias occurs when we select and implement interventions. As natural as this bias may be, we have encouraged practitioners working within a cognitive-ecological framework to move away from a self-centered stance to one that is client-centered. To be effective with clients, we must move away from reliance on perceptions where our expectations, inferences, feelings, evaluations, and judgments are highly rooted in ourselves and our own experiences, to one where our perceptions, interpretations, and decisions are carefully referenced to our clients' perceptions, experiences, and feelings about their world.

It is often at the point of intervention planning and implementation that our mindful application of practice theory breaks down. As with other activities in life, we are inclined to settle into using a limited set of problem-solving or problem-managing methods, familiar methods that we believe to be useful. We have all heard the adage that when all one has is a hammer, everything begins to look like a nail; we can easily become "technique-driven" in our work, rather than working hard to apply those interventions to our clients based on a thorough assessment of them. It is easy to confuse perfection of technique with practice effectiveness. A cognitive-ecological approach to helping requires that we remain situated in the context of the client's goals and assessment as we plan our interventions.

In this chapter, we will first discuss a cognitive-ecological perspective on intervention planning and implementation. Specifically, we will discuss some of the ways through which the practitioner and client can work as collaborators at this stage. We will discuss perspectives and steps aimed toward strengthening a learning and empowerment agenda in the context of intervention planning and implementation. Closely related to these objectives are the underlying models of helping and change that client and practitioner hold, and how these are related to intervention. Finally, we will explore in further detail cognitive-ecological roots of problem solving, with particular emphasis on change within the self-system and niche as central regulators of well-being and social functioning.

What we will not be offering in this chapter is a comprehensive primer of intervention planning and implementation. There are a number of books presently available that provide excellent guidance in this respect, and we will refer to several of these. Rather, our focus is on an existing gap in the practice literature: on the development of cognitive-ecological methods as they apply to the phases and components of practice. As we indicated earlier in the book, our primary focus will be on translation of social cognition theory, findings, and methods as they support practice. Therefore, in this chapter we will focus on these factors as both impediments and resources in intervention planning and implementation.

COLLABORATING FOR CHANGE

The professional helping relationship is a unique one. As we have noted in previous chapters, it shares some of the attributes of a number of other relationships in life (for example, of friend, teacher, confidant, professional adviser), yet should not be confused with any one of these. The specific nature of the professional relationship will vary as a function of numerous factors, such as the type of service provided, the attributes of the client, and the anticipated type and length of the intervention. A practitioner, working in a prison, for a crisis hot line, with an oncology unit at a children's hospital, or at a community mental health center, will need to adapt the helping relationship in ways that are appropriate to that service context.

In the previous two chapters, we spoke at length about qualities important in the working relationship. We have emphasized that the relationship is subservient to achieving the goals of intervention—that the tenor of the relationship be respectful, collaborative, and "humanely businesslike." Practitioners as well as clients approach the helping process with social and emotional needs. It is at times easy to lose perspective of the client's goals, and to become overly embroiled in developing the relationship as an expression of the practitioner's mission and importance. A useful litmus test to help us as practitioners avoid centralizing our own social or emotional needs is to ask precisely how our actions both empower clients and assist them in meeting their intervention goals. Without a commitment to empowerment, helping itself can become another form of oppression (e.g., deciding for clients what interventions they will receive; pursuing emotional intensity or intimacy without clarity about how this will strengthen clients' problem-management outcomes), and therefore reinforcing clients' feelings of powerlessness (see Gutierrez, 1990; Stensrud & Stensrud, 1981; Swift & Levin, 1987, for further reading on empowerment principles in practice).

At the point of intervention planning and implementation, thinking of ourselves as consultants is a useful image to keep in mind. That is, we need to think of ourselves as having been brought in to promote the self-interest of the client in specific ways; we are brought in to work for a specific purpose for a limited length of time. We take a variety of roles, such as listener, observer, collector of data, reporter of observations, instructor, trainer, supporter, challenger, and advocate. Yet, the responsibility for "running the business" ultimately remains with the client (Egan, 1990, p. 79). This is not to suggest that we do not at times strenuously urge directions that are different from those of the client. Indeed, pointing out alternatives, costs and benefits, boundaries, and a variety of undetected or discounted factors is part of the professional role.

Thus, while we are striving to consciously use the social influence component of the professional relationship to guide the client, we are also maintaining an explicit collaborative framework to support the clients' rights, self-responsibility, and self-efficacy. An overall goal of empowerment is to actively help clients perceive themselves as being powerful enough to bring about desired changes. Clients are helped to obtain the desired knowledge, skills, and resources necessary to realize their desired changes, and to render realistic their perceptions of being powerful. The following principles are necessary to incorporate an empowerment objective into the conduct of practice (Kopp, 1989; Solomon, 1976):

1. To help clients see themselves as causal agents in solving and managing the problem(s) at hand.
2. To help clients view the practitioner as having knowledge and skills that they need (and, of course, the practitioner must possess this knowledge and skill).
3. To help clients accept the self-responsibility that goes with self-determination and to see the practitioner as a collaborator or partner in the problem-solving effort (although the specific form this takes may be quite variable).
4. To help clients perceive various power structures in their lives as being multipolar: that different circumstances offer differing opportunities, and thus, unique appraisals are needed for each individual circumstance.

In the following section we will discuss how to translate an empowerment perspective into action for intervention planning and implementation.

There is an additional, very pragmatic, reason to develop a collaborative approach to helping. The realities of counseling and clinical service today reveal many constraints. The actual length of service is very often considerably shorter than is needed to bring to full completion change goals, particularly with complex problems and when focusing on changes in clients' self-system and niche are involved. Phillips (1988), for example, recently reported that the national average number of psychotherapy sessions is between five and six. Contacts for other types of helping practice are generally similar, if not more limited; and even within longer-term helping, such as case management, the majority of the real work of change must take place outside of session, in clients' everyday lives.

The actual length of available time will vary, of course. But today, more than ever, each session must be pointedly oriented toward helping clients continue the therapeutic and change gains begun in formal helping. If the process of translating assessment and goals into intervention possibilities is left mysterious and inaccessible to clients, they will be at a serious disadvantage when undertaking this process in their own behalf. For all of us, envisioning alternatives and figuring out viable ways to "get there from here" are extraordinarily difficult when we are embroiled in the midst of disturbing and discouraging circumstances. In this next section, we turn to processes that help clients know more about how to help themselves as a step to making choices and taking action.

PROBLEM MANAGEMENT SKILLS
AS EMPOWERMENT AIDS

We define professional practice as efforts to enhance the well-being and problem-management capacity of clients. In some cases, the nature of presenting problems is sufficiently delimited that they can be literally solved, in a definitive sense. In most cases, however, the practitioner is working with clients to set them on a viable course, to assist in the acquisition of new information, skills, and supports that will enable them to better grapple with the challenges and problems that they will continue to encounter throughout their lives. (For similar perspectives on the role of professional practice on clients' lives, see Carkhuff, 1987; Egan, 1990; Germain & Gitterman, 1980; Janis, 1983; Kanfer & Schefft, 1988; Hepworth & Larsen, 1990; Watson & Tharp, 1989.) What is emphasized is the fundamental orientation of a cognitive-ecological model to fostering changes that will strengthen clients' abilities to work with their current and future problems in living.

There are a great many parallels between the process of helping and the targets of change. That is, the target of practice typically includes helping the client become a better problem manager or problem solver. The methods for achieving this overall goal have also been conceptualized as a problem-solving process (see Cormier & Cormier, 1991; D'Zurilla & Nezu, 1982; Heus & Pincus, 1986; Spivak, Platt, & Shure, 1976). We will use the term *problem solving* because of its greater usage, but do so with the qualification that *problem management* is a more realistic and flexible term. For example, we saw in Chapter 6 the problem-solving steps for defining the nature of the specific problem used in assessment. In Chapter 7, we saw the beginning stages for formulating a problem-solving plan by identifying desired goals, and the incremental steps for achieving them. In this chapter we see the subsequent problem-solving steps for formulating and implementing a plan toward these goals and objectives.

Too often, the work of specifying a plan of action gets short-changed by both practitioners and clients. It can feel unnatural to specify exactly what tasks or actions are seen as necessary to accomplish desired changes. After all, we rarely operate on such a studied, sequential basis in real life. This is indeed part of the problem. The fact that problems have reached that point, where clients feel they are no longer able to cope with them effectively, signals that clients' natural methods of problem solving are insufficient, and that they need new methods and outcomes. Thus, by making the process of constructing and trying out new problem-solving or problem-managing methods easily observable to the client, the process itself serves as a model and an opportunity to practice and incorporate these new methods into their routines of daily life.

Creating, Strategizing, and Sustaining Goals

There are three elements of problem solving or problem management that particularly relate to effective intervention planning and implementation: creating, strategizing, and sustaining. *Creating* has to do with creativity, with breaking out of the confines of more routinized ways of thinking that are so often part of the breakdown of problem solving (Heus & Pincus, 1986). A number of tools can be employed to model and encourage creative thinking in the intervention-planning process, such as brainstorming, use of stimulating prompts and probes, moving away from a "right way" perspective, and providing new information or training (see Barlow, Hayes, & Nelson, 1984; Cormier & Cormier, 1991; Egan, 1990, Kanfer & Schefft, 1988; Kirschenbaum, 1985). The point is to use the process of formulating an intervention plan as an opportunity to model, encourage, and practice with the client an imaginative, generative capacity to see oneself, one's world, and one's future in different ways. Note that this again reinforces one core theme in this book, of helping clients appreciate that experience and perception (of themselves and events in their lives) are constructions. Rather than the truth, these constructions are more usefully seen as one version of the truth. This recognition can be useful in feeling less stuck, in believing that it may indeed be worthwhile to think about possibilities that previously seemed out of reach.

Strategizing refers to the ability to step back from the problem in order to make a reasonably objective judgment about the strategies that both appear best for the problems at hand and are ones that the client can commit to. Criteria for selecting procedural strategies, to "get there from here," are naturally related to the criteria for goal-setting. For example, is the strategy sufficiently clear and detailed to provide guidance about what to do and when to do it? Is the strategy sufficiently strong and under the client's and/or practitioner's control (that is, do they have the power to enact it)? Is it consistent with the client's values and capabilities? Once an initial direction has been selected, further detail is needed in developing a procedural plan for how to initiate and sustain the strategies. For example, what are the incremental steps, what kind of time frame will they likely involve, and how will practitioner and client communicate about difficulties or concerns?

Sustaining, the third element of effective problem solving, is where contingency plans are identified. Intervention planning is rarely a linear process: Plans provide initial guidance and are modified with feedback and changing circumstances. Thus, intervention planning, much like assessment, is not a one-shot activity, but rather continually evolves throughout the course of the helping relationship and the change efforts. Contingency plans address two aspects of the problem-solving process: how to anticipate and cope with ongoing challenges, and how to get back on track when a breakdown in the new niche and self-system is encountered. It is one thing to be motivated to initiate desired changes in the early excitement of the helping process. It is quite another to persist through barriers, setbacks, tedium, and fatigue in the longer-term work required for durable change.

Encouraging persistence is a necessity to reinforce clients' sustained change efforts beyond their involvement in formal helping. When we take seriously the basic tenet of the cognitive-ecological model—that all components of the niche must adjust when one component changes—it becomes apparent that clients' desired changes will nearly always necessitate changes in their significant social relationships as well. These changes may or may not be welcomed by others in the niche. Yet, generally, others must adapt for clients' changes to be maintained. The use of motivators such as encouragement, incentives, contracts, and progress monitoring, which are used within the context of the helping relationship, can be extended into the client's life as well (see Egan, 1990; Kanfer & Schefft, 1988; Kirschenbaum, 1987; Monroe, 1988). The adaptation needed from others may range from a little to a lot, and may be met with anything from eager acceptance to bitter resistance. Our point is to underscore the importance of facilitating real changes in clients' niches to sustain longer-term change efforts. We will discuss examples of how to foster changes in clients' significant social supports later in this chapter.

When clients get help learning how to generate and select strategies, and how to generate contingencies when needed, they become better observers of their own lives. Guidance in this form will help clients know how to begin to get back on track when inevitable setbacks, confusion, and new problems arise. It is extremely important not to dismiss the skills of strategizing as obvious, simplistic, or basic. The lack or loss of capacity to create, strategize, and sustain alternative possibilities are universal barriers to growth and change. Strengthening these capacities represents a major step toward self-determination and positive adaptation. Later in the chapter we will discuss this issue in more detail with respect to constructing and reinforcing alternative possible selves and possible niches.

PROBLEM-SOLVING ROOTS WITHIN THE NICHE AND SELF-SYSTEM

Intelligence, in the sense of intellectual ability, has not been found to be significantly or consistently related to adjustment and success in living (Felsman & Valliant, 1987; Sternberg & Wagner, 1986). This is not meant to minimize the realistic importance of intellectual ability in our society, or the additional struggles faced by those of low intelligence. Rather, our intent is to look more closely at another aspect of intelligence that does appear to be significantly related to adjustment and success in living—that of practical or social intelligence (see Cantor & Kihlstrom, 1987, for an analysis from a social-cognitive perspective, and Sternberg & Kolligian, 1990, for an analysis from developmental, social, and clinical perspectives). One important component in this more practical intelligence appears to be the capacity for, and use of, constructive and generative thinking. This includes both the capacity to creatively develop and search for alternative solutions to problems, and the inclination to frame problems or goals in additive and constructive terms.

This attribute of *generative thinking* certainly involves an element of optimism and a self-enhancing bias (to be able to let go of what we have in order to envision what could be, we need to believe that we always have options for ourselves). It does not mean, however, that coping, striving, and adjustment exist without a healthy dose of reality testing. There is a balance to be struck here. Findings indicate that the happiest, best adjusted people tend to hold exaggerated views of how positively others view them, how positive the future will be, and how powerful they are (Taylor & Brown, 1988). Yet, unbridled optimism and self-confidence create problems of their own. It is important to acknowledge when clients perceive that there are many factors in their lives over which they have little or no control, and change efforts must be undertaken within this context. As Epstein and Meier (1989, p. 345) point out, adaptive behavior requires a compromise among basic needs, such as maintaining a favorable pleasure-pain balance, a favorable level of self-esteem, and the ability to maintain predictability in the world by being grounded in the events of daily life.

In short, an important empowerment objective is to assist clients to creatively and optimistically solve problems within a framework that reckons with, although may not necessarily accept, the constraints and requirements of the external world. Therefore, we include one's ability to observe and assess oneself and one's environment when we discuss problem-solving abilities. What we will discuss in the remainder of this chapter are intervention guidelines related to promoting these appraisal and problem-solving abilities. Consistent with a core theme of this book, we will focus discussion on how recent theory and findings related to normative social cognition, self-development, and social transactions can be translated into guidelines for breaking maladaptive cycles and for fostering adaptive ones.

As we have discussed previously, intervention goals are the concrete reflections of the possible selves and possible niches that clients desire and seek assistance in obtaining. Given what we know about the mind and memory systems, efforts to help clients achieve their possible selves and niches are best viewed as an additive, reorientation process. This includes:

1. Adding needed components to the individual's problem-solving repertoire
2. Reorienting ingrained habits to make better use of this enhanced repertoire
3. Enhancing clients' abilities to continue and mobilize supports for change goals and efforts outside the supportive, yet artificial, framework of formal helping

As we have discussed previously, significant, durable change in fundamental beliefs about and habits regarding oneself, one's future, and one's social world are exceptionally difficult to accomplish. In part, this is accomplished by helping clients translate abstract world knowledge into more compelling self-relevant, self-definitional knowledge. For example, we have great stores of information about the physical and social world. We know what "assertiveness," "confidence," and "patience" mean. We recognize these qualities in others when we see them. But having this social knowledge in general terms is not immediately applicable to ourselves if it is not explicitly encoded as self-relevant. It may be a potential resource, but until it has been incorporated into the self-system and into the routine patterns of one's immediate social niche, we will not be able to effectively act upon these qualities when desired. As Guidano and Liotti (1983, p. 95) have stressed, an essential element for a durable reorganization of one's attitude and approach toward reality involves the individual's construction of personal identity and place within that reality.

Throughout this chapter we will be addressing the interrelatedness of social cognitions and social transactions, the self-system and the niche, and change aids and the ways in which they are used. Because we are not addressing ourselves to specific problem domains or fields of practice, we must necessarily talk in broadly applicable terms. To anchor this discussion in concrete factors and functions, we will return to our earlier description of the human memory and information-processing system as the physical bedrock of self-knowledge, social knowledge, and their effects. We have found that much of the following can fruitfully be shared with the client in metaphorical terms rather than the relatively technical level on which we speak to the practitioner here. For example, the distinction of a working self-concept from a single true, monolithic self provides a normalizing answer to the paradox of how people can have contradictory views of themselves at different times yet still be quite normal and have an appropriately intact identity. Similarly, differentiating knowing-how procedural knowledge from knowing-about declarative knowledge helps clients understand why new skills and response styles do not automatically come with insight and verbal learning; that procedural knowledge comes from the longer, slower road of practice, experimentation, feedback, and more practice. Practitioners, however, require more than metaphor to inform well-grounded planning and intervention. So, we next turn to the groundwork for accomplishing different types of change in the appraisal and problem-solving methods of clients, focusing on the fundamental ways through which people strive to make sense of themselves and their world. Applying this model to specific clients will require the practitioner to determine which elements are most relevant, and then make intervention choices accordingly.

KNOWLEDGE (MEMORY) STRUCTURES:
BUILDING BLOCKS OF INTERVENTION

When discussing the properties of memory and information processing, one must make the important distinction between cognitive content, cognitive process, and cognitive products (see Hollon & Kriss, 1984; Ingram & Hollon, 1986, for extended discussions). *Cognitive content* refers to the information stored within the central nervous system, organized in schematic and propositional (e.g., "if-then") knowledge structures. Because these knowledge structures are stored in memory, we will use the terms *memory structure* and *knowledge structure* interchangeably. *Cognitive process* refers to the rules or systematic means through which this information is manipulated for use: how it is perceived, encoded, stored, sought, retrieved, and modified. *Cognitive products* are the cognitive results of the application of these processes to the cognitive content: the attitudes, beliefs, judgments, expectations, and evaluations that we hold (see Figure 8.1).

One reason these distinctions are important is that evidence suggests that clinical populations systematically differ from nonclinical (normal) populations with respect to cognitive content and the resultant cognitive products, but not with respect to cognitive processes (see Hollon & Garber, 1988; Ruehlman, West, & Pasahow, 1985, for reviews). Given the relative comparability of cognitive processing between clinical and nonclinical populations, and the fact that cognitive products are so dependent on process and content, the Achilles' heel of adaptive psychological functioning may be the cognitive content of a clinical population. Combined with the considerable power of cognitive structures in memory functioning and information processing (see Chapters 2-4), this suggests that cognitive content structures should be a fruitful focus for intervention effort across a variety of specific problems in living.

These findings are consistent with the theoretical framework we outlined earlier in the book. That is, within nonclinical populations, the essential processes that govern memory functioning and information processing tend to be intrinsic and are highly comparable across individuals. This is not to say that normal cognitive processing habits are necessarily optimal. We saw in Chapters 4 and 5 how normal processing that may work satisfactorily in general can introduce significant risks in clients and in the practitioner role. In addition, well-functioning people have not been found to be necessarily more accurate, undistorted, or

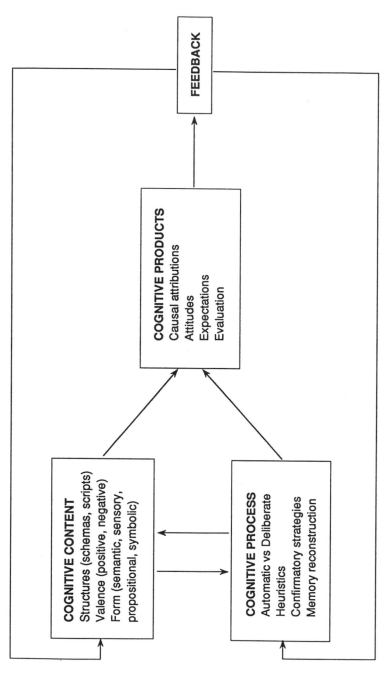

Figure 8.1. Differentiating Cognitive Content, Process, and Products, With Examples of Each

rational in their outlooks and processing habits than ill-functioning people (Lewinsohn, Mischel, Chaplin, & Barton, 1980; Taylor & Brown, 1988).

It appears that realism per se is not the goal. Rather, the keys to optimal functioning are in one's ability to (a) maintain the correct degree and type of distortion needed to promote self-enhancement, (b) maintain compatibility with the social and physical environment (i.e., maintain one's niche), and (c) monitor and manage fluctuations in the niche when they arise.

What do we know about how to change cognitive content in the desired direction and degree? In Figure 3.3 we distinguished declarative knowledge from procedural knowledge. In Chapter 3 we also described how complex, automatic, and mindless our use of these cognitive structures becomes with familiarity and repetition. The same cognitive processes that supply positive schemas with optimistic or self-enhancing inferences, judgments, and expectations also supply negative schemas with pessimistic or self-injuring inferences, judgments, and expectations.

Key differences between accessing self-enhancing versus self-injuring schemas involve (a) the total store of knowledge (memory) structures that each has developed over time (that is, the number and nature of these structures), and (b) the subset that tends to be most frequently activated and thus drawn into working memory at the moment. Recall that a large and diverse collection of self- and other-schemas may exist in long-term memory, which is the storehouse of the repertoire of schemas amassed over time. However, if certain schemas are not readily accessible for use in situations where they are particularly desired or needed, then these schemas are not functionally working for the individual and may even be exacerbating a sense of confusion or inauthenticity.

A LOOK AT CONTRASTS:
THE CASES OF MARTINA AND TERESA

We will discuss these phenomena and effects more fully later in the chapter. First, let us see what an example of how the two key differences described above might look like for two clients. Teresa has come for help with what she calls low self-esteem and long-standing problems in maintaining intimate relationships. Using the assessment strategies described in Chapter 6, one finds that self-schemas of being uninteresting, unattractive, and unlovable, and possible selves and niches of being abandoned and growing old as a lonely, bitter woman have become intertwined to form a cluster that is habitually activated within the context of intimate relationships. This working self-concept cluster shapes Teresa's behavior in these situations, often contributing to responses from partners that make break-ups more likely, which then tends to confirm her theories and expectations of herself and others.

In Figure 8.2, we see a graphic representation of Teresa's overall repertoire of self-schemas, as well as the subset that is easily triggered in intimate relationships (and particularly when anxious or self-conscious). This graphic is, of course, simplified for purposes of the present illustration. It does not reflect, for example, the ways in which information is organized within each structure, nor the complex sets of pathways (interrelationships) among the memory structures, nor the strength of any given structure or pathway relative to others. Although difficult to represent pictorially, these latter factors influence what information gets drawn upon, how readily, and in combination with what else. These are factors we will be addressing as we examine each component of the memory and information processing system.

Now let us look at a very different picture to help illuminate the contrasts. Martina is a client who participated in one of our agency's prevention-oriented relationship enrichment groups, which provided a context for gathering an assessment picture of her self-system. In Figure 8.2 we see that the knowledge structures that are most highly developed and interconnected within the romance/intimate relationship domain of Martina's memory system are positive in nature. She does have a considerable number of negative knowledge structures, as do all of us. Yet, their relative proportion, their likelihood of being activated, and their strength once activated are considerably less than the positive structures. The opposite is true for Teresa. Though she does indeed have a number of positive structures about herself (e.g., "a giving person," "loyal," "a good conversationalist,") their proportion, accessibility, and strength are outweighed by the negative self-knowledge she has amassed.

In addition to the relative proportion, accessibility, and strength of one's memory structures, many structures can be evaluated and can affect behavior differently, depending on the context within which they are accessed. For example, "a giving person" schema that is embedded within a working self as unworthy, unattractive, lonely, and incomplete-without-a-partner will have a different interpretive and behavior-guiding function than the same schema embedded within a working self as self-respecting, content, and lovable. Thus, we see that troublesome

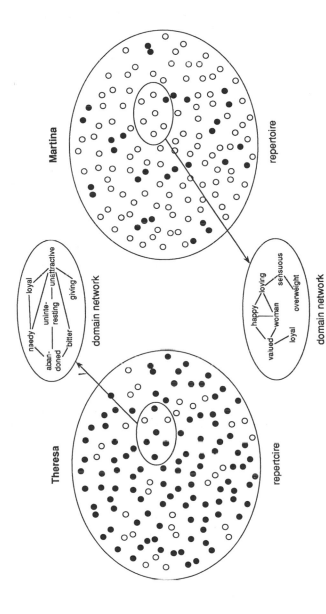

Figure 8.2. Contrasting Self-Schema Repertoires and Networks Related to the Domain of Intimate Relationships

beliefs and responses may not be bad per se. The goal may well not be to purge oneself of certain beliefs, attributes, or habits, but rather to change the broader social and cognitive context within which they are embedded (including how and when they are activated). As is so often the case, elements of a problem can also be seen and drawn upon as assets and resources.

Core Strategies of Unlearning and Relearning

One objective of the interventions with Teresa is to help her revise her cognitive content (i.e., the nature of well-developed schemas regarding herself and her options that are salient in the moment) to foster a more positive and self-empowering bias in her working self-concept. Interventions will involve Teresa's cognitive processing habits as well as her social interactive patterns. To revise the cognitive structure composition as quickly as possible, we would work with Teresa in a kind of accelerated unlearning and relearning process.

Unlearning will include shifting from a mindless or automatic mode of information processing to a mindful or conscious one to help identify and break old habits. *Relearning* will include shifting back to a more automatic and more spontaneous mode of information processing, using new, more adaptive knowledge structures. This strategic use of new cognitive content regarding preferred possible selves and niches, through purposeful manipulation of cognitive processes (what is expected, noticed, and interpreted), will help strengthen new cognitive products and response patterns (that is, a changed sense of self-worth and self-efficacy, and the use of different types of coping and problem-solving strategies). Change at the building block level of increasing and enriching positive self-schemas, combined with mindfulness exercises toward actively drawing upon these new schemas, will generate the desired felt effect of increased sense of self-worth and self-efficacy, and the use of coping and problem-solving responses more consistent with the new positive self-schemas.

Ultimately, we would help Teresa draw disproportionally upon her new, positive knowledge structures, and less upon her long-standing, problematic knowledge structures. As we noted previously, it is very rare indeed to lose one's undesirable knowledge structures per se. We have all had the feeling of dismay when an old self we thought we had managed to escape pops up again, often when we feel least prepared to deal with it. It is more realistic to think in terms of strengthening desired knowledge structures relative to undesired ones, and developing a normalized perspective such that the reemergence of troublesome self-schemas and social-schemas signals not failure but the need for renewed mindfulness strategies.

The term *unlearning* is a bit of a misnomer. This process really involves making the client more mindful of the original steps taken to learn the behavior in the first place. Think of someone relearning appropriate dating behavior after separating from a partner he was living with for many years. After a few awkward dates, feeling rusty and at sea, he first unlearns the outdated rules for social interaction he had been following automatically on these dates. Then, after examining these rules and interaction patterns, and after some trial and error, he can change them to more functionally fit the current situation.

AN ONGOING REMINDER:
IT'S NOT ALL "IN THE HEAD"

It is important to remember that there are a host of both environmental and personal variables that serve as backdrops to the end products we have examined above. Our cognitive processes, content, and products are shaped equally by internal and external factors. We know, for example, that socialization pressures often incline women to measure their self-worth by their attractiveness to men. We know that a variety of social and commercial messages are designed to denigrate the typical woman's sense of attractiveness. Moreover, sociopolitical influences create a power imbalance in personal relationships and in the role of possibilities encouraged for males and females (Cox & Rodloff, 1984; Deaux & Major, 1987). Parallel points can be made for negative societal bias regarding race, class, age, sexual preference, disability, and a number of other stratification and stigmatization factors. In focusing on self-system change, we are not arguing that a universal goal is to change the person to accommodate to a flawed situation. Yet even when changes in the environment are called for, people will still need to change aspects of their knowledge, beliefs, expectations, and skills in order to sustain external change efforts. The fundamental components of change that we describe here apply to learning in general, whether the focus is on oneself or one's social environment.

To design remedial and preventive interventions, one must be able to describe and analyze the role of cognitive content, processes, and products in the development and continuance of presenting problems. The obvious danger with this approach is to only see the person part of the person-environment interaction. It is easy to fall into victim-blaming and explanations based on character defects for behaviors that are products of the person's niche. It remains important to maintain the view that all behaviors (including thoughts and feelings) are products of the niche, and that clients' problem-solving processes remain functional in certain situations. This is the essential yet difficult balance that a cognitive-ecological perspective requires.

Let us now look at several different aspects of this unlearning-relearning process. There are a variety of specific techniques that can be applied to accomplish intervention objectives, depending on the setting, the attributes of the client population, and the time and resources available. Our goal here is to specify guidelines for how interventions link to the cognitive-ecological model.

We will organize these guidelines in terms of the major components of the memory system, as presented in Figure 3.3. The following is an encapsulation of points. For further details, see Ashcraft (1989), Hollon and Garber (1988), and Nurius (1993a, 1993b). As we discuss each component of the memory system, we will discuss its relation to enhancing the client's problem-solving capacity. We will end this chapter with a discussion of meta-memory, or the awareness of one's own memory functioning, as an aid to enhancing client self-awareness and capacity to strengthen her or his efforts toward creative and constructive long-term change.

DECLARATIVE MEMORY AS
AN INTERVENTION TARGET AND RESOURCE

To introduce and enrich alternative knowledge structures (i.e., regarding new self-conceptions, more adaptive coping methods, changed or different life circumstances), the client needs the ability to construct clear, detailed, and retrievable images of what these new structures look like and what they involve. Remember that declarative memory consists of that which we can "declare"; it can be identified within ourselves and articulated to varying degrees. Recall that one component of declarative memory about an attribute, action, or situation can be thought of as semantic facts about ourselves, others, and the world, based on general knowledge. Semantic-based knowledge structure can be fostered in individual or group treatment by providing descriptions, examples, and models through direct discussion, observation, or reading about what it includes (as in bibliotherapy).

A second component of declarative memory is episode-based, which adds an autobiographical form to the more universal or general semantic-based knowledge. Clearly, the two types are interrelated, yet consider the difference between the more abstract, dictionary type knowledge we draw upon when someone asks us to define a term or concept (like assertiveness, patience, confidence, and the like) versus the more vivid, personally relevant knowledge we draw upon when asked to convey our own experiences related to these same concepts. Semantic knowledge gives us a conceptual beginning point of understanding, but episodic knowledge is key to incorporating the knowledge into one's self-concept.

It is important to insure that both aspects of declarative memory are built into interventions. For example, providing information about child development, principles of anger management, and models of effective parenting will all be important in the process of helping maltreating parents build new semantic knowledge about themselves as parents and about how family members can interact. Yet, individual experiences (both simulated through role-plays, and in real life through session homework) are also needed to help generate episodic knowledge of oneself using the needed knowledge.

Cognitive Rehearsal to Enrich Memory Repertoire

One important way that information gets written into long-term memory is through cognitive rehearsal. This involves repeatedly thinking about and cognitively practicing a specific set of images, such as those just illustrated for a maltreating parent. Cognitive rehearsal is the same process we use whenever we learn new information. We repeat simpler things in our mind to help commit them to memory, like phone numbers, names of people, new words in a foreign language. We may use little tricks of association to help us remember them, to help link the new information to more familiar or meaningful existing memories, to help us have that "Ah-hah, that's it!" experience when we try to retrieve the information later.

For more complex and self-relevant learning—as in developing new schemas—it is most effective to rehearse new concepts and self-images in a reflective, purposefully aware and tuned-in manner. This reflectiveness should include identifying one's emotional responses and cognitive associations. This will help link the new knowledge structure with other knowledge structures already stored in memory. Think of this type of learning as analogous to weaving new threads into an existing tapestry. The more you can build upon the strength of the fiber and the existing patterns in the weave, the more coherent and better integrated the new threads will be. This will not happen haphazardly, but rather takes careful attention and effort.

Developing new schemas is best accomplished neither through rote learning nor through passive reliance on therapeutic insight. Instead, schema development is achieved through purposefully drawing upon the richest aspects of memory (images, feelings, symbols, hoped-for and dreaded possibilities), and building them into routines and habits of how we think about and respond to particular situations.

To develop a new self-schema about "competence," for example, reflective learning strategies might include searching for many different examples and models of competence (using the media and other people, for instance); focusing on our feelings associated with competence (perhaps pride and security when we are seeing ourselves as competent; anxiety and self-doubt when we are questioning our competence); selecting symbols and cues to help us activate our notion and goal of competence (that we become attuned to in our environment); and re-peatedly returning to personalized images of our future possible selves as we experiment with new ways of behaving and interacting in relation to competence.

Let us return to our earlier example of Teresa to examine what these strategies and change processes might involve. Teresa may want to present to others a conception of herself as "an interesting person." This abstract self-conception needs to be operationalized in order to discover what this means to Teresa and how it relates to her larger goals. Through this process, she will also expand her perspective through observing and getting input from others: What do interesting people do, how do they do it, how do they reflect on themselves, what are some positive and negative examples? Clarifying and enriching the concept of an interest-ing person is part of semantic knowledge building that helps crystallize Teresa's "interesting person" schema into more specific images and in more flexible and expanded terms (e.g., rather than seeing one best way to be interesting, she can realize that there are many ways to be interesting to both herself and others). Through this process, Teresa is helped to translate her vague and tentative wish into a clear and indi-

vidual goal state—into personalized possible selves and possible niches—
that can more effectively guide desired changes.

Experiential Strategies to Enrich Autobiographical Memory

Episodic or autobiographical knowledge building will certainly take
place as part of these observations, discussions, and cognitive rehearsal.
Yet, to achieve compelling autobiographical memory, reflective rehearsal must go beyond the artificial confines of the helping session and
relationship. It must also be incorporated into the client's social interactions and daily life. One technique to begin this process is through
role playing with the practitioner or with others in a treatment group.
This then needs to be extended by experimenting within relationships
of daily life—for example, through between-session visualization and
enactment assignments, inviting significant others into the agency,
going into the client's home, workplace, and so on. Teresa may then
begin using people, situations, and events from her social niche as part of
her rehearsal ("be interesting in X ways with my new reading group, in Y
ways with the people I work with, in Z ways with the person I'm dating
now"). Thus, cognitive rehearsal is practiced first with the practitioner,
expanded to behavioral rehearsal in the practice setting (role playing), and
then ultimately practiced with members of the social niche.

By first defining the qualities of a possible niche or possible self,
experiential stepping stones (i.e., instrumental goals) become more
envisionable and then doable. Discussion, brainstorming, guided im-
agery, observing models, self-observation with recording, and role-
plays with feedback are examples of ways to undertake these change
goals. By building self-monitoring skills into these change efforts, the
practitioner will help clients challenge themselves by examining barriers and setbacks, as well as reinforce themselves by noticing and taking
pride in small but important steps of change.

Connecting Knowledge (Memory), Situation, and Change Strategies

The elaboration of new schemas is best undertaken within a context
similar to target situations. That is, there are often certain situations that
tend to automatically trigger problematic schemas (such as schemas of
oneself as incompetent, embarrassed, and emotionally out of control when
receiving feedback from authority figures). Even when desired schemas

do exist in the individual's repertoire, if they are not activated and drawn into working memory, they do not benefit the client. Thus, rehearsal of preferred schemas (e.g., calmly and constructively handling criticism) is most effective when the conditions that characterize problematic (e.g., threatening) situations are simulated as closely as possible—through realistic role-plays, group enactments, and incremental experiments in natural situations.

We will discuss the issue of developing schemas under targeted circumstances in further detail under the section on working memory that appears later in this chapter. Part of the point here is to begin the process of associating new knowledge structures to the thoughts and feelings that typify problematic situations. One goal of developing new self-schemas is not just to add them to the data bank, but to make sure that they are accessed when needed. To accomplish this, it is important to work with the client to reframe their old cues as red flags or as signals to help them activate new, desired schemas and knowledge. For example, Teresa presently finds that her feelings of anxiety about rejection tend to trigger a network of images of herself as boring, dumb, and rejected. Here, for example, anxiety is reframed to be a cue to shift into mindfulness. Thus, in contrast to usual confirmatory emotional and cognitive responses to the anxiety ("Oh, no, I'm losing it. He thinks I'm a total idiot"), the anxiety becomes a red flag to trigger a new set of cognitive and behavioral responses. Prior observation, discussion, cognitive rehearsal, and practice with feedback, help make this shift more manageable, even during the moment of anxiety. So, when Teresa feels anxious on a date, instead of automatically feeling rejected and hopeless, her anxiety triggers thoughts such as: "This is what we've been talking about in counseling. He doesn't necessarily think I am being stupid right now. Even if I feel unsure, I need to keep images of the new me in mind and try out some of the things we've been working on."

Knowledge structures continually undergo revision as we learn something(s) new or better, as we add perspectives with maturity, and as we rewrite our personal history to produce more coherent life stories. As we discussed in Chapters 2 and 3, we are very active in what we observe, how we make sense out of it, and how we reconcile discrepancy, conflict, or challenge. Yet, as we discussed above, existing schemas are not easy to purge or delete from memory. When we are in the midst of developing new self-conceptions, for example, the old ones that stand in contrast are neither automatically nor easily removed from memory, or nullified in their influence. Think of how easy it is to step back into the role of being an adolescent when we visit our parents for extended periods of time.

Thus, in addition to teaching clients how to highlight new schemas, training is needed as well in how to dampen maladaptive, discrepant schemas. Specifically, this would entail steps to aid *unlearning,* such as:

1. Becoming more aware of the presence of existing maladaptive schemas and the circumstances under which they tend to exert influence.
2. Using this awareness to reduce the frequency with which maladaptive schemas are activated (in part to be more mindful and attentive to one's own thoughts and feelings under key circumstances).
3. Challenging and revising (reinterpreting, relabeling) maladaptive schemas when they have become active; including recognition that memories do not necessarily reflect facts, and that we can exercise editorial license regarding the story lines of our past, present, and future selves and situations captured in memory.

Steps to aid *relearning* include:

4. Simultaneous to reducing the frequency of activating maladaptive schemas, increasing the frequency with which preferred schemas are activated.
5. Purposefully embellishing and reinforcing these preferred schemas through emotion-laden and autobiographical content (by oneself and with others).
6. Intensively repeating through practice and rehearsal these efforts to strengthen both the interconnections between the new schemas and preexisting knowledge, and the pathways to access them, until their activation becomes more automatic.
7. Periodically returning to these mindful unlearning and relearning efforts when future events disrupt newly reestablished responses.

A variety of techniques can be used toward achieving the above objectives. For example, education for clients, and relevant others in their social niche, about processes of unlearning and relearning will be important. Techniques related to thought stopping, to relaxation training, to visualization and individual rehearsal, to self-instruction and cognitive restructuring, and to a variety of role-playing and enactment approaches are well-suited to these unlearning and relearning processes (see Cormier & Cormier, 1991; Granvold, 1993; Hepworth & Larsen, 1990; Kanfer & Schefft, 1988; Mahoney, 1991; Meichenbaum, 1977; Williams & Long, 1988; Watson & Tharp, 1989, and others for detailed discussions of these techniques).

THE IMPORTANCE OF SOCIAL INPUT AND SUPPORT

It should be obvious by now that social supports are exceedingly important to the changes we have been discussing in developing possible selves and possible niches and in changing problematic patterns of responding and problem solving. It is largely through our interactions with our social environment that we experience the schema-activation cues, as well as feedback that challenges or reinforces our constructions of reality. We gain semantic knowledge by observing others and by attending to the information in our environment. We gain episodic knowledge through our experiences with, and introspection upon, our interactions. Individuals in one's niche influence the development of new declarative knowledge by providing semantic content, by prompting for preferred schemas in specific situations, and by giving feedback that reinforces the value of these alternative responses. This social-self link within unlearning and relearning is partly why it has been argued that group settings are a preferred method of intervention for many individual and interpersonal problems (see Garvin, 1987).

We will further discuss intervention approaches in the following section. There is considerable overlap in the techniques and methods one may choose. For purposes of description, analysis, and guidance, we have dissected the memory and information-processing system; but in reality, it is an integrated whole. As one implements some of the techniques to build declarative memory for new schemas (by gaining information and perspectives, observing models, using cognitive rehearsal followed by role playing, for example), the foundation is also laid for building new procedural memory and sensory-perception habits. However, it is important for the practitioner to attend to development across each of the components we describe here. As was discussed in the previous chapter, durable change requires changes in all aspects of the memory system. For example, a cornerstone of durable change in clients' actual functioning lies in going beyond a declarative level of learning to acquiring solid procedural mastery or expertise. Without this latter procedural knowledge, individuals' gains in insight, alternative images, motivation, and understanding influence of social and background factors are unlikely to be sustained when faced with challenges and constraining forces beyond the support of the professional practice setting.

PROCEDURAL MEMORY AS
AN INTERVENTION TARGET AND RESOURCE

Because procedural knowledge is the how-to skills base of the memory system, how-to instruction and guidance is most effective for change. The single most important factor in building and automating preferred procedural knowledge is behavioral practice, which should not come as a surprise; it takes repeated and concerted practice to become proficient in any skill. A certain amount of how-to knowledge can be abstracted from declarative knowledge. But, it is repetition under guidance that makes the "if-then" ("if this condition, then that response") guidelines more detailed, more likely to be activated, and more effectively competitive with long-standing maladaptive habits and "action rules."

Consider, for example, trying to learn to drive a car, downhill ski, gain fluency in a foreign language, or paint landscape scenes solely through talking, reading, and observing about the activity, with little or no experience in the activity. Even though we think it silly to imagine that we could become skillful in activities such as the above without practice, we do often assume that skill in perception, interpretation, feelings, and imagination should be intuitive, that they should somehow come naturally once one has recognized the problems and made the decision to change them. But ironically, these covert activities are often more difficult to learn, and certainly to unlearn and relearn, than are more visible motor activities. Repetitive practice is essential to building, strengthening, and incorporating procedural knowledge into new self-conceptions, outlooks, and problem-solving capacities.

The Subtle Procedural Skills of
Feeling and Knowing

It is in procedural knowledge that rules are stored for how to appraise situations and interpret events, for how to react emotionally, and for how to be or to manifest attributes. It may seem odd to consider that we have, essentially, procedural guidelines for how to first notice an expression and then how to know what it indicates, for how to experience emotional states such as confidence or patience, and for how and what to feel under different circumstances. All of this knowledge seems so much a part of us. We would often be hard-pressed to come up with rules for why we say one person is manipulative and another is honest, or rules for how we experience suspiciousness, elation, or shyness. While it is true that we experiences innate physical changes—such as in heartbeat, breathing, skin temperature, and so forth—we need interpretive and perceptual rules to allow us to interpret these physical responses as more distinctive emotional states and feelings.

It is far clearer to articulate what we do and do not know about overt or motor-based activities, such as how we learned to play a musical instrument. Yet many of our more subtle and covert activities are learned as well and, as such, are stored as rule-based skills. Clearly, everyone does not have rules or skills for all covert activities any more than they do for all overt activities. We see big differences, for example, in the range of emotional experiences people are able to express, in their capacity to temporarily step outside their known reality, or in their abilities to solve problems in creative ways. People can recognize that there are a great many types of emotional responses theoretically possible in response to specific situations. But if they have never had the experience or developed the rules for how to distinguish between these responses and then enact them, this possible range of emotions will not progress beyond a theoretical understanding.

In short, these covert emotional and cognitive operations are skills to be acquired, or revised. As with more overt behavioral skills, they are best incorporated or strengthened when they are broken into component parts. They are incorporated and strengthened when practiced intensively, and when adjusted and reinforced through specific, constructive feedback. One of the mistakes practitioners sometimes make is to assume that awareness of one's procedural knowledge (one's patterns and implicit rules) is sufficient to promote change. Too often we think that if we can only get our clients to recognize their incongruities or self-defeating errors, and alert them to alternatives, they will begin to make different choices and changes in their lives. Instead, social cognitive research findings indicate that awareness is a necessary but insufficient step (or set of steps) in the change process. Providing awareness alone is akin to providing declarative knowledge without the complimentary procedural knowledge that will translate the abstract into the practical.

Strategies for Enriching and Revising
Procedural Knowledge

Let us now consider some of the ways to foster procedural knowledge. Procedural knowledge is far more likely to be activated in a given situation when it is specific and seen as appropriate to the situation than when it is presented as abstract, broad rules. Rather than offering global rules, such as "If I feel really angry, then use relaxation methods," it is more effective to use a more specific rule, such as "If I feel my anger rising above (a certain prediscussed level), then be 'S.O.L.I.D.' " Note that we have also introduced the usefulness of mnemonic aids to help clients recall clusters of desired information in the heat of the moment. For example, S.O.L.I.D. helps the client cognitively and behaviorally walk through a series of alternative coping steps (*S*low my reactions way down; *O*bserve my own thoughts and the behavioral acts/requests of others; review my *L*ist of options; *I*dentify my choice of options; *D*eclare my action choice and act upon it).

The specific fashion in which steps and guidelines are developed for each client will depend on his or her need (as determined during assessment and goal-setting). For some people it will be necessary to begin with smaller initial steps. This may include first learning how to recognize the experience of anger as well as how to distinguish its form at different levels (i.e., mildly irritated to enraged). Learning how to anticipate high-risk situations, how to self-observe, and how to reduce automatic or mindless reactions are additional examples of translating broad procedures into specific and self-referent rules to enable the client to truly make them their own. Consider what new cognitive and emotional procedural skills our prior case example, Teresa, would benefit from. In addition to strengthening behavioral, social, and relationship skills, what new procedural knowledge is needed for her to know how to be "an interesting person," how to experience or manifest better self-esteem, and how to think differently about herself in intimate relationships?

Accessing Clusters of Associated Knowledge

The above mnemonic (S.O.L.I.D.) was developed to help cue a cluster of self-schemas associated with the goal of being "solid": of being calm, strong, dependable, and self-controlled under challenging circumstances. As we noted in Chapter 3 and will discuss later in this chapter, there is a limited amount of information that active working memory (consciousness) can handle at any given moment. But research shows that experts appear to be able to access more information than novices. Thus, expert chess players can visualize at once whole sequences of moves and positions, while novice players can only see what is immediately before them on the board and can only envision one move at a time. One of the keys to being able to hold onto more information at one time and being able to handle it more quickly is that experts seem to access clusters of associated information, as compared to novices who access information in more discrete bits, processing it one bit at a time. It would follow, then, that people who are experts at anger control are able to access a greater amount of information and more personally usable information than novices. By using clustering schemes, such as the S.O.L.I.D. mnemonic, and through practice that promotes expertise, more complex information can be recalled and handled in the moment. Given that the target circumstances typically tend to be highly emotion-laden, it is particularly important to help clients create aids for envisioning and mentally walking through their desired alternatives, with as many connections already made as possible.

Procedural knowledge tends to become task specific, and does not readily transfer to new tasks. For instance, the S.O.L.I.D. mnemonic example represents a relatively generic sequence of "then" steps that the individual would have to replace with much more specific, individualized steps that work in specific situations. These more specific steps for how to deal with anger will not necessarily match new circumstances (such as how to deal with confusion or panic) and thus will have limited generalizability. Thus, it is important for clients to learn how to restart the process of building their own new response routines by beginning with something they already know—such as their familiar mnemonic that can be adapted to match their new circumstances. It is important to teach clients how to construct more adaptive production rules on their own as they encounter threatening situations in the future.

As we noted earlier, the initial work to develop procedural knowledge for how to behave differently will often feel contrived and unnatural. This is particularly true when compared to what feels very natural to the client, even when the client realizes that the old procedures or rules are problematic. This is where the metaphor of unlearning and relearning (and the difficult shifts from mindless to mindful and back to mindless modes of processing) become particularly useful: The metaphor can help normalize what feels like a highly abnormal and tedious undertaking. For the new knowledge structures to become elaborated and activated, relative to competing maladaptive structures, frequent activation and practice are essential.

Let us now take a moment to consider the implications of the above. We know that it is generally not possible to simply lose maladaptive schemas from the memory system. It is, however, possible to revise them. With long-standing and deeply held beliefs and understandings, however, the job of revision can be very complex, and a number of relabeling, reframing, resocialization, and cognitive reconstruction techniques can be useful. Thus, an essential addition to revising and changing maladaptive schemas is to develop alternative schemas. Let us look at this in more detail.

We know that those schemas that are activated most frequently and most reflectively become easier to activate in the future. We know that those schemas that become elaborated with salient experiences and with personal details are more likely to have a greater impact on how situations or events are perceived and responded to. We know that practiced use of a schema tends to make it more condensed and embedded within an accessible cluster of information (the chess-playing schema for a champion is physically more compact than for a novice), thus making much more detail accessible in the working self-concept at any given moment. Repeated practice also tends to make a schema more routinized (one does not have to think about each act of tying a shoelace once one has learned it) and more linked or associated with other schemas. One set of social cognition findings indicates that activation takes place in a fan-like method. Thus, when any given schema is activated, the activation fans out to touch those other schemas that are most closely associated with it. The fanning effect quickly wanes, so the reach into the network or cluster does not usually go very far. However, routinization of desired responses will strengthen the likelihood of desired schemas being activated and desired rules being fired.

Taking all of this into account, it cannot be emphasized enough that practice of new schemas with immediate, specific, and constructive feedback, practiced within real-life situations is essential to help clients successfully develop and then routinely access adaptive schemas and behavioral responses.

With respect to enhancing overall problem-solving or problem-managing aptitude, recall that the crucial step of procedural knowledge planning is very often short-changed. That is, we often develop goals and images of our preferred selves and niches, but the practical, procedural planning for how to operationalize these goals within the context of the social niche, and planning for inevitable setbacks and impediments, are often left to the devices of our clients. The difficulty is that the natural impulse for all of us is to maintain what is known and familiar, and then feel even more frustrated since we now have a better sense of what we should be doing differently. The procedural side of realizing goals is essential on both a cognitive structure level and on a social problem-solving level. Aiding clients to become more effective self-counselors, problem solvers, and change agents requires helping them establish new procedural knowledge and the skills to flexibly adapt this know-how knowledge to new situations. This is one of the most fundamentally important empowerment supports we can offer.

WORKING MEMORY AND
THE SENSORY-PERCEPTUAL SYSTEM
AS INTERVENTION TARGETS AND RESOURCES

In several respects, working memory is the real workhorse of intervention efforts. In contrast to our vast capacity to store memories, we have a substantially more limited ability to hold in our working memory a subset of memories that we use at any given moment or situation. In addition, as we have stated, the cognitive processes typically used to perceive information and to retrieve knowledge into working memory tend to be biased. As we discussed in previous chapters, it is far more likely that we will notice what we are familiar with, and overlook or discount information that we are not familiar with or have not previously determined to be relevant to us. We are far more inclined to recall memories that are vivid or atypical, as compared to those that are actually more normative (e.g., it is far easier to recall the one schizophrenic man who wrecked havoc in a residential center in our neighborhood versus the hundreds of other mentally ill clients who did not behave dramatically). And we are inclined to pay attention to, and even search for, features that seem to go together, and to overlook, or set aside information that seems odd or discrepant with our working theories (for example, consider the term *histrionic:* what gender, age, and personality attributes most immediately come to mind?).

Yet it is through working memory that we most readily reach long-term memory, particularly with respect to conscious thought and awareness. This is not to say that in the process of learning we are conscious of each and every aspect of what we are experiencing, nor that we always understand what we are experiencing and learning. Rather, working memory serves as something of a two-way transfer station for information into and out of long-term memory. Thus, it stands as an important resource for guiding and managing the unlearning and re-learning therapeutic or change tasks we have discussed.

Fostering Insight About the Change Process and How to Direct it

One of the central self-management tools for guiding and managing the unlearning-relearning process involves meta-cognitive and meta-memory training. Briefly, this consists of awareness of one's memory and cognitive/emotional functioning: recognizing how one reacts to certain situations and people; recognizing one's ability to perceive cues, to make sense of a situation, to respond emotionally and behaviorally. Meta-cognition is similar in some respects to the psychoanalytic concept of *insight:* not only having an awareness of one's own behavior, but understanding its etiology and function in current life. Training toward gaining this awareness is an end in itself, as an extension of self-observation and self-monitoring abilities discussed earlier. This training is also a tool for clients as they undertake the difficult and relatively lengthy process of developing and strengthening new schemas, skills, and social supports consistent with their goals.

Specifically, clients will often need to explicitly negotiate and secure needed supports in their own niches. This work will likely include a combination of obtaining informational supports (e.g., information about options and alternatives; feedback regarding practice efforts), emotional supports (e.g., encouragement; acknowledgment of efforts and gains), instrumental supports (e.g., opportunities to take on new roles and to acquire needed preparation; practical and material assistance), and cognitive supports (e.g., encouragement to broaden and be creative in one's problem solving; reinforcement of statements and behavior in line with the client's goals). Meta-cognition and meta-memory help clients identify and ask for the kind of supports they need related to problem solving and self-concept change. To reduce the dominance of negative cognitive content, and to promote preferred positive cognitive content, the individual needs to repeatedly recruit preferred schemas into working memory and to work with members of the social environment (the practitioner and niche members) to elaborate and validate these positive schemas.

We discussed above how change in cognitive content can be affected by making new schemas available for use in long-term memory in both declarative and procedural form, much like adding new resources to the individual's personal library. Cognitive content can be further changed by strengthening preferred schemas. Metaphorically, one can think in terms of enhancing the text, graphics, and ease of accessing underused library holdings. Through working memory, cognitive content is affected by influencing what is actually retrieved and used in a given situation. Continuing the metaphor, this is analogous to influencing circulation so that the use of certain library holdings is promoted and encouraged, while retrieval of others (maladaptive schemas) is discouraged and constrained.

What is active in working memory will therefore hugely influence the problem-solving steps of task identification and appraisal that we described in Chapter 3. If, for example, working memory in a situation contains schemas of oneself as ineffectual, fearful, and disdained by others, and contains schemas of the environment as based on a status hierarchy where powerful others offer only negative evaluations, the individual will likely appraise the situation and what it permits in very different terms than if her working memory is dominated by more neutral or positive self-knowledge and social knowledge. Therefore, a prime intervention target for working memory and the closely associated sensory-perceptual system, is the circulation desk functions of exerting control over what gets retrieved, how long it is held, and what is discouraged from use.

Our sensory-perceptual system is a prime conduit between the individual's meaning-making system (i.e., memory and information-processing system) and the physical and social environment. The person's bodily experiences are part of his environment in the sense that the biophysical events must be detected and interpreted (e.g., is a "rush" sensation a sign of excitement, illness, anxiety, or low blood pressure?). The sensory-perceptual system is conservatively biased: It detects information that is expected and interprets it in ways consistent with what is known. Given that retrieval of schemas into active working memory is heavily dependent on the cues salient in the moment, it becomes clear that intervention efforts must include habits and inclinations of this conservative sentry—the sensory-perceptual system.

MINDFULNESS AND META-COGNITION

Normally, we rely on our sensory-perceptual system to monitor internal and external information and to alert us when we need to shift from the routine, automatic, mindless mode of processing to a more deliberate, attentive, mindful mode of processing. In terms of intervention, we need to help clients shift in a number of ways. Hollon and Garber (1988) have made the point that to help clients make needed cognitive content changes, we must assist them to temporarily adopt cognitive processes that are not typical of everyday life. Examples of the types of shifts needed toward more learner-oriented and less assumption-oriented processing include:

1. Becoming more data-driven. This includes paying careful attention to the descriptive, behavioral information from the internal and external environment, and being less reliant on inferences or presumptions about what these cues and signs "must" mean.

2. Adopting more multi-causal approaches to making inferences and attributions about events. This involves purposefully considering a variety of interpretations of any given event, including possibilities that disconfirm long-standing theories or inclinations. For example, rather than stopping with the assumption-confirming attribution "She acts that way because she thinks I'm stupid," one would search the situation for overlooked information, such as "She said she had a doctor's appointment and had to hurry. She did say she liked most of my report, and only asked for a small change."

3. Strategic use of cues, such as anxiety or self-denigration, to shift from mood-congruent thinking to more data-based thinking. As we discussed previously, we are inclined to think about past events and future possibilities that are consistent with our current mood. When we are experiencing negative moods or thoughts, this built-in bias fosters a vicious cycle by making negative, maladaptive information easier to recall. So, if we are feeling hurt or embarrassed, it will be far easier to remember painful experiences of being shunned by others (even if this has not been our typical experience) than it will be to think about times when we felt invited and liked by others. We can train ourselves to reframe our emotions to serve as a prompt to make our responses more deliberate, and thereby begin building different associative networks among our schemas.

4. Efforts to incrementally challenge and revise maladaptive schemas. For example, we have discussed the need to sidestep the effect of maladaptive schemas by minimizing their role in information processing. Schemas that are infrequently activated tend to lose their "recallability" and strength relative to those more frequently drawn upon. In addition to avoiding and thus weakening maladaptive schemas, they can

be challenged and changed directly. A key aid to this is to focus greater attention to typically overlooked or discounted information in the environment that refutes maladaptive assumptions. More balanced observations combined with meta-cognition awareness and environmental supports can combine to support relearning and resocialization efforts.

5. Repeated return to deliberate, mindful information-processing strategies versus more habitual automatic strategies. Shifts away from long-standing perception, recall, interpretation, and decision-making habits are fatiguing and difficult to sustain. Thus, progress is often more iterative than it is linear. This will require repeated returns to the more deliberate methods of observing, interpreting what we see, making attributions and judgments, and responding. To truly develop new habits of these fundamental and often subtle thinking/feeling/acting processes takes considerable time. An important foundation can be started in the context of formal helping, but will generally require more time and experience beyond this.

Meta-cognition is a form of insight about how one's niche and self-system function, and the potential assets and impediments presented by this functioning. And while these factors constitute the nuts and bolts of our perceptual processes, they are by no means "all in the head." Throughout this book we have emphasized how our cognitive processes are intimately tied to our social environments, and particularly as they relate to the development and ongoing functioning of the self-system and the maintenance of the niche.

BELIEFS AND EXPECTATIONS
OF THE HELPING PROCESS

We have emphasized an empowerment objective in our practice recommendations throughout this book, noting that the form and degree of this emphasis will vary as a function of differences across cases and practice settings. However, we should note that empowerment is by no means a universal goal held by either practitioners or clients. Inherent within the concept of empowerment is client self-responsibility, along with the rights and supports to decide one's own fate and pursue one's chosen goals. Yet one of the reasons clients come in for assistance is that this orientation toward self-governed living has been impeded, broken down, or was never in place. For a number of reasons (e.g., overwhelming environmental pressures, exhaustion, fear, lack of confidence, lack of skills), clients may approach the practitioner with a vision of the expert helper solving their problems, or with fixed (and unreceptive) sentiments about taking on the challenges that will be necessary to make significant changes.

We have talked about the extraordinary importance that people's cognitive constructions of reality (about themselves and their world) play in their well-being and social functioning. We have also spoken of the mind's abhorrence of uncertainty, and the propensity to fill in informational gaps by generating expectations based on existing schemas of oneself, of others, and of how the world works. It should come as no surprise that neither the client nor the practitioner approaches the process of helping devoid of beliefs and expectations about that process. In this section, we will discuss a number of cognitive-ecological predispositions that affect both practitioner and client in their selection and pursuit of intervention options.

One very basic factor in the selection of interventions is the nature of one's ideas of how change takes place. For example, some view change as a decisive turning point in their lives, while others envision and approach change as something that develops slowly and cautiously (Guidano & Liotti, 1983, p. 126). Clients are often much clearer about what they do not want than they are about what they do want. Thus, for some, changes are represented more in terms of ridding themselves of certain events, stressors, or self-images, or of getting other people or situations to change. For others, changes may be represented in radical and subtractive terms, rather than in incremental and additive terms (for example, believing that to achieve relief, one must sacrifice the sense of self, or submit to extraordinary intrusions). As was discussed in Chapter 6, assessment includes understanding how clients view changes in their life. Using this information helps the practitioner understand how to present intervention options, how to guide the client through desired changes, and how to minimize struggles when practitioner and client hold different views and expectations of how the helping process should work.

Models of Helping

Note that we raised the issue of models of helping in the previous chapter when we discussed the importance of actively dispelling the myth that professional practice will solve all of life's problems. Brickman et al. (1982) and Karuza, Zevon, Rabinowitz, and Brickman (1982) offer a useful framework for distinguishing different implicit models of helping. These authors distinguish between *past-focused attributions* about responsibility for the cause of the presenting problem and *future-focused attributions* about who should be responsible for solving the problem. High attributions of self-responsibility for the cause reflect a view of personal responsibility for one's actions and/or outcomes. Low self-responsibility attributions reflect greater emphasis on external causes, such as other people, events, and features of the environment.

Beliefs regarding who and what is responsible for solutions are often not explicitly acknowledged, or even recognized, by either client or practitioner. Some of these beliefs will be based on cultural values and norms. As we can see in Figure 8.3, these beliefs incline us to think along certain lines about the character of the target person (in this case, the client) and about the appropriate actions to take, which greatly shapes decisions about intervention strategies.

Contrast, for example, differences between what has been called the Compensatory Model and the Medical Model of helping. Both are based on low attributions of client responsibility for problem cause, although for different reasons: one on the basis of victimization or deprivation, and the other on the basis of illness. Because of these differences, practitioners drawing upon a Compensatory Model would be inclined to expect and foster client assertiveness and mobilization of resources, both within the client (e.g., skill building) and within the external environment (e.g., with family members and/or allied agencies). Because of the orientation toward responsibility on the part of experts to solve the problem, practitioners drawing upon a Medical Model would be inclined to expect and foster client acceptance of, and compliance with, treatment directions of the experts.

Part of the practitioner's challenge is to learn what model of helping the client may implicitly hold. Many clients, for instance, have not had much experience with mental health or counseling practitioners, and draw upon their experience with other helpers to imagine what to expect. Experiences with doctors, dentists, attorneys, and tax advisers are likely to incline clients to anticipate a Medical Model, where the expert practitioner tells them how to improve their condition or how to solve the problem. Experience with religious groups or peer support groups, such as AA, will likely incline a client toward an Enlightenment Model, wherein a benevolent authority figure or group is viewed as having the needed wisdom and strength to advise individual decision making. Experience with motivationally oriented groups—such as est

Attribution of person's
responsibility for solution

	High	Low
Attribution of person's responsibility for problem		
High	*Moral model*	*Enlightenment model*
View of person	Lazy	Guilty
Actions expected of person	Striving	Submission
Others besides person who must act	Peers	Authorities
Actions needed by others	Exhortation	Discipline
Low	*Compensatory model*	*Medical model*
View of person	Deprived	Ill
Actions expected of person	Assertion	Acceptance
Others besides person who must act	Subordinates	Experts
Actions needed by others	Mobilization	Treatment

Figure 8.3. Underlying Assumptions in Four Models of Helping and Coping

SOURCE: Adapted from Brickman et al. (1982).

and some career consultants or popular lay advisers (columnists, phone-in programs, some family and friends)—may incline the client toward a Moral Model of thinking.

Nurturing Positive Expectancies

As we have discussed and illustrated, changes in the self-system and the niche require considerable effort, vulnerability, and discomfort. Part of the practitioner's role is to encourage the motivation, persistence, flexibility, and affirmation needed to take on and maintain one's personal objectives. Which model of helping is best will depend on the case, the context, and the goals. What is needed, however, is sufficient understanding between client and practitioner. As we noted in Chapters 6 and 7, it is generally best to include discussion of expectations of one another as part of the groundwork to establish norms, rules, and a collaborative relationship. At other times, talking directly about the developing professional relationship will be useful in clarifying and negotiating different perspectives. This involves use of "you and me" talk or interactions of the moment to check out resistance, conflict, or impediments between client and practitioner related to differing models of helping.

We invite the readers to resist the impulse to place themselves in the grid presented in Figure 8.3, or to categorize each of the models according to their relative merit. We join Rabinowitz, Zevon, and Karuza (1988) in maintaining that each model may have merit, depending on the circumstances of the case and the goals of the client. Instead, the challenge for practitioners is to identify and mindfully manage their own models of helping in order to match them to the needs of the case. Part of what makes this challenge so difficult is that the practice arena has tended to draw membership lines on the basis of theoretical orientation. For example, practitioners are often expected to define themselves according to a given school of thought or therapeutic approach (e.g., behavioral, psychoanalytic, cognitive-behavioral, Rogerian, Adlerian, feminist, existentialist). To do so limits how we perceive the sources of helping in treatment, which necessarily leads to favoring some intervention strategies over others, regardless of client needs.

Practitioners tend to view clients' capacities for change and improvement more negatively than they view people not seeking formal help, and more negatively than clients view themselves (Batson, O'Quin, & Pych, 1982; Wills, 1982). This suggests that within our role as practitioners we use different models of helping for individuals categorized as clients than for people not engaged in treatment or related forms of planned change (see Lerner, 1980). This may have the effect of making us frustrated and feeling burned out, particularly when a client resists an intervention approach deeply tied to our professional identities. As practitioners, then, we must represent our professional identities in broad terms. In the cognitive-ecological model we describe, we have stressed the importance of linking clinical assessment, goal-setting, intervention, and evaluation to well-supported theories of human behavior in the social environment. These theories must undergo modification and development as the knowledge base grows. Subsequent practice activities should be expected to reflect these modifications and developments. We have emphasized cognitive-ecological factors in our formulation of human behavior in the social environment as a means to redress a gap in the practice literature. We emphasize again that we are not proposing that this formulation is all-inclusive or sufficient in and of itself. Rather, it must complement other general human behavior knowledge (such as biological development theories) and problem-specific knowledge (such as research on schizophrenia or family violence).

EMPOWERMENT TOOLS FOR DURABLE CHANGE

Professional helping is a privileged but not a private activity. By this, we mean that all practitioners have an inherent and formal responsibility to be accountable to a social environment beyond the helping relationship. We have underscored in a number of ways the significant potential for influence that the practitioner has in work with clients. We have argued that a cognitive-ecological approach orients the practitioner to work toward the enlightened self-interest of the client, and to do so from a position that has both conceptual integrity and empirical support. One guideline that is a useful barometer for practitioners is to maintain the image of having one's work scrutinized by a sympathetic yet critical public. Practitioners must be able to articulate their reasoning, planning, and behavior at any point in the helping process. Practitioners are in danger of abusing their role when they are embarrassed, ashamed, or defensive about disclosing what they said or did with their clients.

This is, of course, an ideal; there are a host of factors that render such a utopian goal difficult. On the other hand, keeping the sympathetic-yet-critical-public image in mind is a useful strategy to keep oneself accountable and responsible. Furthermore, there are quite a number of ways to build supports toward this goal into the professional relationship. In the next chapter we will discuss the importance of ongoing feedback and efforts to strengthen clients' abilities to maintain their gains after termination. We will frame this as a natural extension of a cognitive-ecological, empowerment approach to each phase of the helping process.

Evaluation is often approached as an artificial, add-on component of practice, often geared toward the informational needs of others rather than those of the practitioner and client. We will emphasize the opportunities to use monitoring and evaluation to assist clients in achieving their short-term and long-term goals and to facilitate our learning from and about cognitive-ecological practice.

SUMMARY

In this chapter we detailed some of the ways in which the interpersonal and human memory concepts defined in earlier chapters can take concrete form in intervention planning and implementation. We have used the analogy of the practitioner as consultant, in which a practitioner offers many different types of help, yet the responsibility for running the business is the client's. To enhance clients' personal efficacy in making desired changes, we noted the need to help clients:

1. See themselves as causal agents in solving their problems and achieving their goals
2. View the practitioner as having needed skills and knowledge
3. Accept the responsibility that goes with self-determination and see the practitioner as a partner in this process
4. See power structures affecting their lives as multipolar; to look at a number of different causative as well as problem-solving factors associated with different situations

The bulk of this chapter was devoted to a detailed discussion of problem solving as a universal framework for intervention planning and implementation. Because much of the work necessary to generating sustainable changes in complex problems of social functioning takes time and effort, we focused on intervention approaches that train clients and their social support networks in how to effect and maintain desired change. Three key factors include:

1. Adding needed components to the client's problem-solving and self-concept repertoire (i.e., enhancing cognitive content)
2. Reorienting ingrained habits (i.e., existing cognitive processes and products) to make better use of the enhanced repertoire
3. Supporting clients' ability to transfer these efforts into the relationships and routines of daily life

As the central regular of social functioning, the self-system and its place within clients' niches are primary foci of intervention. Both targets and methods of intervention were discussed. Drawing upon our earlier discussions of the human memory and information processing system, methods of stimulating change related to: (a) knowledge structures, (b) declarative long-term memory, (c) procedural long-term memory, (d) working memory, and (e) the sensory-perceptual system. A primary training agenda in stimulating and sustaining desired change focuses on enhancing mindfulness about the operations of one's memory, and developing the skills to use this awareness to accelerate the processes of unlearning and of relearning.

We ended the chapter with a discussion of social-cognitive factors that influence the helping process. The next chapter will describe how we can help our clients maintain their positive changes as they translate their gains from the practice setting into their everyday life.

Chapter 9

FEEDBACK AND FOLLOW-THROUGH

This chapter will focus on enhancing the feedback given to clients regarding progress toward achieving their goals. It will also focus on ways to help clients continue their work and maintain their gains after terminating the formal helping relationship. We will identify additional ways to foster mindfulness regarding the change process, as well as productive feedback loops to solidify newly established patterns of interaction and problem management.

We will first discuss major roles and goals of feedback aids. This will be followed by a discussion of types of information that constitute the essentials of providing ongoing feedback to clients across various phases of intervention. We will end the chapter with a discussion of two key elements of postservice follow-through: preparing for termination and helping clients plan for their continued work to achieve, maintain, and expand their goals. As in previous chapters, our emphasis will be on cognitive-ecological factors that bear upon feedback and follow-through, and on fostering client self-determination.

ROLES AND GOALS OF FEEDBACK AIDS

One of the reasons that people seek professional help with personal problems is that our ways of regarding ourselves and our environments become so routinized (mindless) that we can lose our awareness, flexibility, and effectiveness to manage daily life problems. Colloquially, we hear this difficulty cast in terms of getting stuck in a rut and losing sight of the forest for the trees. An ongoing balance must be struck between interacting in characteristically routine ways and remaining flexible to the nuances of change in daily life. Once entrenched in maladaptive patterns, it is difficult to undergo the unlearning and relearning process we discussed in Chapter 8. Not only is it difficult to shift from assumption-driven information processing ("I don't have to try it; I know I'll look like a fool and everyone will think so, too") to data-driven information processing, it is difficult to obtain adequate data upon which to build new self-concepts or social concepts, new coping or problem-solving habits, and new social networks. This is particularly true when we are being most mindless. Further complicating the situation, feedback from the environment is often vague, delayed, ambiguous, and at times obstructive in nature—none of which effectively supports positive change.

Thus, one goal for the maintenance and follow-through of positive change is to help both clients and practitioners obtain higher quality information at each phase of the professional relationship. We can conceptualize a continuum of information needs useful in typical practice settings. This continuum reaches from information obtained for the highly individualized clinical needs of the client, to the macro-level information obtained for the organization and profession. Let us consider some specific roles and goals that feedback aids offer.

1. Enhancing clients' awareness of their own information processing and response patterns as well as enhancing attention to neglected information in the social environment.

As described in earlier chapters, the vicious cycles of distorted perceptions, erroneous inferences, and discounted cues are an integral part of the forces maintaining current problems in living. A first step to changing these patterns requires a capacity for perceiving the broader picture in more objective and complete terms.

2. Supporting a self-adjusting form of cognitive-ecological practice; adjusting and fine-tuning interventions on the basis of an ongoing stream of feedback regarding client functioning and goal attainment.

The observation, inference, and judgment tasks of the practitioner can be extraordinarily difficult. Moreover, these are often conducted under circumstances of fuzzy or incomplete information, of time and resource constraints, and of serious risks and consequences. Thus, feedback aids become very important regarding what is not working well and what needs adjustment, and where the client stands at any given point (in relation to risk, to their goals, and to changes in intensity of services).

3. Aiding practitioners to detect and correct their own biases and oversights inherent to memory functioning and information processing (e.g., the inclination to seek information that would confirm preexisting beliefs).

We have discussed many ways in which all people are susceptible to perceptual and cognitive bias, and how this can pose problems for counselors in their practice reasoning and judgment. A difficult balance needs to be struck between fostering professional expertise (which naturally involves a certain amount of selective thinking and predisposition) with a true openness to a variety of possible explanations and practice approaches. The risks of bias are exacerbated by the pressures of contemporary practice, based on such things as time, privacy, and resource constraints. Yet, as discussed in Chapter 5, there are also a number of aids available to help support goals of validity, reliability, and relevance in our methods of assessing, monitoring, and evaluating cases.

4. Providing self-observation tools that the client can continue to use after termination to strengthen in vivo gains, to transfer learning to other situations or problems, and to help clients proceed following slips and setbacks.

As we have seen in many of the case examples, client problems have often built up over considerable periods of time, or are associated with life events that impose considerable disruption. Much of the needed awareness, tools, and supports can be realized within a time limited framework. Yet the fuller integration of major changes into one's niche and self-system often takes considerable time beyond the limits of formal intervention.

5. Making more explicitly interrelated the information priorities across organizational levels to make practice more effective.

The conduct of cognitive-ecological practice and sound clinical reasoning should not be an ancillary goal pursued by individual practitioners. These are professional values and responsibilities that can unify practice across agency levels around the shared goal of providing services that are effective. One barrier to this unification has been that different kinds of information are prioritized for questions at different levels (e.g., regarding program evaluation for administrators, personnel performance for supervisors, individual client progress for direct practitioners). One step toward fostering organizational unification is the development of feedback aids that are of clinical utility to the line

practitioner, but that can also be aggregated and analyzed for the broader questions of supervisors and administrators (e.g., measures of problem severity, service intensity, or goal attainment).
6. Building a richer, more detailed, and more systematic practice knowledge base (e.g., by operationalizing and documenting observed relationships among background factors, specific interventions, progress indicators, and case outcomes).

The knowledge base of the helping professions is constantly changing and expanding. Yet the economic, ethical, and practical constraints of conducting controlled clinical research impose limits on this growth. An important complement is naturally occurring research contained within agency-based practice. As part of daily agency functioning, information is routinely collected on clients, their problems and goals, interventions provided, and outcomes. If the tools used to collect and store this information were to be carefully developed, this routine paperwork could become the basis for a clinical database to help address practice questions beyond the outcome of single cases. This could involve, for example, analyzing case outcomes as a function of high-risk factors, analyzing the type and intensity of interventions offered, or analyzing outcome differences based on clients' backgrounds. It could also aid organizational planning by observing how services sought and provided shift over time.

Questions of how to make service more effective by blending clinical and management information needs are gaining increasing attention in mental health service research. (For detailed discussions on these questions, see Binner, 1988; Patti, Poertner, & Rapp, 1987; Nurius & Hudson, 1993; Wells & Whittaker, 1989).

ESSENTIALS OF FEEDBACK THROUGHOUT
THE HELPING PROCESS

The specific forms of feedback that are most appropriate and meaningful will naturally vary across cases and practice settings. In the following section we will illustrate a variety of possibilities. There are, however, a number of general principles and questions that are fairly universal. One principle focuses on the direct links between progress-monitoring aids with other aspects of client intervention. Feedback tools and efforts should complement planned interventions as fully as possible. In some circumstances, immediate and accurate feedback is sufficiently important to ensure that intervention plans build around it—such as when severe risk of neglect, harm, or deterioration is involved. More typically, however, indicators for monitoring client progress or functioning can be tailored to suit the needs of the case and situation.

Another feedback principle focuses on the correspondence between the feedback aid and the desired outcome goals of the case. Practitioners must determine whether to use a standardized measure or a client-tailored rating scale, whether to focus on contents of the client's thinking or on behavioral changes in their social interactions, and whether to closely follow small degrees of change in a client's functioning or to step back and get a more global overview of client functioning. These are neither arbitrary nor standard decisions. Rather, they should flow from the goals established as priorities with clients, from the initial assessments that suggest the strengths and limitations of clients and their niches, from gaps in the assessment picture, and from the types of intervention strategies proposed or under way.

By and large, as discussed in the first chapter of this book, we have been assuming an intervention context that permits repeated contact with clients over time. Yet, these contacts do not have to continue over an extended period of time. As we noted earlier, the national average for length of psychotherapeutic treatment is between five and six sessions. Furthermore, many agencies are imposing time restrictions as a cost-containment effort to spread limited resources across clients seeking services. Thus, while we will generally speak within a "time-series" framework of gathering feedback across the various phases of practice with clients, we will also discuss ways in which these principles apply to one-shot contacts (in emergency rooms, or crisis hot lines, for example), circumstances in which several workers are involved in a case (for case management, or medical setting teams), and when services other than psychological counseling are the mainstay of intervention (in adoption or discharge planning).

As we have repeatedly emphasized, interpersonal practice is rife with inferences, judgments, and decisions that must be made. We have argued for the importance of a conceptually and empirically grounded framework from which to operate that allows practitioners to articulate their rationale for decisions and plans for action at each point in the professional relationship. As practitioners, we are constantly engaged in a form of hypothesis testing: gauging this client's level of functioning relative to others we have seen, correlating attributes we observe with attributes we suspect, making causal attributions for both problems and changes in a case, and so forth. This testing takes place throughout the entire professional relationship, constituting an ongoing assessment. Yet the nature of the questions for which we need feedback changes with shifts in the phases of the helping process.

Five key questions that reflect how information needs shift throughout treatment can be identified (summarized from Nurius & Hudson, 1993):

1. Have I validly and adequately captured the client's baseline functioning?
2. Is the client progressing toward identified goals?
3. Is this progress meaningful and sufficient?
4. What attributions can I make about the cause of observed progress (or the lack thereof)?
5. What generalizations can I make to the future of this case or to other cases?

Whether explicit or not, we make constant judgments about these and other questions. But much like the importance of increasing client mindfulness, greater awareness of the information and inferences upon which these judgments are based is essential to the practitioner. Note the sequence of the questions and their extensions beyond a particular case. With each case, we accumulate practice knowledge upon which we draw for decision making in later cases. If earlier judgments are based on error, bias, or inadequate information, the consequences for clients can be significant. This may occur, for example, when practitioners prematurely begin interventions based on insufficient assessment, when indicators of risk are unrecognized or glossed over, when lack of progress is erroneously attributed to client resistance, or when outcomes with a limited or homogeneous client sample are overgeneralized to other practice settings.

Let us now look at some of the types of feedback aids that would be useful for each major question.

1. Have I Validly and Adequately Captured the Client's Baseline Functioning?

Baselines refer to the level of functioning that best represents clients' pre-intervention status. To get a representative picture of preintervention status, multiple observations or types of data are important. We have all experienced the mistake of developing erroneous first impressions of an individual based on a single, limited observation. The difficulty is compounded in the context of professional practice where clients are asked to reveal highly intimate information or a confusing situation to a stranger under circumstances of considerable personal stress and intrusion.

Part of the importance of obtaining a representative baseline has to do with its role to guide assessment, goal-setting, and intervention selection. Practitioners often feel pressured to begin something almost immediately, in the hope of bringing relief to their clients. While speed is certainly important, interventions based on inadequate formulation of problems and resources are likely to be less well focused, less useful in relationship building or as a teaching aid for clients, and less effective (Hayes, Nelson, & Jarrett, 1987). Working collaboratively with clients to bring their natural environment and their characteristic response patterns into the artificial confines of treatment is one powerful way to enhance the validity of assessment.

It is not our intent to survey the armament of potential assessment and feedback aids available to the practitioner. A number of books exist that describe these measures as well as their measurement and scoring guidelines (see Barlow, Hayes, & Nelson, 1984; Bloom & Fischer, 1982; Blythe & Tripodi, 1989; Corcoran & Fischer, 1987; Gambrill, 1983; Nurius & Hudson, 1993). Rather, we will focus on a few feedback aids to illustrate their potential within a cognitive-ecological framework to support the six levels of information feedback described in the previous section.

One example of a well-used feedback aid is the structured journal. A structured, self-monitoring log, accompanied with careful instructions for how to use it, can direct clients to focus on specific details associated with their presenting problems. This could include social transactions (what people did and said before, during, and after a target event) as well as specific perceptual and cognitive processes involved in the social interactions (what images or thoughts they had, the intensity of their feelings). A log serves as a mechanism to get specific snapshots of clients' niches (albeit highly filtered through their perceptual lens), while initiating training for clients in becoming more mindful and objective observers of their own behaviors. This same feedback aid can later be modified to direct clients to note alternative responses they might imagine, and to record their thoughts and feelings associated with their attempts at new responses.

Thus, we can see that the process of working closely with the client to obtain a baseline involves clinical opportunities to foster client education and insight. Getting a clearer picture of clients' baseline functioning is also important to goal-setting. For example, based on their current functioning, what are realistic ultimate goals? Relative to their individual baseline, what are realistic interim and instrumental goals? Are current levels of functioning normative? Has there been any clear trend in their preintervention level of functioning (for better or worse) that may tell us something about contributing factors (positive or negative) going on in their life? As we saw in Chapters 6 and 7, an important component in helping clients become better problem solvers is the ability to gain a more objective view of present functioning (and often the functioning of others important in their niche, such as their children or partners).

Finally, clients' preintervention baselines serve a critically important role as a clinical referent. Specifically, when we look at later questions, such as whether clients have progressed and whether this progress is meaningful, the baseline serves as a primary standard against which evaluations and judgments are made. Evaluations at the point of terminating or phasing out formal helping are useful for more macro questions, such as determining which interventions appear most effective for different types of client problems or under certain conditions. However, for feedback to be useful to the practitioner's and client's need to stay focused and effective, assessment and feedback must be ongoing and immediate.

Are the above activities related to what many practitioners already do naturally? We would argue that these activities do reflect an expansion of practitioners' natural activities (see Brower & Mutschler, 1985; Brower & Nurius, 1985). That is, when we observe, gauge, infer, and evaluate client functioning, we are doing measurement in our minds— though at varying levels of explicitness. When we try to describe our clients to colleagues, we are using evaluation concepts. By encouraging the use of more systematic and specific efforts to obtain and document baseline functioning, these natural processes are made more explicit, and equally important, more mindful. Because it is so easy for us to be influenced by our preexisting clinical schemas—concerning types of situations, kinds of people, and diagnostic categories—great care is needed to ensure that our clinical inferences and decisions are as valid as possible.

Paradoxically, some of the very tools practitioners apply to gather and interpret information about their clients' problems and functioning can impede clinical judgment. A major element here is a reliance on categorical frameworks. This would include reliance on problem and symptom checklists and use of classification systems (such as the *Diagnostic and Statistical Manual III-R*, soon to be revised as DSM IV). The DSM III-R has been found to be the single most frequently consulted professional reference (Kutchins & Kirk, 1986). Categorical systems do help us organize, recall, and deal with a flood of information, but they also impose great costs. For example, look over the forms one currently uses for intake, clinical assessment, or case disposition. Are they constructed in a fashion to support validity and to minimize bias? Do they encourage the consideration of: (a) alternative explanations, (b) disconfirmatory information-gathering strategies, (c) noninferential evidence, (d) triangulated consistency (i.e., a consistent picture emerging from multiple types of information from differing sources), (e) environmental contributions to problem development (combating the fundamental attribution error of inferring individual causes problems)?

As we saw in Chapter 3, individuals can store vast amounts of information in long-term memory, but can recall only a fraction at any given moment. Thus, a valuable aid to both practitioner and client is prompts that help us avoid overlooking important information, rather than prompts that foster theory confirmation and bias. This should be the purpose of intake forms and social history questionnaires.

In addition to use of prompts and aids that broaden the scope of information gathered, use of tools to minimize reliance on memory is also important. Arnoult and Anderson (1988) argue that because information is both forgotten and incorrectly remembered, practitioners should not depend solely on their memories for important judgments and evaluations. Rather, efficient means are needed to keep varied sources of high-quality clinical data available. What might these look like? Examples include (but are by no means limited to) the use of:

- Global rating scales (e.g., of social functioning or psychiatric status)
- Broad-range inventories (e.g., of problem behavior clusters or performance of social roles)
- Problem-focused standardized measures (such as the Clinical Anxiety Scale)
- Psychophysiological measures (such as heart rate and muscular tension)
- Ratings by self or others based on direct observation of actual or simulated (role-play) events
- Client-tailored measures (such as self-reported intensity of anger measured on a 1-7 scale based upon client language and experiences)

- Measurement of the physical and social environment (e.g., types and degree of economic resources, social supports, and life stressors)
- Observation of problem-related products (such as weight, injuries, substances in the bloodstream, medications not taken)
- Interpretations of projective instruments (such as complete-a-sentence and draw-a-picture exercises)
- Multidimensional standardized tests (such as the MMPI)
- Carefully documented problem-oriented record keeping (i.e., clearly specifying behavioral observations of the client, identifying patterns in relation to critical incidents)

To strengthen validity and to provide educational examples of information-driven, rather than assumption-driven, approaches to assessing a problem and situation, tools such as these can be helpful for gathering, recording, triangulating, and interpreting baseline and ongoing progress data.

2. Is the Client Progressing Toward Identified Goals?

We have previously discussed the importance of fostering hope and motivation through the professional relationship. One aid to accomplishing this is the recognition of incremental progress. Progress on clinically significant problems is seldom as fast or as linear as we would like. It is all too easy to apply unrealistic expectations ("I'm an adult, therefore I should be able to pull myself together and be done with this problem") and to lose sight of real progress attained.

As discussed in Chapter 7, it is important to document incremental progress because of the tendency we have to revise history in directions consistent with our current beliefs and expectations. For example, Hollon and Garber (1988) describe clients' tendency to "forget" prior lower levels of functioning, to have difficulty discerning the progress actually attained, and to minimize or discount incremental successes as meaningful ("I guess I wasn't as bad off as I thought I was"). External indicators of incremental progress thus provide additional resources to challenge client distortions and to help galvanize motivation.

Monitoring aids also help the practitioner model for the client ways to retrain oneself. Here we are talking about some strategies to help clients in their efforts to shift from reliance on maladaptive assumptions and expectations to an active search for multiple sources of information available in the moment or situation. Learning how to identify appropriate indicators of change, to observe these over time, and to use the feedback to inform one's decision making ("This does not seem to be working, so I need to change the way I'm going about it" or "This is awfully hard work, but I can see steady improvement so I need to hang in there") are tremendously important for all of us in our quests for change. There are many ways to establish indicators of meaningful progress (or maintenance of gains). For example, practitioners can explore the notion of acceptable evidence (Barlow, Hayes, & Nelson, 1984). That is, what are some of the ways clients would like to see their life different, that although not perfect, would be acceptable to them? Does the practitioner also see these changes as acceptable and meaningful indicators of sufficient change in the needed direction?

As we have identified previously, clients often have a far clearer image of what they wish to avoid than what they wish to accomplish. This is generally true of all of us when in the midst of difficult, confusing, threatening, and fatiguing life circumstances. Moreover, clients very often carry with them an idealized image of their desired goal state, one that they believe they should be able to accomplish. The notion of acceptable evidence helps clients visualize in realistic terms what they would view as acceptable change in the desired direction. In essence, acceptable evidence helps clients develop more clear and attainable possible selves and possible niches.

For Teresa (last chapter's case example), acceptable evidence of becoming more interesting may include participation in group activities or volunteer work that interest her, greater initiation of conversations and greater ability to sustain them, greater awareness of environmental cues about her as a person of worth and interest (which requires less minimization of such cues), and greater self-reinforcement of her worth and abilities. Acceptable evidence related to her goal of more satisfying intimate relationships would likely overlap with the above, but would also tap into other specific domains of her life. These may include fewer thoughts and feelings of desperation about being able to hold onto a man, greater comfort in living independently, greater participation in a variety of social and friendship relationships, greater clarity about what needs would or would not be satisfied by an intimate relationship and the qualities that would be needed in a suitable partner, and greater clarity about the skills important for maintaining this type of relationship. Again, through the process, Teresa is helped to clarify her possible selves and possible niches concerning her image of herself as interesting and involved in a satisfying relationship. As compared to affective, behavioral, and environmental factors, clients tend to discount the role played by their own perceptions and cognitions. That is, we tend to look for concrete explanations for our problems and our discomforts. Because we underestimate cognitive factors, we are more inclined to attribute failure to incompetence, to character defects, to other people, or to constraints of the situation. All of these other factors may indeed be part and parcel of the problem. The issue is that because we tend to experience our observations and thoughts as facts, and because we are generally unaware of the power of our information and memory processing, we are inclined to overlook the role of our own beliefs, attributions, and expectations, and therefore we miss opportunities for change.

Thus, intervention should involve the active preparation of clients to monitor their cognitive change. Anger management interventions provide one example of how cognitive change goals can be monitored. Clients often learn about the nature of anger, and how their thinking, observations, and feelings work hand in hand. They learn how to slow down their explosive reaction patterns and ask themselves certain questions (such as, "What exactly did the other person say?" "What did I think she meant and how did I feel?"). As a function of this self-regulation, they become better prepared to observe their cognitive processing (concerning their schemas about themselves and others and their subsequent expectations, beliefs, and attributions). This is one example of how meta-cognition and self-monitoring can combine toward therapeutic and empowerment goals.

Monitoring progress is an essential aid to staying focused on identified priorities and goals. It is also one of the bases for self-adjusting practice—that is, of adjusting interventions as a function of what appears to work or not work. Once again, we see the benefit of the practitioner making explicit and visible the specific tools that will aid the clients in becoming more effective in their self-observations and problem solving.

We noted in the prior section that there is an immense array of measurement aids to assist assessment and case monitoring. Regardless of the aids used, instrumental and ultimate goals should include specification of how these indicators or measures fit in. For example, for clients pursuing improved self-concept, what kinds of indicators fit well with their notion of acceptable evidence? If they are monitoring self-statements and response patterns in situations where they have tended to feel most threatened in the past, what levels of change would they be satisfied with? At what point would they feel the first stage of goals had been attained?

3. Is This Progress Meaningful and Sufficient?

Determining what constitutes meaningful and significant change for any given client requires that we take into account a number of factors specific to the individual (or couple, family, group). For example, case-specific referents include clients' preintervention baselines plus their intervention goals. In combination these provide two clinical indices unique to each client within which to interpret present levels of functioning.

Consider Figure 9.1, for example, a graphic case profile for Mrs. Thomas, a depressed woman in her early sixties. Her baseline is made up of two retrospective points (her recollections about how she would have responded 2 months prior to admission), and two scores taken during the first two treatment sessions in which intake, assessment, and goal-setting were undertaken. In articulating her goals, Mrs. Thomas recognized that everyone has occasional feelings of depression. Thus, her ultimate treatment goal was to experience swings that were largely within the normal range (0-30 on the Generalized Contentment Scale that was being used).

Given setbacks and the normal difficulties in achieving clinical change, Mrs. Thomas identified some of the ways she would like to be living and feeling differently on a daily basis (examples of acceptable evidence of change) that reflected movement toward her ultimate goals. This discussion aided the client and the practitioner in developing a shared image of what changes or evidence would reflect a return to a level of functioning that Mrs. Thomas found sufficiently satisfactory to discontinue clinical intervention (or to focus on different issues).

In some cases, this kind of discussion will reveal schema deficiencies as discussed in Chapters 4, 6, and 8. That is, the persons may not have images of what their possible self and possible niche look like, and will have great difficulty in trying to generate images to clarify their pictures. This, of course, is part of the assessment process informing the practitioner of what underused, but nonetheless existing, knowledge structures the client may have in memory. In cases where progress is anticipated to be slower and more modest, increments of change need to be correspondingly smaller, and indicators need to be more sensitive to smaller degrees of change.

Another source of input to determine meaningful and sufficient change is to use clinical norms. This is one advantage of using standardized measures and instruments. That is, in the process of formally validating the measure, norms for both clinical and nonclinical populations are typically established. Standardized norms provide clinical cutting scores that help users determine low, medium, and severe levels

Figure 9.1. Depression Profile of Mrs. Thomas

Generalized contentment scale

- - - - - = Clinical cutting score;
Client goal = stable in 0-30 range

2 mos   2 wks   Intake,   Assmt,   1   2   3   4   5   6   7   8
Retrospective   Assmt   Goals
                              Individual counseling

of problem behavior (such as for depression, or being at risk for aggressive behavior toward others). Let us add two clinical cutting scores to our prior example of Mrs. Thomas. We see that a score of 70 or more constitutes severe depression and a clinically significant risk of suicide among depressed individuals, as measured by the Generalized Contentment Scale (GCS); a score of 30 or less indicates the nonclinical level. Of course, such cutting scores will not hold true for every individual, and it is important to use norms appropriate to one's client (for example, a GCS score of 50 may be experienced as grave and disabling for a given individual and as moderate for another, and the norms for the elderly may be different than for younger adults). Yet, if the norms are based on careful validation research, they will reflect the functioning parameters of most individuals, and can provide a useful guideline to use as a beginning point for interpreting client data.

Therefore, even with the use of standardized measures, practitioners need to use their own judgment in order to standardize the standard measure to the individual client. (As discussed in previous chapters, norms and normality are defined differently for different situations.) To do this, scores should be compared to other established clinical indices—in this case, Mrs. Thomas's vegetative signs, her level of affect in the interview, and her ability to enjoy activities that she used to enjoy. Mrs. Thomas's baseline score of 50 on the GCS needs to be anchored to real behaviors that exist in her daily life for the score to be meaningful in the work with her.

Judgments of the significance of client progress are also intimately related to intervention planning. For example, practitioners often need to determine when to increase or decrease their intensity of services, or when to shift from one problem or intervention to another. Use of feedback aids to monitor progress can help not only to make this determination but also to model this process of decision making for the client. The same holds true for establishing a point to phase out and terminate intervention. As suggested in Chapter 7, the service contract should stipulate the termination date and number of sessions antici-pated. Additionally, termination readiness involves an examination of how fully the intervention goals have been attained.

We have discussed judgments regarding significance solely in terms of practical or clinical significance. It is important to note another form, that of statistical significance. *Statistical significance* refers to the likelihood that observed changes or patterns have occurred due to chance. Statistical significance involves calculating the probabilities that normal or random factors deriving from a variety of sources could account for the client changes or patterns. With Mrs. Thomas, for example, the question a practitioner must ask is: Given the variability in her functioning at baseline, what is the likelihood that she would have made the changes, observed at the point of termination, if she had not received professional help?

The question of whether the degree of change is real, in the sense of not being attributable to random factors or those already in place at baseline, involves statistical significance. The question of whether the degree of change observed is enough, in the sense of meeting clients' goals and/or reflecting what practitioners believe to be adequate healthy functioning, involves *practical significance*. Evaluating each type of significance helps address different kinds of questions. Thus, each serves complementary goals, toward different types of feedback.

In practice, one rarely has the opportunity to have "controls"—clients receiving no intervention or services—who can serve as a planned basis of comparison. However, we would like to suggest that more advantage be taken of the naturally accruing clinical database generally in place in our practice settings. Almost all settings routinely collect information about clients—generally from intake forms, evaluation or termination summaries, quarterly reports, and the like. It is not often the case, however, that our settings make systematic use of these data, particularly for clinical purposes. Think back to the six levels of feedback we enumerated under roles and goals of feedback aids, and consider ways in which the database at your practice setting might be used for these purposes. For example, could simple rating scales of problem severity, service intensity, and client satisfaction be developed for use on every case, to help provide more clinical referents for program evaluation? Could criteria be developed to help operationalize degrees of successful outcomes for such activities as discharge planning, crisis intervention, and evaluation with referral? Could agency norms or clinical cutting scores be established to help differentiate groups of clients believed to be different in one's agency? (Brower, 1989b, and Nurius, 1992, provide further discussion on how practitioners can develop ways to make use of their agency data.)

4. What Attributions Can I Make About the Cause of Observed Progress (or the Lack Thereof)?

In the first of these five key questions that discussed baseline functioning, we spoke of *measurement validity*: To what extent am I actually tapping the factors I believe I am tapping through my various information-gathering methods? In considering the question of attributions about causality, we are talking about a different type of validity—*internal validity*. That is, in virtually all aspects of professional practice, the practitioner is engaged in a form of experimentation. After initial data is collected, hypotheses are generated regarding the factors creating the problem, the factors maintaining the problem, and the intervention factors generating the desired level and type of change. The practitioner introduces the chosen independent variable (the intervention, or agent of change) and then observes the dependent variable (the problem, or target of change) to determine if the expected change occurs. If these changes are not forthcoming, the practitioner either changes the intervention or addresses factors that may be blocking, suppressing, or diluting the effects of the intervention.

Clinical research indicates that when changes are observed, practitioners tend to attribute client changes to factors consistent with their expectations and preconceptions of psychopathology; generally, attributing positive change to the intervention, and negative change to client or environmental factors (Kayne & Alloy, 1988). This is by no means a tendency unique to practitioners, but nonetheless has serious implications for how we evaluate our clinical work (see Jordan, Harvey, & Weary, 1988, for an overview of attributional issues in clinical decision making).

Internal validity related to attributions about what caused change concerns the degree to which alternative explanations of change can be ruled out. Rarely do we find in practice the kinds of naturally occurring controls needed to confidently rule out alternative explanations. Instead, in clinical research, the best we can hope for is to try to impose some control over the intervention process to help reduce the effects of confounds and to monitor alternative explanations of client change.

Keep in mind that the issue of internal validity is not a rarefied concept that concerns only hard-core researchers. Instead, it stands at the heart of developing clinical knowledge for individuals, agencies, and for the profession. How do we decide which interventions serve as likely sources of change, support, and relief for our clients, and how much confidence can we place in these interventions? What limitations or qualifiers should we consider? Were our clients receiving forms of support or input from sources outside of treatment that contributed to their change? Did normal maturation contribute to change? Were those clients who dropped out taken into consideration in the evaluation of the intervention?

Determining internal validity is a matter of degree. While practical and ethical considerations limit the kinds of controls we can impose on intervention, we can incrementally introduce safeguards into the treatment process to foster confidence in our attributions about clinical changes. We have already discussed one safeguard: explicitly and routinely considering alternatives to our favored theories, as well as gathering and interpreting information to explicitly disconfirm our hypotheses. Before we work to improve an unemployed client's interviewing skills, for example, we must rule out economic and environmental constraints as the important factors determining that person's unemployment.

Another internal validity safeguard involves careful measurement of the intervention itself. To answer questions about client change, we must have information about both the presumed independent variable (intervention) and the dependent variable (the client or environmental target of change). Yet rarely is information about interventions recorded, or even articulated, with much specificity or detail. Think again at the forms in one's practice setting, this time with an eye to how interventions are conceptualized and recorded. Typically, some form of categorical designation is used on planning and termination forms. For example, one is instructed to check whether clients received individual counseling, family therapy, group work, information and referral, advocacy, or the like. The question is, how useful are these very general categories to understanding the interventions administered?

The most common reporting scheme—narrative case recording—does often include descriptions of interventions used. Yet, these narratives, more often than not, are only loosely structured and highly individualized. Nevertheless, we recommend that case notes are one important place where interventions can be more specifically and systematically elaborated. It is not that most practitioners have not spent a great deal of time thinking (and talking to their supervisors) about what they do with clients. Rather, the issue is that this seldom becomes recorded information in a manner that permits a practitioner, supervisor, or administrator to really learn from an agency database. Rarely does case recording include ways to gauge important qualities of interventions, such as the level of effort, the intensity or strength of the intervention, the integrity of specific strategies (i.e., the extent to which we actually did what we had planned to do with the client), or the overall quality of the service provided (see Blythe & Tripodi, 1989; Yeaton & Sechrest, 1981, for a discussion of these factors). Anyone who has inherited a thick case file about a client, and then had to wade through sheet after sheet of marginally legible and relatively vague recordings, can appreciate the need to have systematic recording procedures for gaining a comprehensive picture of both the functioning profile of the client and the specific kinds of interventions that have been applied. Clearly, then, a significant challenge of practice is better articulation, measurement, and evaluation of intervention. If we are unable to clearly articulate and document the components of the services we offer, our causal attributions regarding our professional practice rely on little more than biased and unsubstantiated leaps of faith.

Finally, a number of criteria can be presented for inferring causality and for protecting against known threats to internal validity. First, it is important to understand that causality can never be fully established; it is instead always a matter of finding degrees of confidence with which one is satisfied. Questions the practitioner would want to consider include: Did changes only occur after the intervention? Were changes observed fairly quickly (that is, time lags increase the likelihood that other or additional factors are causal)? Are observed changes consistent with expectations (according to theory and one's experiences)? Are there other plausible explanations for the change? Have these been ruled out, or do ways exist to rule them out? Are there nontreatment factors—such as maturation, experiences outside of treatment, receipt of multiple interventions, or expectations regarding intervention—that may be contributing to the outcomes? Are there interfering effects—such as the influence of being observed and asked questions; cultural, class, gender or age factors; natural biases in the perceptions of the practitioner—that may be influencing outcomes?

Familiarity with these questions, and their incorporation into our clinical reasoning habits, will greatly help to reduce erroneous causal attributions. They will help us build an individual and professional knowledge base in which we can have increasing confidence. Several useful sources exist for the further discussion of how to enhance internal validity in practice (see Bloom & Fischer, 1982; Cook & Campbell, 1979; Barlow & Hersen, 1984).

5. What Generalizations Can I Make to the Future of This Case or to Other Cases?

We turn at this point from internal validity to *external validity*; from feedback about attributions of cause and effect in a particular case, to feedback about the range of applicability of observed effects across cases. The bad news relative to external validity is that we all are exceedingly prone to overgeneralization (as we have discussed throughout this book). It is only marginally comforting to know that this is not unique to practitioners. We are also inclined to view our personal experiences and observations as accurately reflecting broader reality and broad-based norms for others (Dawes, 1986; Unger, Draper, & Pendergrass, 1986). The good news is that there are a number of feedback aids to help temper this inherent inclination, not the least of which is the feedback we gain as a function of the prior key questions we have discussed thus far.

The effective use of a clinical information system across clients can be invaluable here. For example, to what extent are the activities from one practitioner's experience supported by the experience of others in the same setting? Yet even when one can address this question, the generalizability issue is not fully solved. Knowledge development within practice settings is still at risk of being nonrepresentative of any other setting. Practitioners within settings tap clients from the same general pool; clients coming to one setting may very well have more in common with each other than they do with clients from another setting. Practitioners must keep current with their professional literature, if for no other reason than because it serves as an additional referent point for judging the extent to which their experiences generalize to clients broadly.

Judgments of generalization are an excellent example of the importance of integrated practice thinking. That is, to make valid generalizations, practitioners must be able to draw upon (a) theory and findings about human behavior generally, (b) the specific problem at hand, (c) the specific interventions applied, (d) the characteristics and data of this specific case, and (e) the principles of clear analytic thinking.

Generalization judgments require practitioners to distinguish between samples and populations. For example, the particular clients we see are a sample of the larger and more varied pool of individuals who seek help with that problem. The people who seek help are a sample of the larger and more varied pool of people who have that problem but do not seek help. The people who have that problem and are suffering negative effects are a sample of the larger and more varied population who have the same set of symptoms but do not suffer negative effects (or are able to manage them successfully, such as partners of addicts who could not reasonably be assessed as codependent; grown children of a parent with a serious drinking problem who are far from the popularized Adult Children of Alcoholics image; child abuse victims who develop into healthy, nonabusing parents; and so on).

When determining the generalizability of a case, one must consider demographic characteristics of clients and practitioners. There are obviously a host of normative differences among clients. Among the most obvious are differences among clients' culture, race, age, gender, socioeconomic resources, and sexual preference. Although sensitivity is growing as to how these differences affect professional practice, there has been a problematic trend in the past to make superficial changes in one's approach based on these differences, or to overgeneralize on the basis of stereotypic characterizations (i.e., assuming all African-Americans will react to treatment in the same way; see Cousins et al., 1985; Franklin, 1985). Similarly, there are a number of practitioner characteristics, which include the same normative features noted above, that may well influence how an intervention is provided and experienced. Further, research demonstrates that these client and practitioner characteristics themselves interact in specific ways (see Brower, Garvin, Hobson, Reed, & Reed, 1987). And, there are obviously also practice-specific practitioner differences—such as belief systems, and interpersonal style—that influence the conduct of intervention. Thus, it may be more prudent to start from the assumption that assessment profiles, client reactions, or case outcomes from one case will not generalize to other cases. The burden then is on the practitioner to justify why these outcomes do generalize.

As we mentioned previously, one crucially important factor that is often underspecified in records involves the nature of the intervention itself. Exactly what did it consist of? What sequence of services were provided, in what manner, and with what degree of intensity? We often make the mistake of believing that others use buzz words, or professional jargon, in the same way that we do. This implies that terms like *humanistic, behavioral,* or *psychodynamic* practice, *re-parenting, cognitive restructuring, structural family therapy,* and the like, can be assumed to be highly uniform—a clearly risky and unrealistic assumption. To generalize from case to case, we must specify our interventions in precise and clear behaviorally descriptive terms.

Finally, generalizability must be assessed with respect to the nature of the problem in the environmental context within which it appears. What, specifically, do problems like depression, family enmeshment, undersocialization, and hysteria mean for specific segments of the population, at this point in our cultural and political history? Green (1982) has stressed that use of such cover terms—terms that cover or contain a great deal of implicit meaning—must be carefully defined to avoid misinterpretations, miscommunications, and misleading assumptions.

Collectively, two themes emerge as useful guidelines regarding external validity. The first is simply being as specific as reasonably possible. That is, rely more on descriptive detail and less on jargon, categories, cover terms, and labels. The second theme has to do with replication. If the same essential set of relationships and outcomes is repeatedly observed across clients, practitioners, and settings, the greater the assurance of generalizability.

Again, we see the fruitful possibilities to use routinely collected information. The potential exists for virtually any professional practice setting to also serve as a natural clinical research center. We are not talking here about research in the sense of running controlled experiments, nor are we advocating the conversion of service-provision centers into research labs. Rather, we wish to emphasize the opportunities for the clinical database that naturally accrues across clients to address many of the broader practice questions raised. Yet this is possible only if sufficient planning is done to make documentation and feedback procedures provide useful information to practitioners and clients.

FOLLOW-THROUGH: A BRIDGE BETWEEN FORMAL HELP AND SELF-HELP

Part of what makes durable behavior change hard is that it is difficult to sustain the prolonged effort needed to make real changes in our lives. We have all experienced the surge of energy, motivation, and optimism that often comes with the initial commitment to tackle a challenge, only to later see our rate of progress decline as our enthusiasm and energy wane. This kind of entropy is normal and widely experienced, yet like so many factors that we have spoken about, it can seriously undermine clients' views of their capacity for real change.

The vulnerability to discouragement, fatigue, and complacency is particularly marked once the prompts, guidance, and supports of helping interventions are withdrawn. This is one of the reasons to incorporate training and practice with problem-solving skills into both change and maintenance-oriented practice. This vulnerability is also one of the reasons we have emphasized the importance of focused efforts to help clients recognize and accept their personal power and responsibility in terms of becoming their own practitioners.

It is encouraging to note that evidence exists documenting how client self-attributions about their therapeutic change are important to the continuation and maintenance of their changes (Brehm & McAllister, 1980; Colletti & Stern, 1980; Sonne & Janoff, 1982). In models of helping where the clients are viewed as not responsible for their solutions or as incapable of successful problem management, the clients are dependent on powerful others to effect desired changes in their lives. There are certainly times when we must realistically give up a considerable degree of decision making and personal control (for instance, when seeking advice and expert services from a diagnostic and surgical team). It is also true that the degree and nature of clients' self-responsibility depend on their capacities and the context of the intervention. However, within these practical constraints, it is important to provide as much opportunity as possible for clients to determine their own fate and to exit professional practice well prepared to take over the practitioner functions themselves.

The point of termination is, as Zaro, Barack, Nedelman, and Dreiblatt (1982) have pointed out, often a compromise between changes that are hoped for and constraints arising from various sources (such as financial, time, energy, and emotional costs). This is a situation that some practitioners find very difficult to accept. We are not suggesting that practitioners become inured to the limitations blocking individuals from receiving needed help. Rather we are highlighting the potential problem of the overprofessionalization of life. That is, all of us could theoretically benefit from therapeutic intervention throughout our life spans. There are always issues one could explore, problems one could work with more effectively, and additional goals toward which one could strive. But this perspective distorts the reality that learning, growth, and development are ongoing parts of life itself; that life is not a race to nirvana; and that normal life is difficult and even terrible (as well as wonderful) at times. Economic constraints aside, this kind of minimization of individuals' abilities to make their own way unaided by us, the aggrandizement of the importance of counseling and therapy, and the perpetuation of the myth of mental health equaling constant happiness, is self-serving at best, and exploitative at worst.

Egan (1990, pp. 399-400) has encapsulated a number of principles to use in both determining the point of termination and preparing for it:

- Make sure that the values espoused regarding empowerment and ecological practice are behaviorally manifest throughout the entire helping process, from initial contact to termination. This will help keep communication open and make termination planning a joint consideration.

- Long-term relationships belong in the social niche and everyday lives of clients. Subordinate the professional practice relationship to helping achieve specific client outcomes goals, client self-efficacy, and mobilization of social and physical resources in the client's natural environment.

- To the extent possible, incorporate discussion of ending points as part of initial intervention planning and contracting. This would include contracting for "digestible" blocks of sessions and for specific levels of goal attainment that are acceptable as points to phase out the professional relationship.

- Limit input to those areas of clients' lives that both need remedial action and reflect agreed-upon points of intervention. The balance between empowering help and inappropriate intrusion into clients' personal lives is a delicate one. If the practitioner's view of what clients need is different from their own, explain the kind of help one believes is needed and work toward a mutually agreeable contract.

- From the beginning, help clients find and develop the resources they need in their niche to manage their problem situations and to pursue their goals. Work to incorporate gains achieved in helping (new perspectives, possible selves and niches, skills) into clients' natural environments.

- Keep in mind that the one-to-one professional relationship is merely one form of helping, and one that should, for the most part, be short-term in nature. As needed, work to incorporate forms of helping that are closer to clients' everyday lives and that broaden the sources and forms of support (such as therapeutic, educational, support, or self-help groups; training and preparation for new roles; interest and activity programs).

PREPARING CLIENTS FOR TERMINATION

Let us now consider a number of ways to prepare clients for termination. First, consider that the niche and the self-system are systems that both galvanize and resist action and change. One of the basic premises of the cognitive-ecological model is that the introduction of change into either the self-system or the individual's niche necessitates change in other elements of the system (since all other elements will have to adapt for the change to stick, and for the niche to survive). Thus, clients can be prepared for termination by identifying the kinds of obstacles they are likely to encounter that hinder broad changes in their niche. In several respects, this is an extension of the same kind of activity practitioners and clients engage in as they undertake initial intervention planning. What are the goals for intervention, and what are the strengths and limitations in the niche and self-system, relative to their goals? Given this, what intervention options look most promising? What underused resources could be mobilized, and what factors (e.g., people, information-processing habits, social-structural variables) are likely to impose obstacles? Many of the experiences shared in the process of helping services can provide a useful beginning point for this forward-looking analysis and planning.

Through these efforts, we are helping the client to anticipate and role-play (behaviorally and cognitively) future events. Within these role-plays, the client can try out several approaches to problem solving. Since life rarely progresses down a straight and narrow path, the point will not be to only practice with clients specific reactions to anticipated events, but rather to help clients foster (a) environmental analysis abilities, (b) foresight about facilitating and restraining forces in the environment and in the person, (c) creativity in approaches to dealing with them, and (d) planning and practicing how to cultivate support and cope with impediments.

To help transfer these planning, analysis, and simulation activities into clients' postintervention patterns, several writers have advocated the use of *think rules* or self-prompts to help one remain task-focused and action-oriented. Think rules are a written form of questions clients can pose to themselves on how to analyze their environment, how to anticipate and prepare for challenges, how to recruit support from themselves and from others, how to identify manageable incremental steps for goal attainment, and how to remain flexible and creative in their problem solving (for further discussion, see Carkhuff, 1985; Kanfer & Scheftt, 1988). Clients should be encouraged to take their red flags seriously: to understand that basic life issues are never solved once and for all, but rather are confronted again and again in different forms throughout life.

Research on this type of preparatory cognitive simulation of events and responses indicates that it holds significant clinical utility (Taylor & Schneider, 1989). However, the cognitive-ecological approach encourages attention to key social transactional factors and relationships in the client's niche, meaning clients' actions must be developed within their social context and supported by their social niche.

Over the past several years, a great deal has been learned about social support. Social relationships have both positive and negative features. They can be comforting and supportive, as well as stressful and demanding (Coyne & DeLongis, 1986). Simply increasing the number of people within one's social network is not necessarily an advantage to the client. Moreover, relationships are two-way exchanges. Changes that bear upon relationships often involve some kind of negotiation pertaining to this change, and the process of negotiating changes in the social niche itself can be taxing.

Social support also takes many forms. Many people automatically define social support as emotional in nature, and construe emotional support rather narrowly to mean sympathy, acceptance, and being nurtured. It is important to remember that social networks also provide such things as *instrumental aid* (providing needed actions or materials such as child care, transportation, money), and *informational aid* (communication of facts or opinions, advice, directions, feedback, and constructive challenge) (House, 1981; Jacobson, 1986; Turner, 1983).

Two important dimensions to consider in fostering effective social support are to provide the type of support needed, and to help clients appraise the support constructively. First, the type of social support must meet the needs of the client. Expressions of sympathy, for example, may not only be insufficient, but may be experienced as frustrating if what the client most needs is instrumental aid (such as finding alternative lodging or a loan to return to school) or informational aid (such as prompts to become more positively assertive, information about how to receive certain resources, or skills to compete for a new job). Clients must be helped to identify the kind of support they need from their environment, how to request and use that support, and how to reinforce and maintain their support network.

Second, social support is only effective when it is perceived as such by the client. As became clear in Chapters 1 through 4, our social reality is a function of our social transactions and our cognitive constructions of these transactions. Consistent with this, social support appears to influence health outcomes as a function of appraisal processes. Thus, it is not social activity per se that promotes health, as much as it is how that activity is perceived and interpreted (Heller, Swindle, & Dusenbury, 1986).

More formalized sources of social support—such as self-help groups and helper-assisted training groups—can also provide needed aid to clients following termination. In some problem domains, group input is extremely important; for example, among work with a variety of addictive behaviors, victims of violence, and people who share such traumatic experiences as death of a child and serious illnesses. Group input is also often useful to accelerate and solidify self-concept change. The extensive practice, feedback, and esteem-enhancement required for self-concept change is well suited to the social microcosm of a problem-focused group. Groups can provide opportunities to exchange socioemotional and corrective feedback, as well as opportunities to practice and reinforce the development of new schemas (Garvin, 1987; Rose, 1977). Finally, providing an open-door policy to clients allows for further work when struggling with new phases of life. Booster sessions, for example, can help clients get back on track, or help them experiment with new behaviors within their natural environment. Booster sessions are conceived as just that: very brief and focused contacts that build upon prior work. Of course, a client may elect to return for more extensive help for a variety of reasons—encountering a new type of problem in living, or experiencing a crisis or significant setback. Under these circumstances, the phases of assessment, goal-setting and contracting, and intervention planning need to be repeated for the newly introduced problem.

SUMMARY

In this chapter we have focused on methods and tools for pulling together information in ways that guide the practitioner and client toward their respective goals. Many of the points made in this chapter have themselves been pulled together after having been initially introduced in previous chapters. We identified a continuum of information needs and practice goals for which feedback aids would be useful. Examples from this continuum include:

1. Enhancing clients' awareness of maladaptive habits and patterns through self-observational and feedback aids.

2. Adjusting intervention on the basis of ongoing monitoring of client functioning and goal attainment.

3. Helping practitioners to detect and correct inevitable biases and oversights through ongoing use of prompts and memory aids.

4. Aiding clients to transfer gains achieved in practice beyond the treatment relationship through prompts and self-regulation aids.

5. Harmonizing the information collected for practice and for other purposes in the practice setting (e.g., planning, program evaluation) through use of

effectiveness-oriented measures of problem severity, service intensity, or goal attainment.

6. Making better use of the above sources of clinical data by using aggregated case-focused data to develop databases within the setting that can answer practice-relevant questions.

We identified and discussed information needs across the course of treatment and ways to meet these needs. Five key questions reflect these information needs:

1. Have I validly and adequately captured the client's baseline functioning?
2. Is the client progressing toward identified goals?
3. Is this progress meaningful and sufficient?
4. What attributes can I make about the cause of observed progress (or the lack thereof)?
5. What generalizations can I make to the future of this case or to other cases?

We noted that bridges are often neglected between professional practice and clients' social niches following termination, making difficult the transfer and maintenance of gains achieved in practice. Guidelines were identified for determining the point of termination, and for preparing clients to generalize their gains to their everyday lives:

1. Ensure that the values regarding client empowerment and cognitive-ecological practice are behaviorally manifest throughout intervention.
2. Assure that the professional relationship helps clients achieve self-determination, self-efficacy, and the mobilization of needed supports in their niche.
3. Plan for endings from an early point through use of such aids as contracts.
4. Limit practitioner input to those areas that both need remedial action and are agreed-upon targets of intervention.
5. From the onset, concentrate on transfer of gains to the niche (such as extensively practicing and processing real life situations), and on developing resources and supports to sustain these gains.
6. When possible, expand forms of helping across domains of the clients' niches (through training and education, self-help groups, friendship networks, and so on).

Changes in the self-system and changes in the niche go hand in hand, and clients will benefit from long-term supports that take both into account. But, while we strive to make human service intervention play a significant role in helping our clients make niche and self-system changes, we should strive equally hard not to make professional relationships a permanent feature of their daily lives.

EPILOGUE

In this book, we have focused on how we construct meaning in our worlds and how we create a coherent life story from the events and interactions in our lives, a life story that helps us make sense of ourselves, our surroundings, and ourselves within our surroundings. Our life story charts the path from our history of experience, through our current niche, to our future life goals. We have emphasized that, in order to help our clients, we must develop our abilities to see the world as they see it, and to feel how they feel within their own worlds; we must develop the ability to bridge between their worlds and our own.

Four core themes have pervaded the thinking in this book. The first has been to explore and understand the normative, daily, social-cognitive processes and social transactions of our clients as a way to understand the problematic behaviors presented to us. We have discussed that the processes underlying both problematic and normal behaviors and interactions are similar. Instead of looking for pathology in clients, we have encouraged practitioners to look for how normal cognitive and social processes and interactions sometimes work toward undesired ends.

The second theme running through this book is a social constructionist one: We construct our social realities through our perceptions and interpretations of ourselves and the world. We selectively notice certain cues in our environment and ignore others; we are finely attuned to specific thoughts and feelings and tend to overlook or de-emphasize others; and we use our past knowledge and experience to help us make sense of our current situations and interactions. As we have discussed, we work hard to confirm our schema-based reality, and work equally hard to disconfirm information that is counter to our schemas. We live much of our lives within the routines that we forge through our interactions with our surroundings. We have discussed through several chapters that our reliance on our routines and schemas is both a help and a hindrance to us: They help us respond to information and situations quickly and easily, and they can also blind us to new knowledge and new ways of interacting. And this is as true for our clients as it is for us as professional practitioners.

The third theme organizing this book sees behaviors as our best efforts to address problems and strive for goals in our lives. Thus, when clients encounter problems, the problems are best seen as the result of clients doing the best they can, given what they know in the situation. As we have discussed throughout the book, presenting problems can best be understood within the context of the client's niche, and as a solution to some other problem, or set of problems, that exists in the niche. Yet, as we have discussed, this everyday problem solving or goal-striving is not always conscious or within clients' awareness. We very often behave in mindless, routine, or automatic ways in our day-to-day lives. The problems we are trying to solve, and the goals we are striving for, are often implicit, and the routine methods we employ to address them may or may not be in our best interest.

Thus, the fourth theme of this book has been that the process for behavior change helps clients first become more mindful about their lives, and then helps them become more mindless again: Clients are first helped to understand how their current behaviors are reasonable and understandable, given their niches, and how their behaviors are structured around their daily life choices. They are then provided the environment and the resources within the helping relationship to practice new behaviors, and are also provided the assistance and support to introduce these new behaviors into their daily lives. Clients are encouraged to practice these new behaviors enough so that the behaviors can again be enacted mindlessly—that is, in a routine and second-nature manner. Furthermore, the roles of mindlessness and mindfulness are important concepts for professional helpers: Just as our schemas can blind us to new ways of perceiving events and interacting with others, our professional schemas can blind us to complexity and novelty in our clients. We can easily stereotype them and treat them in routine ways. We must be vigilant to our own biases and schematic judgments in our professional relationships,

just as we encourage clients to do the same in their lives. The professional relationship is a collaborative one that should foster client self-
determination; the practitioner must build into it safeguards against
undue bias and influence, and must demonstrate through action the
collaborative and social-interactionist nature of the change process.

We have introduced several new concepts in this book. First, the
niche and the *self-system* were highlighted and described in detail as
the two elements of attention when applying the cognitive-ecological
model to practice settings. The niche describes that portion of the
environment within which the person lives. It contains the people and
situations with which the person comes into routine contact, and
describes the intricate network of interdependent factors that shape
behavior. The niche has been discussed as the basic unit with which to
work in the practice setting: assessment, goal-setting, and intervention
planning are directed at the client's niche.

The self-system has been discussed as that portion of the person that
is most influential in his or her interactions with the environment. It is
defined as the system of *self-schemas* that the person uses to store and
retrieve information about the self; it is used when we make sense of
self-relevant cues in the environment. We emphasized that people
activate a subset of self-schemas to allow interaction with particular
situations, and that this subset can be described as the *working self.*

When we project ourselves into the future, we do so by creating
possible selves and *possible niches.* These future-oriented representations
organize our (positive and negative) images of ourselves and our surroundings—they contain our thoughts, feelings, dreams, and fears about
where our lives are headed, and where we wish our lives were headed.
We have discussed possible selves and possible niches as concrete
representations of our *life goals*, and that a critical aspect of goal-setting
is to help clients both envision life goals and then translate them into
treatment goals. We have discussed how life goals and treatment goals
can be used as yardsticks to measure progress in the change process.

Finally, we identified the processes of *procedural* and *declarative*
memory, and the *perceptual-sensory system* to describe cognitive and
affective functioning in human memory. These memory processes were
themselves described as working as a system. We described how various problems that face clients can be understood by examining each of
these memory processes as well as their relationship to each other.

The development of the cognitive-ecological model, and the application of social cognition and information processing to direct practice,

is only at a beginning stage. Much more work needs to take place to develop the model for wide-ranging client groups and problems.

It may be that the areas in which the cognitive-ecological model can be developed can themselves be organized into two broad areas: those that relate to the development of the model per se, and those that relate to the limitations of the model itself. With respect to the latter, it may be said that the cognitive-ecological model does a better job to describe what is cognitive than to describe what is ecological. Many of the most obvious practice applications suggested by the case examples and in the chapters describing problems and appropriate interventions, are focused on the individual. We have argued that interventions directed toward the client's niche, and toward the environment generally, are not only necessary and important but required for the maintenance of behavior change. Nevertheless, it is difficult to ignore the fact that intrapsychic processes are given center stage in our discussions of the role of perception and interpretation in social interaction. One central issue discussed within social cognition itself has been that the social aspects are often overlooked (see Fiske & Taylor, 1991). In fact, a special issue of the journal, *Small Group Research*, is devoted specifically to the question of what is social about social cognition (Nye & Brower, 1994).

It is our view that the environmental and/or social aspects of the cognitive-ecological model are critical, but also underdeveloped. The theory certainly claims that these aspects are critical to human behavior, yet many studies have not made them central to their research. Instead, much of the work has focused on the internal aspects of memory processing, schema development, storage, and activation, and the like. It may very well be, then, that the language of symbolic interaction-ism—from which social cognition has borrowed heavily—is more ame-nable to the development of research that explores the social aspects of social cognition. In any event, it is our hope that this book will spark readers' interests in pursuing these broad-ranging questions.

In terms of areas of development that pertain to the cognitive-eco-logical model per se, it will be important to examine its use in a wide range of settings and with a wide range of clients. How will the model of assessment need to be adapted when working with children, or for clients with severe mental illnesses? How will the notions of life goals as possible selves and niches need to be altered when working with involuntary clients, or those suffering from severe depressions? How can a cognitive-ecological perspective help us address the social prob-lems that will face us with increased frequency in the near future:

helping clients cope with AIDS, cancer, and other fatal medical illnesses; helping clients face lives increasingly filled by the pressures and demands brought on by limited resources and opportunities, and of having to make the difficult choices between home and work; helping clients face increasing poverty rates and widening social and economic divisions in our country?

The call for services that are appropriate to our increasingly fast-paced and globally interdependent world will likewise shape how practice models generally, and the cognitive-ecological model in particular, develop in the future. The growing trends emphasize services that are solution-focused and short-term in nature, that demonstrate cost-effectiveness, that emphasize acute needs and populations over chronic concerns, that handle multiple problems in centralized service centers rather than in specialized settings, and that employ interventions that address problems at many levels simultaneously. Trends in service delivery are emphasizing self-help and community-based models, and services themselves are increasingly being dictated by managed-care models.

No single practice perspective can address all of society's problems. Yet the extent to which a cognitive-ecological model can be helpful will be the extent to which it provides direction and guidance for understanding and working with problems such as these. We have had some success teaching students and practitioners how to use the cognitive-ecological model in diverse client settings and for diverse problems. We are in the process of developing a casebook that illustrates such uses.

One final issue should be discussed, that of how a cognitive-ecological model might be integrated into one's practice setting. Just as we have argued that our client's niche must change in order to sustain desired changes, it is also true that agency norms and practices will either support or present obstacles when a practitioner makes efforts to use a new practice approach.

For example, does the information sought on case-relevant forms (such as on intake and social history questionnaires, or problem specification and goal-setting materials) sufficiently attend to the client's niche and his or her interactions and interdependence with that environment? Do they provide opportunities for client collaboration? Do the forms incline practitioners toward routinized and mindless use of client information? Similarly, what kinds of supports exist for practitioners' professional growth and ongoing supervision? Are in-service and supervision formats compatible with practitioner mindfulness and empowerment practice (i.e., how are agency decisions made, and how are practitioners included in this process)? Does groupthink exist, regarding a personal pathology orientation, or toward specific syndromes? Are agency policies compatible with the notion that clients move in and out of their need for professional service, offering such programs as booster sessions and community support groups?

We do not mean to argue that all agencies should adopt procedures that support a cognitive-ecological perspective. On the other hand, without concrete institutional or work environment supports, it is difficult, at best, to incorporate and sustain changes in one's helping approach, regardless of that approach. If one is constantly fighting with the agency, can effective services be delivered to clients?

We hope this book can add incrementally to the definition of the person-environment interaction, and its application to direct practice. We have advocated and demonstrated the importance of taking an integrative and conceptual approach to practice: of both thinking broadly about clients and their problems and teaching the skills necessary to apply broad theoretical concepts to specific cases and problems. We believe that such an approach leaves practitioners less vulnerable to fads in the practice literature that lead one to "syndromatic thinking"—seeing "the child within" in every client one meets, or viewing everyone as codependent. Such an approach leaves the practitioner less vulnerable to being technique-driven in one's work—treating all problems as "nails" because one has only a "hammer." It is only though the development of a broad-based and sufficiently detailed practice theory that one can remain firmly grounded when making practice decisions.

We have aspired to develop a practice model that emphasizes the connections between formal helping and collaboration, between concrete problem solving and empowerment. We have aspired to advance a practice perspective that has both its feet grounded in the real world, and its head in the clouds of our human affinity to hope and dream. Our clients' life stories are unique and ever-changing, providing us with constant challenge and continued promise.

Appendix

CASE STUDY: *Jeanne*

The following extended case example illustrates a number of features of the cognitive-ecological approach to practice. Although we have illustrated many of these same features in the body of the book, we believe it is also useful to walk through a case from start to finish to present a more integrated and coherent feel for what we have discussed in each of the prior chapters.

This case study was developed from the report of an alcohol and drug counselor who was supervised by one of the authors. It was edited only for clarity and to protect the client's anonymity. At the end of each major section (that is, after Assessment, Goal-Setting and Contracting, and Intervention Planning and Follow-Through), some commentary is made concerning how the case illustrates particular points of the cognitive-ecological model.

The reader will note that this case is not meant to represent a perfect example of how a cognitive-ecological approach can be used. In fact, the reader is encouraged to identify areas in which the assessment, goal-setting, and intervention processes could have been developed further, or where greater parsimony or focus is warranted. It is hoped that this case can stimulate discussion and debate about the application of the cognitive-ecological model to a complex practice situation.

ASSESSMENT

Background, Demographic Information, and Face Sheet Information About the Case

"Jeanne" is a 22-year-old white woman, the mother of two daughters: "Trista" (age 3½) and "Kay" (age 1½). She did not graduate from high school, and is not now employed outside of the home. She supports herself financially through AFDC and food stamps. She volunteers 4 hours per month with mentally retarded adults at a nearby residential treatment home. Jeanne has never been married, and currently has a boyfriend, "Kevin," who is the father of Kay. At the time of the agency contact, he had been moved out of their apartment for approximately 5 weeks. Prior to this they had been living together for several years.

Jeanne's mother died from alcohol complications when Jeanne was 7. Her father is living, and is 60 years old. She has four sisters, ages 30 to 35, and she has one brother, age 34. Jeanne's father has been sober for approximately 6 years. All her siblings have been or are currently chemically dependent. Jeanne, her siblings, and her father all live in the small, rural town in which she was raised.

Jeanne has been in 12 inpatient chemical dependency treatment programs, starting when she was 13 years old. Her last stay was 3 years ago. At that time, Trista was 6 months old and was taken away from Jeanne and put into foster care. After 3 months, Trista was returned to Jeanne's care, at first under supervision and then independently. Jeanne did not drink for 2 years following this inpatient stay; the case was considered a success and was closed at that time. She had continued to remain sober until approximately 6 months prior to the current incident.

1. Identification of Presenting Problems

Jeanne's father called the local police to report that Jeanne had called him to say she wanted to "end it all." She said she had a gun in the house, and he reported that she sounded like she had been drinking. When the police arrived at Jeanne's home, they found that Jeanne had been drinking and was quite upset. The kids were sleeping in their beds. The police reported that they did not find a gun anywhere in the house. Jeanne became quite upset that the police were there. Because they thought Jeanne was a threat to herself and others, the police decided to take Jeanne into custody for the night. Since no family members were immediately available to care for the kids, they were placed into temporary foster care. This, not surprisingly, escalated Jeanne's anger and panic. Jeanne was released the next day, but the kids remained in foster care until an updated alcohol and drug assessment could be completed for her. Jeanne admitted that she had begun drinking again; that she was feeling somewhat depressed; and that she was having problems with Kevin, who had recently moved out. She was afraid that her kids would be taken away from her permanently, and so she agreed to receive professional help. She requested to be assigned the same alcohol and drug counselor that she had had in her previous alcohol treatment 3 years ago. This counselor was available and was assigned to her.

In their first meeting, they listed the following presenting problems together:

1. Jeanne's drinking and alcohol abuse
2. The kids having been removed
3. Kevin's departure and the state of their relationship
4. Jeanne's depression

2. Identification of Situations in Which Problems Exist

1. Jeanne's Drinking and Alcohol Abuse. Jeanne drinks once or twice per week until intoxicated. On the nights she plans to drink, she will first bring her kids to a family member for the night and then pick them up the next day after she recovers from her hangover. She sees herself as a "mean drunk": When she drinks, she feels depressed, and she picks verbal and physical fights with Kevin and others she has gone out with. If she then finds herself alone, she will more often than not have a one-night stand to avoid being alone. She sees herself as losing control and judgment when she is drunk.

2. The Kids Having Been Removed. Having Jeanne's kids removed from the home led the counselor to assess Jeanne's parenting style and skills. Jeanne generally meets her kids' basic needs, except for the obvious fact that she leaves them with relatives several times per week since she has again begun drinking. She reports feeling overwhelmed and frustrated at times, trapped and alone with the kids. She reports trying to engage in fun activities with the kids, taking them out to dinner, a movie, or bowling (the counselor did note that these activities were more specifically social activities for Jeanne, with the kids brought along). Jeanne feels that her kids are the most important part of her life;

being a mother is the most important part of her self-identity. She believes that kids should not see their parents drinking and fighting, which is how she was raised. Her solution, then, is not to not drink, but to arrange for family members to care for her kids while she drinks. If a family member is unavailable, Jeanne will postpone her drinking for the evening. In this way, Jeanne sees herself as doing a better job of parenting than she received from her own parents. The counselor noted that Jeanne was probably correct in this judgment.

   3. Kevin's Departure and the State of Their Relationship. Kevin moved out 5 weeks prior to Jeanne's current incident, mainly because of their frequent fights and Jeanne's infidelities when she was drunk. Jeanne states that they often fought because Kevin was complaining about the amount of time and money she spent on bowling and bingo (about $20 a week). When confronted by him, she would get angry and resentful, and then feel depressed. She states that she felt bored and restless sitting around their apartment every evening (Kevin works shift work and therefore does leave Jeanne alone many evenings), and she began going out more and more frequently with her drinking buddies. Jeanne said she was suspicious that Kevin was having an affair, though he denied this. When Kevin left, he said he would not return until Jeanne was sober again.

   4. Jeanne's Depression. Jeanne defined her depression as self-pity and a lack of direction in life. She sees herself as socially isolated, except for Kevin, her kids, her family, and lately, her drinking buddies. She states that the primary roles important to her are mother, sister, and daughter; at the same time, she states that her family relationships are not entirely satisfying. She seeks help and emotional support from her sisters and father, and then gets angry when they tell her how to lead her life. She sees herself as very often backing down from arguments with family members because she needs them for child care and emotional support. She loves them a lot, but also feels sometimes like she is too dependent on them. She would like to feel "more like her own person," but does not want to risk losing their love, which she feels like she would do if she "made waves."

   Jeanne had two suicide attempts as a teenager, neither seriously life-threatening. She states emphatically that she does not want to kill herself currently. The counselor noted that it was difficult to assess disturbances to her eating and sleeping due to her alcohol abuse. Her appearance and dress were appropriate.

   (*Note:* In Chapter 6, the third step is outlined as "Identifying the client's characteristic reaction and problem-solving patterns." This practitioner chose to incorporate this step into the one identifying daily routines, described below.)

3. Identification of the Distal and Proximal Environment and the Distal and Proximal Person Factors

1. Distal Environment: Twenty-two years old, white, female, never married. Jeanne did not graduate from high school. Her income is from AFDC and food stamps. She lives in the small, rural town in which she was raised. She was raised Protestant, but states that she has no real religious affiliation currently. Jeanne states that she would like to be financially independent and not on public assistance, but also wants to be able to stay home with her kids until they are in school full-time (another 4 or 5 years). She feels guilty and stigmatized for being on welfare, and believes she has the skills and abilities to be employed full-time. She has no work history, but does currently volunteer at a local residential treatment home, taking care of mentally retarded adults.

2. Proximal Environment: Very involved with family; father and siblings all live nearby; Jeanne has daily contact with them. These relationships are characterized as conflictual and enmeshed. She states she was raised by her oldest sister after her mother died. Jeanne depends on her family emotionally and for child care, but also feels trapped by them since they tell her what to do. All family members currently abuse or have abused alcohol, though her father has been sober for past 6 years, with the help of AA. His attitude is that he pulled himself up by his bootstraps, and that his kids should do the same. Jeanne describes him as having a know-it-all attitude.

Jeanne's primary social outlets are her bowling league, weekly bingo, and (lately) her drinking. Kevin is a long-standing boyfriend. He does not drink and has recently moved out due to their fighting and her drinking. Jeanne again stated that her children are the most important things in her life.

Jeanne believes that her life would have been different if her mother were still living—she would have prevented her from "running the streets," drinking, and her adolescent delinquency. Jeanne states that her mother would have protected her from the verbal and physical abuse she received from her father. (The counselor noted here that this was the first time any mention of childhood abuse was made. The counselor also noted the fantasy elements of this wish for her mother's presence: Mother died from alcohol complications, and she was unable to protect Jeanne from father when she was living.)

3. Distal and Proximal Person Factors: Jeanne has reasonable parenting skills, she is friendly, personable, humorous, and can be open and honest. She is sincere about wanting help, albeit motivated by her desire to have her kids returned to her. She did successfully complete her previous chemical dependency treatment and then remained sober for almost 3 years. Previous test results in Jeanne's file indicate that she has low-average intellectual functioning, consisting of concrete thinking and limited abstract reasoning skills. The current assessment indicates that Jeanne has poor self-esteem, often demonstrates a lack of self-awareness, and is often dependent on others for direction in her life. She was raised in a home where alcohol was abused routinely and daily. She is still surrounded by alcohol abuse.

4. Identification of the Client's Daily Routines, Life Tasks, Possible Selves and Niches, and Characteristic Reaction Patterns

Jeanne's typical day is as follows: When her kids are home, she will get out of bed when they awake, usually around 7 a.m. or so. She fixes them breakfast, and they eat in front of the TV. After breakfast and putting away the dishes, she will most often go over to the home of one of her sisters, or call a sister to come to her home. Once together, they will just "hang out": talk, watch TV, sometimes go to a park if it is nice outside. They will all have lunch together, and then Jeanne will do errands, sometimes taking the older daughter with her while the younger one naps under the sister's supervision. By the late afternoon, Jeanne and her kids will return home, and she will begin to fix dinner. After dinner, Jeanne will usually go out—either to bingo, bowling, or (lately) to a bar. She will arrange to drop her kids off at a family member's home for the night. The next day, if she did not get drunk, she will pick up the kids for breakfast. If she did get drunk, she might not pick them up until late morning.

Jeanne states that the TV is almost constantly on, providing background noise, regardless of whose house they are in. Jeanne states that they will watch it off and on.

Jeanne also states that things were a lot better when Kevin lived with them, it was "more like a real family." Now she feels "kind of lost" and directionless. "Every day is the same—boring."

Jeanne states that she wants to have another child in 3 or 4 years. She wants to be off public assistance and have a full-time job, preferably working with mentally retarded adults (which is what she does now in her volunteer job). She wants to parent her kids until they reach adulthood. She would like a satisfying relationship and would like to be involved in satisfying activities. She states her goals as being a "good mother," remaining sober, and reestablishing her relationship with Kevin. She would like to feel more independent, and also be available to her family to help them when she can. She would like to keep her kids out of foster care, and be free of the "system" (the courts, welfare).

5. Determination of How Client's Presenting Problem Is Best Understood Given Her Niche

The counselor presented the following description of Jeanne's niche and how the presenting problems fit within it: Her current drinking and depressed/angry mood can be viewed as the coping mechanism of least resistance (i.e., it is most familiar and mindless in the sense of being very patterned and automatic), as a reaction to conflicts between the client's goals, values, and priorities and her daily routines and relationships. The counselor noted that Jeanne's possible selves and possible niches were very conflictual: She would like to be employed full-time and free of the "system," but she is making no plans to do so. Furthermore, she states that she wants to stay at home until her kids are in school full-time, yet if she has another child, this would mean prolonging going to work for several more years. She states she is being overwhelmed by two children; adding another may be too much to handle. She speaks of wanting to reestablish her relationship with Kevin, but this may be out of her control; he has refused to be included in any counseling she receives.

Her drinking therefore serves to help her cope (albeit to avoid coping in more direct problem-solving ways) with stresses in her life—the boredom and lack of direction, her normal frustrations with the kids, the conflictual relationships with family—and, possibly, in response to the difficulties connected to her feelings of loneliness, isolation, her breakup with Kevin, and her presumed grief over the loss of her mother and how she was raised. Her drinking is a way to cope with the hurt, pain, and fear in her life.

Jeanne's general life's "directionlessness" can also be understood as her characteristic way to make decisions in her life. Even though she does not always like the directions her life takes, by being buffeted along by others, she is able to avoid her fears that her current life is all she can ever hope for. She has dreams of getting better, and knows what this means in the abstract, but does not know how to achieve these goals (i.e., she has the beginnings of images of possible selves and niches, but does not yet have the procedural knowledge to achieve them). She furthermore does not have the supports in her niche to help her take the appropriate steps to better her life. Instead, her niche encourages and supports her drinking and current patterns of coping.

The major disruption in her niche—the reason she appears for professional help and is motivated now (and therefore the potential leverage for change)—is that her kids have been removed from her custody. It is speculated that if it were not for the fact that the kids were removed, Jeanne's niche would have remained stable, albeit dysfunctional, and she might not have sought professional help for her stated life dissatisfactions, unless precipitated by an incident similar to this one. And it appeared inevitable that an incident would have occurred: Although Kevin may not be her perfect mate, she does state that things were better with him, and that she has been spiraling downward since he has been gone. She is therefore motivated to reestablish a relationship with him, potentially on his terms of sobriety. Last, Jeanne's self-image and desire to be a good mother are strong and compelling for her. With further definition and development, this possible self can be supported and encouraged to serve as a clear goal toward which she can work.

*   *   *

NOTES ON ASSESSMENT

By understanding Jeanne's niche, we can understand both her drinking behavior and her motivation for assistance. What is instructive in this case example is how the alcohol and drug counselor began to put the pieces of information together to understand Jeanne and her niche, to understand what Jeanne's life feels like and how she constructs, understands, and experiences it. Some of this work was done through posing the kinds of questions identified in the steps of the assessment process. Other work was done through questions aimed at putting information together that appeared inconsistent on the surface—such as understanding Jeanne's resentful dependence on her family of origin.

The strongest interpersonal theme present in her niche is her involvement with her family—both to her daughters and to her siblings and father. This involvement creates for Jeanne a sense of order and routine in her life, albeit routines that are less than functional. We see that alcoholism touches every member of this family, and we can view Jeanne as making an almost heroic effort to not damage her own kids in the ways that her parents damaged her. But while she is able to make some efforts to protect her kids from seeing her drunk and getting into fights, and while she is able to at least verbalize her view of a better life (i.e., where she is free of the "system," where she is economically self-sufficient, where she is connected to her family but not obligated to them), it is unclear at this point how well-developed this possible self is. It is unclear, therefore, how much she would be able to take the appropriate steps toward making her possible self a reality without outside help. She can see where she wants to go, but does not have the resources to get there, does not envision and take action on the steps necessary to achieve her possible self, and does not have the supports in her niche to help her along the way.

While it is true that all niches are resistant to change, it is likely that Jeanne's niche will be more intractable than most: Any changes that Jeanne makes toward the realization of her possible self will be met with resistance in the form of guilt-inducement from her sisters ("How come you never come around any more? Don't tell me you're becoming high-and-mighty like Dad . . . "), and feelings of social isolation. These will be very powerful sources of resistance for Jeanne. Her niche appears intractable, too, in that it is assumed that it has functioned much as it does now for many years. It may be that crises, like this one, crop up on occasion, but for the most part the daily routines function more or less smoothly, and with enough flexibility to accommodate daily changes (if one sister is busy, another is available, and so on) to allow family members to maintain their drinking and life-styles.

After understanding Jeanne and her niche through this process, the counselor understands that Jeanne will need much support and compassion from the treatment relationship. It is also likely that Jeanne will react to treatment using the interpersonal schemas, scripts, and skills she knows best, namely by being conciliatory and somewhat dependent while at the same time resentful: not wanting to be told what to do, even as she is asking for help from the counselor, in exact replication of her interactions with her family. Jeanne will need to be shown by the counselor that other modes of interpersonal relationships exist, namely that the counselor can demonstrate no-strings support and can reinforce Jeanne's efforts toward self-determination. From the assessment of Jeanne's niche, the counselor understands that Jeanne is vulnerable to social isolation and will therefore need to be alert to interventions that put her at odds with the rest of the family, without also providing her with some substitute social supports. This assessment also tells the counselor how highly Jeanne values being a mother, and a good mother at that. This, then, provides a whole arena for framing interventions to support and elaborate Jeanne's view of what a good mother does, as well as provide another caution to avoid interventions that even appear to set her against her children.

The cognitive-ecological assessment, therefore, provides the counselor with a view of the client's niche and her problem-solving framework relative to the current problems that concern her most, and with a way to understand the presenting problems within the context of this niche and evolving framework. With this information, the counselor is in a good position to develop with the client intervention goals and plans, and to develop the treatment relationship in ways that are consistent and compatible with the existing aspects of the client's life that are most functional.

* * *

GOAL-SETTING AND CONTRACTING

Based on the counselor's assessment, the overall focus of the professional relationship will be for Jeanne to achieve more consistency between her life tasks and self-schemas on one hand, and her daily routines on the other: She seems to present adequate tasks and schemas, and has already developed reasonable possible selves and niches, but she does not possess the procedural knowledge to "get there from here." Four problems were identified during the assessment phase: (1) Assessing current alcohol use and chemical dependency; (2) Returning Jeanne's two children to her custody; (3) Dealing with Kevin's recent move out of the home; (4) Assessing Jeanne's depression. Discussion of each of these problems will focus on how goals and a contract were established.

These problems were explored during the assessment phase, with the counselor and the client determining together that the two main problems of immediate urgency were to help Jeanne get her kids back, and to help her stop drinking. Thus, these two problems were addressed first. The relationship and depression problems were therefore assigned a secondary priority: During assessment, it was determined that Jeanne's depression was not serious enough to pose a risk to her own or anyone else's safety. The decision on goal priorities was based on safety, in the case of the sobriety problem, and on the client's motivation, in the case of getting the children back from foster care. These two problems (her drinking and temporary loss of child custody) are themselves related, in the fact that the courts will not award custody to Jeanne until she demonstrates her sobriety.

1. Assessing Current Alcohol Use and Chemical Dependency

The first step in addressing this problem was to state the ultimate goal as how the courts required it (for Jeanne to get her children back): "Jeanne's total abstinence from drinking alcoholic beverages." Jeanne was referred to the _____ Family Center to complete a chemical dependency (CD) evaluation, and if recommended, to complete a CD treatment program. It was recognized by both Jeanne and her counselor that Jeanne's niche and her social isolation both supported her drinking. Instrumental goals would therefore be formed to address her drinking behavior directly, and to address social and relational gaps in her niche.

After the evaluation was completed it was recommended that Jeanne enter a CD treatment program. This instrumental goal (i.e., completing CD treatment is instrumental to maintaining sobriety) was further defined as follows:

1. Complete outpatient treatment at the _____ Family Center. This treatment will consist of 6 weeks of four times a week group treatment (to be held on Monday, Tuesday, Wednesday, and Thursday evenings), and twice per week sessions with an individual CD counselor. By the end of the 6 weeks, Jeanne will have completed at least 8 of the 12 steps specified in the CD treatment program operating at _____ Family Center. In addition, Jeanne will have identified an AA sponsor for herself. If she has not achieved these objectives, the length of her CD treatment will be extended.

2. After the 6-week period, an aftercare plan will be initiated that consists of attending once a week post-CD treatment groups at _____ Family Center, attending at least two AA meetings a week, and having regular contact with her AA sponsor.

To support Jeanne's sobriety, another instrumental goal was established, that of having Jeanne complete a psychological evaluation at the _____ Human Development Center. The purpose of this evaluation will be to determine Jeanne's current skills, abilities, and vocational interests, and areas of psychological strength and weakness. Jeanne and the counselor both felt that the additional information obtained from these evaluations would support Jeanne's desires to do more with her life, thus leaving her less reliant on her drinking and her old patterns of interaction with family and friends.

Jeanne appeared genuinely motivated to remain sober. The counselor felt that the primary reason Jeanne began drinking again was due to her isolation, lack of support, and the deterioration in her relationship with Kevin. She did well previously in an outpatient CD program, which was the primary reason outpatient treatment was prescribed again. Note that the counselor specified in great detail the criteria used to evaluate whether Jeanne successfully completed her treatment program. These criteria were designed to provide not only support and encouragement but also clear and attainable steps to maximize success and accomplishment.

2. Returning Jeanne's Two Children to Her Custody

The goal established to address this problem was stated as follows: "Jeanne's children will be returned to her care at the time of completion of psychological and CD evaluations, if no recommendations to the contrary are made." The following instrumental goal was developed to facilitate this goal:

1. Arrangements were made for Jeanne to have her 18-year-old niece, "Sherry," reside in her home to help baby-sit the kids, act as a safety mechanism for the kids, and offer support and companionship to Jeanne. Sherry will live with Jeanne for 30 days to bolster Jeanne's ability to keep to her treatment program and therefore maintain her sobriety. Kevin agreed to be available in Sherry's absence.

Sherry is sober, recently graduated from high school, is not currently employed, and has baby-sat for Jeanne's kids in the past. She was willing to be available in this capacity to help Jeanne avoid having her kids remain in foster care. The option of having Sherry come into her home to care for her kids came up when the counselor and Jeanne discussed the possibility of needing to attend an inpatient CD program. Both the counselor and Jeanne agreed that they would like to see her children be able to come back home as soon as possible. But the counselor needed to assure the court (thus, underscoring the need to develop verifiable goals) that Jeanne would remain sober and that her children would be adequately cared for while she was attending the inpatient program. Even though it was ultimately decided that Jeanne would complete an outpatient program instead of the inpatient one, Jeanne was very enthusiastic about having extra help and companionship at her home. She made arrangements with Sherry for how much she would pay her for her baby-sitting and other tasks.

2. A second instrumental goal was to refer Jeanne to weekly parenting skills classes to be held at the _____ Human Development Center. As part of these classes, clients are evaluated weekly on how much they are learning.

3. Finally, the State Department of Human Services agreed to provide and/or pay for day care and transportation costs to allow Jeanne to attend meetings related to the treatment plan stated above.

Note here that Jeanne's strong desire to care for her children is respected, with appropriate safeguards to protect the safety of the children and to monitor her sobriety. The options of having Sherry care for the children, and for the Department of Human Services to provide day care, were offered to allow Jeanne some freedom from having to rely on her siblings for support. This respected Jeanne's desire to not be so dependent on them but also to not lose contact with them altogether. It was a fortunate opportunity that Sherry was available in this capacity.

These two ultimate goals and treatment contracts were submitted to the court so that it would drop its dependency petition and allow Jeanne to work voluntarily with the State Department of Human Services without court involvement. (Remember that in addition to wanting her kids back, one of Jeanne's hopes was to be "free of the system.") The court did accept the above goals and objectives as adequately meeting its standards.

During assessment, it was discovered that both of Jeanne's remaining presenting problems—her relationship with Kevin and her depression— were related to her social isolation, her poor self-esteem, her characteristic patterns of overdependence, her dissatisfaction with the lack of direction in her life, and her characteristic patterns for expressing her emotions (both her current emotions and those attached to her schemas, resulting from the suspected physical abuse committed on her when she was growing up). To summarize briefly from the assessment, Kevin moved out because of Jeanne's drinking—when she drank she picked fights with him and then often became involved in one-night stands with men she would meet at the bars. Jeanne's depression consisted of her feeling stagnant and without direction in her life: She would like to be employed, but also valued being a full-time mother to her children, and had neither completed high school nor had the training necessary to engage in the employment she thought she was interested in. Jeanne's social and economic environment did not offer many choices or real power. She did not like who she was or what she did day-to-day, but did not know how to make the changes she desired.

Based on this assessment, the two presenting problems of Kevin's absence and Jeanne's depression were addressed by the following three goals:

3. Explore Effects on Current Life of Having Been Raised in a Dysfunctional Home

Jeanne had begun expressing her feelings about having been raised in an alcoholic home, and had just begun alluding to being physically abused when she was young. The counselor expressed her opinion that these proximal environmental factors might very well play a large role in her self-esteem and in her choice of partners. Jeanne did accept these observations as ringing true for her, but at the same time was not willing to change her view that if her own mother had lived, Jeanne's life would have turned out better—that her mother was all good and would have protected her and kept her in line. The counselor did not want to push too strongly for uncovering these possibly traumatic feelings, and so a goal was defined as follows: "Jeanne will talk about feelings and memories about childhood if they come up and if she feels comfortable doing so. The counselor will not raise these issues in a session unless Jeanne has initiated the topics." When these topics do come up, the counselor will help Jeanne explore them, and will provide additional information about adult children of alcoholics and survivors of child abuse through recommendations of books on the subjects. If Jeanne becomes interested in working further on these topics, the counselor will make referrals to groups for adult children of alcoholics and for adult survivors of abuse.

4. Explore Career and Parenting Interests and Options

Jeanne expressed interest in working full-time, particularly with mentally retarded adults, which she had been doing on a volunteer basis for some time. She would also like to be financially independent, and off public assistance. The ultimate goal was stated in exactly those terms: "To be financially independent by working full-time in a job that

I'm interested in." Both Jeanne and the counselor thought that full-time employment would solve a number of problems, in addition to freeing her from dependence on the public welfare system: It would provide additional social outlets for her, it would allow her to be more independent of her family both financially and socially, and it would give her some direction in her life. At the same time, the biggest barrier to seeking employment was that Jeanne also felt very strongly that she wanted to parent her children until they left for grade school. Jeanne saw full-time mothering also as a valid direction for her life, though she realized that it did not provide her with a salary or necessarily provide additional social outlets. She did, however, decide to put on hold any ideas about having a third child.

With further discussion and clarification on this dilemma, Jeanne decided that she would continue to provide full-time care for her children, but also begin the process of training herself for employment. Her goal was therefore modified to "Become financially independent by working full-time in a job that I'm interested in once my children enter school full-time." At the same time, Jeanne and the counselor continued to view social isolation as a problem, so they made plans to try to increase Jeanne social network through her interests in parenting. The following instrumental goals were established:

1. Since Jeanne would not plan to actually seek employment for several years (until her 18-month-old was in school), it was decided that Jeanne should think of these years as preparation for employment. She could begin to explore her interests and possibly begin augmenting her education and training to make her employable.

Jeanne began this process by signing up for a career interest workshop offered at the local community center. In this 4-week workshop, participants would take the Strong-Campbell Interest Inventory (an easily administered and interpreted instrument that evaluates vocational interests) and then spend the rest of the time discussing its results and its implications for career directions. With Sherry to help care for the kids, Jeanne was free to attend this evening workshop. At the end of this workshop, Jeanne and the counselor would determine what her next steps would be to further her employability.

2. Jeanne's overall self-esteem could be improved by boosting her confidence in her choice to remain a full-time parent. Based on the assessment of Jeanne's niche and her self- and other-schemas, it was decided that the best way to do this was to provide her with as much support, encouragement, and skills as possible. She was already planning

to attend parent skills training classes as part of the goal to get her kids back from foster care. Additionally, when the kids returned home, it was agreed that Jeanne would find a weekly play group that she could go to with them. In Jeanne's town many of the play groups are organized through a volunteer child services office (that is, an organization that is not part of the "system" as such, but instead is run by volunteer mothers who keep track of where groups meet, how many members each has, ages of kids present, and so on). It does not cost anything to join one of these groups—they often rotate meetings at each of the parent's homes. These play groups serve the function of providing support and friendship for the parents as well as providing playmates for the children. It was agreed that Jeanne would begin immediately the process of trying out and selecting a play group, and that by the end of 6 months, she would have found one that she attends regularly.

5. Improve Self-Esteem and Social Skills

The final goal established with Jeanne was to help her "improve my self-esteem and social skills." Jeanne did feel like she wanted to simply feel better about herself, and expressed some hesitation and doubts that she would be able to fit in with all these groups she was now planning to attend. The counselor suggested to Jeanne that skills-training programs were often a very good way to help her feel good about herself, since with better social skills, she can feel less inhibited about meeting new people and knowing what to say. The counselor also discussed with Jeanne the fact that they could practice her new skills in the context of applying them toward more central situations that will arise in her niche; that is, being more assertive with her sisters and father, learning to talk more straightforwardly to Kevin about their finances and relationship, and so on.

Two instrumental goals were established for the purpose of accomplishing this goal:

1. Jeanne and the counselor would begin to practice social and assertiveness skills exercises when they were together. For at least part of each session, they would engage in role-playing exercises focused on meeting new people in unfamiliar situations. These role-plays would continue until Jeanne was able to complete them comfortably and competently. Criteria for performing a successful role-play would be based on those specified by Rose (1977), which relate to clients both carrying out a role-play correctly and correctly generalizing the information learned to other related situations.

At that point, the role-plays would switch to focus on situations involving how to bring up and talk about deep feelings in conversation with friends and family. These role-plays would continue, again, until Jeanne was able to complete them successfully. Finally, a third set of role-plays would focus on Jeanne's abilities to express strong and important positive and negative emotions in appropriate and constructive ways. Again, these role-plays would continue until Jeanne felt confident and successful performing them. It was expected that it would take Jeanne from 3 to 5 weeks to complete each of the three types of role-plays, for a total of 9 to 15 weeks spent on these exercises.

2. The counselor would teach Jeanne relaxation techniques that she could use that would help her center herself when she felt socially uncomfortable and when strong feelings came up. Relaxation techniques would also provide Jeanne with a way to cope with the stresses of parenting and daily life. The techniques to be used were guided self-imagery and progressive relaxation (training oneself to relax selected muscle groups, progressing throughout one's body). Jeanne would be taught these techniques within the first few sessions. They would know whether she was mastering them by her ability to relax herself when she needed to. The definition of how relaxed she could make herself was left up to Jeanne: Since she would have ample opportunity to feel self-conscious and anxious, given all the new meetings and groups she would attend (some might say that Jeanne was encouraged to become a group meeting junkie), Jeanne could report back to the counselor information about her level of anxiety.

*   *   *

NOTES ON GOAL-SETTING AND CONTRACTING

Several questions are raised by the application of the principles of goal-setting and contracting in this case. These questions are described below to serve as points of discussion and thought for the interested reader.

Several things are demonstrated quite well in this case example: The goals specified are done with a great deal of detail and will lend themselves easily to the planning of interventions and to the monitoring of change. At the same time, note that not all the goals fully meet the criteria specified in the chapter on goals. The third goal, for example, to "explore effects on current life of having been raised in a dysfunctional home" fails to meet several criteria: It describes a process rather than a result; it does not specify a timeline; it is not particularly specific or clear (how directly does Jeanne have to initiate these topics for the counselor to ask questions about them?); and it is not necessarily adequate to the problem it addresses (if Jeanne talks about these feelings and memories, will the problems automatically be alleviated?).

Yet this goal is a good example to present precisely because it demonstrates how one takes the theory and applies it to a complicated case. For example, this goal was mutually agreed upon, it was positively stated and motivating for Jeanne, it was realistic in terms of her skills and abilities, it was supported by her niche, it was feasible, and it was consistent with her values and culture. In some respects we can look at this goal as instrumental to the ultimate goal of emotional and psychosocial growth and development that Jeanne will experience when she is able to functionally incorporate these feelings, memories, and experiences into her current life. We can also see, weighing the goal against the criteria of effectiveness, that we need to work further to better specify the goal toward providing better guidelines for these complex goals of growth and incorporation.

As a basis for further discussion, several other goals were specified that may initially appear to reflect client change, but in fact monitor the client's attendance at various meetings and group sessions, with no real feedback about the client vis-à-vis her goals. For example, how might the counselor have developed goals to encourage and monitor changes taking place within Jeanne's niche and daily routines? How will attendance at her CD program, and at the various parenting and support groups, foster changes in her self-system and schemas? Her role playing experiences might have been extended to include observing her interacting with her own kids. In this way, the generalizability of the training she received could have been explicitly extended into her niche. Furthermore, by teaching Jeanne in the unlearning-relearning process, described in the chapters on Intervention Planning and Follow-Through, Jeanne would be in a much better position to monitor her own self-esteem and working self. She could be helped to translate her old thoughts and feelings into red flags alerting her to access her new skills and schemas.

Finally, interventions were developed to hinge on her 18-year-old niece. Particularly, as written, it appears that Sherry will directly assist Jeanne in her sobriety and parenting. Even if this were true, how would it occur? It is true that Sherry will provide companionship and respite for Jeanne, and in these ways alleviate some of the stresses and isolation she feels (which are part of her impetus to drink). But is Sherry expected to do more than this? How might these goals be stated more clearly to both describe Sherry's role and then assure Jeanne's sobriety and improvement of her child care?

*   *   *

INTERVENTION PLANNING AND FOLLOW-THROUGH

Outpatient chemical dependency treatment at _____ Family Center was selected as the preferred sobriety resource because it would provide adequate support and structure for Jeanne and would be less restrictive than an inpatient program. An outpatient setting would allow Jeanne to continue residing in her home and parenting her children on a daily basis (which was very important to her) with the assistance of her niece. This program would also satisfy the requirements of the court to get the dependency petition dismissed. It is likely that Jeanne will need support to keep sober on a long-term basis, and this program provides ongoing aftercare services. Jeanne had previously been in outpatient treatment at this same agency. She believed this program and staff were helpful to her in the past and offered flexibility to meet her needs. More direct, individual time would be available if she needed it. Jeanne felt other programs moved through the information and steps too fast and she would get lost or overwhelmed in the process.

Jeanne successfully completed the CD treatment program. She missed very few individual and group sessions (4 out of 36). Absences were due to illness and no child care. Jeanne reached step 8 out of the 12-step AA treatment model. This level of accomplishment was determined by Jeanne and her counselor, based on her previous participation in their program. Jeanne's counselor felt she had worked hard in the program and was committed to maintaining her sobriety. She developed and contracted for her aftercare plan. She followed through on this plan, including attendance in the Adult Children of Alcoholics (ACOA) group. Jeanne plans to continue attending AA meetings and the ACOA group. Jeanne recognizes her need for support to remain sober and is learning new information about herself through the perspective of being an *affected family member*. Jeanne felt proud of her accomplishments in this program.

Jeanne did get drunk on one occasion (approximately 2 months after completing treatment). She voluntarily informed her counselor and aftercare group members of this slip, even in light of the perceived consequences of possibly having to go back to court, losing her children, and getting kicked out of her group. The counselor's feeling was that Jeanne had changed considerably since their initial involvement by taking responsibility for her behaviors and seeking support to cope with this slip. The counselor believed that this loss of control had frightened Jeanne—she was afraid it indicated that the gains she had made were eroding, and that she was falling back on her prior routines and behaviors. This was understood by the counselor to mean that Jeanne had made healthy changes in her niche: She utilized effective coping skills to deal with her drinking and reaction to a stressful situation, she no longer wanted to hide and isolate herself from fear, and she took positive actions rather than obsessing about the slip and sinking into depression. She reflected upon this incident, was able to go back and reinterpret the situation, to reframe it cognitively to arrive at her own interpretation: that her drinking was done to avoid having her boyfriend move back into her home (remember that Kevin said he would only move back when Jeanne was sober).

Jeanne showed evidence of being more independent and in control of her own life. She began using a day-care provider on a regular basis rather than using her family. She assumed sole responsibility for parenting her children. She was no longer dependent on her boyfriend or family to share this role and responsibility. Jeanne made the decision not to resume her relationship with her boyfriend. She took concrete steps to reinforce this decision. Jeanne followed through on developing sober social contacts and activities (group participation, bowling, and bingo). The professional people in Jeanne's life were still primary supports for her; however, she has other options available to her. The counselor suggested a gradual reduction in the frequency of contacts with Jeanne (once a week to twice a month to once a month) with the purpose being twofold: (a) to create some distance and lessen the likelihood of client-counselor dependency and (b) to give Jeanne the message that she has grown stronger and requires less intensive services, thereby promoting her confidence and independence. At the same time, the counselor made it clear to Jeanne that she would be available between planned contacts if the need arose.

Jeanne's children were returned to her care after the updated assessment was completed and after she began her treatment program (approximately 2 weeks after their placement in shelter care). Jeanne was extremely relieved to have her children back in her care. Her niece, Sherry, resided in the home for approximately 3 weeks until it was mutually decided by Jeanne, _____ Family Center, and the counselor that Jeanne was maintaining her sobriety. Jeanne was appreciative of her niece's assistance and support.

The counselor suggested to Jeanne that she might want to look at an educational parenting skills class to help her learn how to manage her kids and avoid feeling frustrated. Jeanne indicated that she was interested. She took the initiative and found out there was a 10-week parenting skills group beginning in September and again in January. Jeanne chose not to start the class in September, as her schedule was too busy, and elected to wait until the January class. Hopefully, Jeanne will not lose her motivation in the interim (she currently says she plans to attend this class). The counselor will continue to encourage her to follow through on the enrollment by discussing her original reasons for wanting this group and the potential benefits to be gained.

In the process of completing her individual psychological evaluation, Jeanne began talking about being abused as a child in her parental home. It was Jeanne's suggestion that after completion of her treatment and aftercare program, she would like to start individual counseling.

Jeanne's niche appeared to be changing. She has learned to handle situations more effectively, as shown by her sharing her slip and seeking support from her group members. Jeanne has been willing to explore new ways of problem solving and making decisions. She has become more independent, as evidenced by her use of a child-care provider, choosing not to live with her boyfriend, and depending less on her family as her sole source of support. Jeanne has shown that she is motivated to increase her self-awareness. She has done this through attending the ACOA group and individual treatment.

Jeanne's niche has become one of sobriety and one where she tries to effectively cope with stressful situations and the myriad of feeling of which she became aware. Her niche was no longer such a safe haven for her, but instead offered challenges and opportunities for risk-taking for her further growth and development. Jeanne's day-to-day routines and behaviors no longer support drinking: She was busy attending groups and activities that support sobriety, and was less bored and isolated. She was still frustrated with her children's behaviors but enrolled in a parenting class to learn better ways to interact with them.

Jeanne was less depressed about her life and viewed her future more optimistically. She saw the world as less threatening and hostile. She no longer viewed herself as a passive observer in her world, but instead as an active participant. Her current environment, life tasks, and behaviors were changing. Her niche was in flux, but she was working toward a place where stability would incorporate these positive changes.

*   *   *

NOTES ON INTERVENTION PLANNING AND FOLLOW-THROUGH

Characteristics that have been central to the treatment and outcome of this intervention have been Jeanne's need for control over her own and her children's lives. This control was diminished somewhat by her involvement with the court and Human Service systems. Now that court services have terminated, and given the voluntary nature of the counselor's involvement, Jeanne has regained control. She also sees the need to have control over her own drinking—it is a major factor in maintaining and keeping her life together. Jeanne also recognizes the need to become more independent and responsible as an adult peer and as a parent. She has shown she is able to be independent by living on her own, not allowing her family to enable her to become dependent on them, and establishing social activities outside her family.

A major factor that has influenced client change was the relationship established between Jeanne and the counselor. The counselor believes they expressed genuine trust and respect for one another and maintained a health-promoting, future-oriented perspective on their work together.

Throughout their work together, Jeanne sought approval and reinforcement from the counselor. The counselor tried to get Jeanne to identify her own needs and the issues on which she wanted to work. They would mutually come up with a plan to achieve these goals, and the counselor would then support her efforts to implement the plan and make healthy decisions for herself. The counselor would then praise her for accomplishments to help boost her self-esteem and confidence.

Other factors outside their relationship are also likely to have helped compliment Jeanne's outcomes. She developed trusting, supportive relationships with her AA sponsor, CD counselor, individual counselor, and group members. All of these people's efforts complimented each other's, to present Jeanne with a coherent package of services that supported the healthy changes she desired in her niche.

Strategies that were particularly effective included cognitive reframing, person-situation reflection, support and clarification, combined with attentive listening, concern, and respect. It was particularly important that goals were made concrete and clear, that they were divided into small steps to maximize Jeanne's opportunity for success. Techniques that were not particularly effective included confrontation, where she tended to become extremely defensive, and intellectualized discussions of Jeanne's response patterns, which generally did not generate much of concrete use for Jeanne.

In looking back over the course of this case, there were several areas that the counselor could have explored further with Jeanne. Jeanne told the counselor on numerous occasions how satisfied and confident she felt about the volunteer work with MR adults at the state hospital. Jeanne felt she had the necessary skills (a lot of patience and understanding) to work with this population. It appears that the counselor overlooked these cues and that, in retrospect, Jeanne might have benefited a great deal from part-time employment. It may have facilitated the promotion of her self-confidence, self-esteem, and independence, as well as give her job skills to possibly get off public assistance. To pursue this area, it would have been important to assess the skills Jeanne possessed and then provide training where needed.

The counselor also assumed that Jeanne had adequate social skills because she had no problem in establishing the relationship with the counselor and had formed friendships in her groups. Again in retrospect, the counselor felt that she may have failed to recognize the context of these relationships. The social skills Jeanne used to develop these relationships might not generalize to other relationships in her niche. Jeanne and the counselor could have more closely evaluated her social skills and self-perceptions to determine what auxiliary services could have been provided, and then could have done a better job of helping Jeanne translate these skills into other social relationships in her niche.

As was stated earlier, this was the second time the counselor was involved with Jeanne. The counselor stated that she understands Jeanne is initially highly motivated to do well at making positive changes in her life. However, she may not be able to maintain these changes over periods of time longer than 1 or 2 years. Because of this, the counselor made sure to add other aspects of education and long-term community support (parenting class, Adult Children of Alcoholics group, and individual counseling) to the intervention plan—it was hoped that Jeanne would establish a lasting support network independent of county child protective services. The presenting problem of this case was Jeanne's drinking. However debilitating this problem was, from a cognitive-ecological perspective, it was understood to be only one contributing factor in the larger context of her niche. Jeanne's drinking was understood to be a product of several factors in her niche that contributed to her helplessness, dependency, and ineffectiveness. Thus, the overall goal of this case was to effect change in Jeanne's niche. And, while the counselor believes that their involvement was successful in initiating changes in Jeanne's niche, further work needs to be done. Jeanne will need continued support and instruction to improve her parenting, continued support for her sobriety, and additional guidance to address her issues of intimacy and self-esteem. It is the counselor's impression that Jeanne has the motivation, skills, capacities, and resources to make these positive changes in her life.

REFERENCES

Abelson, R. P. (1978). *Scripts*. Address delivered to the Midwestern Psychological Association.

Alloy, C. B., & Abramson, L. Y. (1979). Judgment of contingency in depressed and nondepressed students: Sadder but wiser? *Journal of Experimental Psychology: General, 108*, 441-485.

Anderson, J. R. (1983). *The architecture of cognition*. Cambridge, MA: Harvard University Press.

Arkes, H. E., Dawes, R. M., & Christensen, C. (1986). Factors influencing the use of a decision rule in a probabilistic task. *Behavior and Human Decision Processes, 37*, 93-110.

Arkes, H. R. (1981). Impediments to accurate clinical judgment and possible ways to minimize their impact. *Journal of Consulting and Clinical Psychology, 49*, 323-330.

Arkes, H. R., & Harkness, A. R. (1980). The effect of making a diagnosis on subsequent recognition of symptoms. *Journal of Experimental Psychology: Human learning and memory, 6*, 568-575.

Arnoult, L. H., & Anderson, C. A. (1988). Identifying and reducing causal reasoning biases in clinical practice. In D. C. Turk & P. Salovey (Eds.), *Reasoning, inference, and judgment in clinical psychology* (pp. 209-232). New York: Free Press.

Ashcraft, M. H. (1989). *Human memory and cognition*. Glenview, IL: Scott, Foresman.

Atchley, R. (1989) A continuity theory of normal aging. *The Gerontologist, 29*, 183-190.

Balgopal, D. R., & Vassil, T. V. (1983). *Groups in social work: An ecological perspective*. New York: Macmillian.

Bandura, A. (1977). Self-efficacy: Toward a unified theory of behavioral change. *Psychological Review, 84*, 195-215.

Bandura, A. (1986). *Social foundations of thought and action: A social cognitive theory*. Englewood Cliffs, NJ: Prentice-Hall.

Bandura, A., Lipsher, D. H., & Miller, P. E. (1960). Psychotherapists' approach-avoidance reactions to patients' expressions of hostility. *Journal of Consulting Psychology, 24*, 1-8.

267

Barlow, D. H., Hayes, S. C., & Nelson, R. O. (1984). *The scientist practitioner.* New York: Pergamon.

Barlow, D. H., Hersen, M. (1984). *Single case experiential designs: Strategies for studying behavior change* (2nd ed.). New York: Pergamon.

Bartlett, H. (1970). *The common base of social work practice.* New York: National Association of Social Workers.

Batson, C. D., O'Quin, K., & Pych, V. (1982). An attribution theory analysis of trained helpers' inferences about clients' needs. In T. A. Wills (Ed.), *Basic processes in helping relationships.* New York: Academic Press.

Beck, A. T., Rush, A. J., Shaw, B. F., & Emery, G. (1979). *Cognitive therapy for depression.* New York: Guilford.

Berlin, S. B., & Marsh, J. (1993). *Informing practice decisions.* New York: Macmillan.

Binner, P. R. (1988). Mental health management decision making in the age of the computer. *Computers in Human Services, 3,* 87-100.

Blai, B. (1987). College and university freshman shift values, attitudes, and goals. *College Student Journal, 21,* 194-200.

Bloom, M. ,& Fischer, J. (1982). *Evaluating practice: Guidelines for the helping professional.* Englewood Cliffs, NJ: Prentice-Hall.

Blythe, B. J., & Tripodi, T. (1989). *Measurement in direct social work practice.* Newbury Park, CA: Sage.

Bordin, E. S. (1975). The generalizability of the psychoanalytic concept of the working alliance. *Psychotherapy: Theory, Research, and Practice, 16,* 252-260.

Bower, G. H., Gilligan, S. G., & Monteiro, K. P. (1981). Selectivity of learning caused by affective states. *Journal of Experimental Psychology: General, 110,* 451-473.

Bransford, J. D., Sherwood, R., Vye, N., & Reiser, J. (1986). Teaching thinking and problem solving. *American Psychologist, 41,* 1078-1089.

Brehm, S. S., & McAllister, D. A. (1980). A social psychological perspective on the maintenance of therapeutic change. In P. Karoly & J. T. Steffen (Eds.), *Improving the long-term effects of psychotherapy: Models of durable change.* New York: Gardner.

Brickman, P., Rabinowitz, V. C., Karuza, J., Jr., Coates, D., Cohn, E., & Kidder, L. (1982). Models of helping and coping. *American Psychologist, 37,* 368-384.

Brower, A. M. (1988). Can the ecological model guide social work practice? *Social Service Review, 62*(3), 411-429.

Brower, A. M. (1989a). Group development as constructed social reality: A social-cognitive understanding of group formation. *Social Work with Groups, 12*(2), 23-41.

Brower, A. M. (1989b). *Teaching direct practice students evaluation technologies using microcomputers: The development of client-focused database management skills.* Presented at the 35th Annual Program Meeting of the Council on Social Work Education.

Brower, A. M. (1989c). *Person-situation transactions as the basic unit of assessment in clinical social work.* Unpublished manuscript, University of Wisconsin-Madison.

Brower, A. M. (1990). Student perceptions of life task demands as a mediator in the freshman year experience. *Journal of the Freshman Year Experience, 2*(2), 7-30.

Brower, A. M. (1992). The "second half" of student integration: Life tasks and the power of choice on student persistence. *Journal of Higher Education, 63*(4), 441-462.

Brower, A. M., Garvin, C. D., Hobson, J., Reed, B. G., & Reed, H. (1987). Exploring the effects of leader gender and race on group behavior. In J. Lassner, K. Powell, & E. Finnegan (Eds.), *Social group work: Competence and values in practice.* New York: Haworth.

Brower, A. M., & Mutschler, E. (1985). Database management and data analysis for practitioners: Case examples using computer-assisted information processing. In C. Germain (Ed.), *Advances in clinical social work practice*. New York: National Association of Social Workers.

Brower, A. M., & Nurius, P. S. (1985). A teaching model for the use of computers in direct practice. *Computers in Human Services, 1*(1), 125-131.

Brower, A. M., & Nurius, P. S. (1992). Cognitive schemas and the operationalization of the "person in environment." Presented at the First Annual Conference on Social Work and Social Science, Ann Arbor, MI.

Buss, D. M. (1987). Selection, evocation, and manipulation. *Journal of Personality and Social Psychology, 53*, 1214-1221.

Cantor, N., & Kihlstrom, J. (1987). *Personality and social intelligence*. Englewood Cliffs, NJ: Prentice-Hall.

Cantor, N., & Kihlstrom, J. F. (1989). Social intelligence and cognitive assessments of personality. In R. S. Wyer & T. K. Srull, *Advances in social cognition, volume II: Social intelligence and cognitive assessments of personality* (pp. 1-59). Hillsdale, NJ: Lawrence Erlbaum.

Cantor, N., Norem, J. K., Niedenthal, P. M., Langston, C. A., & Brower, A. M. (1987). Life tasks and cognitive strategies in a life transition. *Journal of Personality and Social Psychology, 53*(6), 1178-1192.

Carkhuff, R. R. (1985). *PPD: Productive program development*. Amherst, MA: Human Resource Development Press.

Carkhuff, R. R. (1987). *The art of helping* (6th ed.). Amherst, MA: Human Resource Development Press.

Carson, A. D., Madison, T., & Santrock, J. (1987). Relationship between possible selves and self-reported problems of divorced and intact family adolescents. *Journal of Early Adolescence, 7*, 191-204.

Chomsky, N. (1972). *Language and mind*. New York: Harcourt Brace Jovanovich.

Cohen, C. E. (1981). Goals and schemata in person perception: Making sense from the stream of behavior. In N. Cantor & J. F. Kihlstrom (Eds.), *Personality, cognition, and social interaction*. Hillsdale, NJ: Lawrence Erlbaum.

Colletti, G., & Stern, L. (1980). Two-year follow-up of a nonaversive treatment for cigarette smoking. *Journal of Consulting and Clinical Psychology, 48*, 292-293.

Corcoran, K., & Fischer, J. (1987). *Measures for clinical practice: A sourcebook*. New York: Free Press.

Corey, G. (1991). *Theory and practice of counseling and psychotherapy* (4th ed.). Pacific Grove, CA: Brooks/Cole.

Cormier, W. H., & Cormier, L. S. (1991). *Interviewing strategies for helpers* (3rd ed.). Pacific Grove, CA: Brooks/Cole.

Cook, T. D., & Campbell, D. T. (1979). *Quasi-experimentation: Design and analysis issues for field settings*. Chicago: Rand MacNally.

Cournoyer, B. (1991). *The social work skills workbook*. Belmont, CA: Wadsworth.

Cousins, P. S., Fischer, J., Glisson, C., & Kameoka, V. (1985). The effects of physical attractiveness and verbal expressiveness on clinical judgments. *Journal of Social Service Research, 8*, 59-74.

Cox, S., & Rodloff, L. S. (1984). Depression in relation to sex roles: Learned susceptibility and precipitating factors. In C. S. Widom (Ed.), *Sex roles and psychopathology*. New York: Plenum.

Coyne, J. D., & DeLongis, A. (1986). Going beyond social support: The role of social relationships in adaptation. *Journal of Consulting and Clinical Psychology, 54*, 454-460.

Davis, L. V. (1984). Beliefs of service providers about abused women and abusing men. *Social Work, 29*, 243-250.

Dawes, R. M. (1986). Representative thinking in clinical judgment. *Clinical Psychology Review, 6*, 425-441.

Deaux, K., & Major, B. (1987). Putting gender into context: An interactive model of gender-related behavior. *Psychological Review, 94*, 369-389.

Durkheim, E. (1951). *Suicide* (J. A. Spaulding & G. Simpson, Trans.). New York: Free Press.

Dweck, C. S. (1986). Motivational processes affecting learning. *American Psychologist, 41*, 1040-1048.

D'Zurilla, T. J. (1986). *Problem-solving therapy: A social competence approach to clinical intervention*. New York: Springer.

D'Zurilla, T. J., & Nezu, A. (1982). Social problem solving in adults. In P. C. Kendall (Ed.) *Advances in cognitive-behavioral research and therapy* (Vol. 1). New York: Academic Press.

Eccles, J. S., Midgley, C., Wigfield, A., Buchanan, C. M., Reuman, D., Flanagan, C., & Mac Iver, D. (1993). Development during adolescence. The impact of stage-environment fit on young adolescents' experiences in schools and in families. *American Psychologist, 48*(2), 90-101.

Egan, G. (1990). *The skilled helper: A systematic approach to effective helping* (4th ed.). Monterey, CA: Brooks/Cole.

Emmons, R. A. (1986). Personal striving: An approach to personality and subjective well-being. *Journal of Personality and Social Psychology, 51*, 1058-1068.

Emmons, R. A., & King, L. A. (1989). On the personalization of motivation. In R. S. Wyer & T. K. Srull, *Advances in social cognition, volume II: Social intelligence and cognitive assessments of personality* (pp. 111-122). Hillsdale, NJ: Lawrence Erlbaum.

Epstein, L. (1992). *Brief treatment and a new look at task-centered approach*. New York: MacMillan.

Epstein, S., & Meier, P. (1989). Constructive thinking: A broad coping variable with specific components. *Journal of Personality and Social Psychology, 57*, 332-350.

Faust, D. (1986). Research on human judgment and its application to clinical practice. *Professional Psychology: Research and Practice, 17*, 420-430.

Felsman, J. K., & Valliant, G. E. (1987). Resilient children as adults: A 40-year study. In E. J. Anthony & B. J. Cohler (Eds.), *The invulnerable child* (pp. 289-314). New York: Guilford Press.

Fiske, S. T., & Taylor, S. E. (1991). *Social cognition* (2nd ed.). New York: McGraw-Hill.

Fong, G. T., Krantz, D. H., & Nisbett, R. E. (1986). The effects of statistical training on thinking about everyday problems. *Cognitive Psychology, 18*, 253-292.

Frank, J. D. (1941). Recent studies of the level of aspiration. *Psychology Bulletin, 38*, 218-226.

Franklin, D. (1985). Differential clinical assessments: The influence of class and race. *Social Service Review, 59*, 44-61.

Franklin, D. (1987, February). The politics of masochism. *Psychology Today*, pp. 52-59.

Freud, S. (1965). *New introductory lectures on psychoanalysis* (J. Strachey, Ed.). New York: Norton. (Original work published 1933)

Gambrill, E. (1983). *Casework: A competency-based approach.* San Francisco: Jossey-Bass.

Garvin, C. D. (1987). *Contemporary group work* (2nd ed.). Englewood Cliffs, NJ: Prentice-Hall.

Garvin, C. D., & Seabury, B. A. (1984). *Interpersonal practice in social work.* Englewood Cliffs, NJ: Prentice-Hall.

Gecas, V. (1982). The self-concept. *Annual Review of Sociology, 8,* 1-33.

Genero, N., & Cantor, N. (1987). Exemplar prototypes and clinical diagnosis: Toward a cognitive economy. *Journal of Social and Clinical Psychology, 5,* 59-78.

Germain, C. B. (1973). An ecological perspective in casework practice. *Social Casework, 54,* 323-327.

Germain, C. B. (1991). *Human behavior in the social environment. An ecological approach.* New York: Columbia University Press.

Germain, C. B., & Gitterman, A. (Eds.). (1980). *The life model of social work practice.* New York: Columbia University Press.

Glasser, P., Sarri, R. C., & Vinter, R. (Eds.). (1974). *Individual change through small groups.* New York: Free Press.

Goldfried, M. R. (Ed.). (1982). *Converging themes in psychotherapy. Trends in psychodynamic, humanistic and behavioral practice.* New York: Springer.

Goldfried, M. R., & Robins, D. (1983). Self-schemata, cognitive bias, and the processing of therapeutic experiences. In P. C. Kendall (Ed.), *Advances in cognitive-behavioral research and therapy* (pp. 33-79). New York: Academic Press.

Goldstein, H. (1973). *Social work practice: A unitary approach.* New York: Columbia University Press.

Gordon, W. E., & Schutz, M. L. (1977). A natural basis for social work specializations. *Social Work, 22,* 422-426.

Gould, K. H. (1987) Life model versus conflict model: A feminist perspective. *Social Work, 32*(4), 346-351.

Granvold, D. K. (Ed.). (1993). *Cognitive and behavioral treatment: Methods and applications.* Pacific Grove, CA: Brooks/Cole.

Green, J. W. (1982). *Cultural awareness in the human services.* Englewood Cliffs, NJ: Prentice-Hall.

Greenwald, A. G. (1980). The totalitarian ego: Fabrication and revision of personal history. *American Psychologist, 35,* 603-618.

Greenwald, A. G., & Banaji, M. R. (1989). The self as memory system: Powerful, but ordinary. *Journal of Personality and Social Psychology, 57,* 41-54.

Greenwald, A. G., & Pratkanis, A. R. (1984). The self. In R. S. Wyer & T. K. Srull (Eds.), *Handbook of social cognition.* Hillsdale, NJ: Lawrence Erlbaum.

Greif, G. L., & Lynch, A. A. (1983) The eco-systems perspective. In C. H. Meyer (Ed.), *Clinical social work in the eco-systems perspective.* New York: Columbia University Press.

Guidano, V. F., & Liotti, G. (1983). *Cognitive processes and emotional disorders.* New York: Guilford Press.

Gutierrez, L. (1990). Working with women of color: An empowerment perspective. *Social Work, 35,* 149-154.

Guterman, N. B., & Blythe, B. J. (1986). Toward ecologically based intervention in residential treatment for children. *Social Service Review, 60*(4), 633-43.

Haley, J. (1976). *Problem-solving therapy.* New York: Harper Colophon.

Hayes, S. C., Nelson, R. O., & Jarrett, R. B. (1987). The treatment utility of assessment: A functional approach to evaluating assessment quality. *American Psychologist, 42,* 963-974.

Heller, K., Swindle, R. W., & Dusenbury, L. (1986). Component social support processes: Comments and integration. *Journal of Consulting and Clinical Psychology, 54*, 466-470.

Hepworth, D. H., & Larsen, J. (1990). *Direct social work practice: Theory and skills* (3rd ed.). Belmont, CA: Wadsworth.

Heus, M., & Pincus, A. (1986). *The creative generalist: A guide to social work practice.* Barneveld, WI: Micamar.

Higgins, E. T. (1989). Self discrepancy theory: What patterns of self-beliefs cause people to suffer? *Advances in Experimental Social Psychology, 22*, 93-136.

Hoffman, L. (1981). *Foundations of family therapy.* New York: Basic Books.

Hollis, F. (1972). *Casework: A psychosocial therapy* (2nd ed.). New York: Random House.

Hollon, S. D., & Garber, J. (1988). Cognitive therapy. In L. Y. Abramson (Ed.), *Social cognition and clinical psychology.* New York: Guilford Press.

Hollon, S. D., & Kriss, M. R. (1984). Cognitive factors in clinical research and practice. *Clinical Psychology Review, 3*, 35-76.

House, J. S. (1981). *Work stress and social support.* Reading, MA: Addison-Wesley.

Ingram, R. E. (Ed.). (1986). *Information processing approaches to clinical psychology.* New York: Academic Press.

Ingram, R. E., & Hollon, S. D. (1986). Cognitive therapy for depression from an information processing perspective. In R. E. Ingram (Ed.), *Information processing approaches to clinical psychology.* New York: Academic Press.

Isen, A. M. (1984). Toward understanding the role of affect in cognition. In R. S. Wyer & T. K. Srull (Eds.), *Handbook of social cognition* (Vol. 3, pp. 179-236). Hillsdale, NJ: Lawrence Erlbaum.

Jacobson, D. E. (1986). Types and timing of social support. *Journal of Health and Social Behavior, 27*, 250-264.

Janis, I. L. (1983). *Short-term counseling: Guidelines based on recent research.* New Haven, CT: Yale University Press.

Jordan, J. S., Harvey, J. H., & Weary, G. (1988). Attributional biases in clinical decision-making. In D. C. Turk & P. Salovey (Eds.), *Reasoning, inference, and judgment in clinical psychology.* New York: Free Press.

Kahle, L.R. (Ed.) (1979). Methods for studying person-situation interactions. *New Directions for Methodology of Behavior Science, 2.*

Kanfer, F. H. (1984). self-management in clinical and social interventions. In R. P. McGlynn, J. E. Maddux, C. D. Stoltenberg, & J. H. Harvey (Eds.), *Social perception in clinical and counseling psychology* (pp.141-166). Lubbock: Texas Tech. Press.

Kanfer, F. H., & Schefft, B. K. (1988). *Guiding therapeutic change.* Champaign, IL: Research Press.

Kaplan, S., & Kaplan, R. (1978). *Humanscape: Environments for people.* North Scituate, MA: Duxbury Press.

Karuza, J., Jr., Zevon, M. A., Rabinowitz, V. C., & Brickman, P. (1982). Attribution of responsibility by helpers and recipients. In T. A. Wills (Ed.), *Basic processes in helping relationships.* New York: Academic Press.

Kayne, N. T., & Alloy, L. B. (1988). Clinician and patient as aberrant actuaries: Expectation-based distortions in assessment of covariation. In L. Y. Abramson (Ed.), *Social cognition and clinical psychology: A synthesis.* New York: Guilford Press.

Kihlstrom, J. F., & Cantor, N. (1984). Mental representations of the self. In L. Berkowitz (Ed.), *Advances in experimental social psychology* (Vol. 17, pp. 1-47). New York: Academic Press.

Kilhstrom, J. F., Cantor, N., Albright, J. S., Chew, B. R., Klein, S. B., & Niedenthal, P. M. (1988). Information processing and the study of the self. *Advances in Experimental Social Psychology, 21*, 145-178.

Kirschenbaum, D. S. (1985). Proximity and specificity of planning. *Cognitive Therapy and Research, 9*, 489-506.

Kirschenbaum, D. S. (1987). Self-regulatory failure: A review with clinical implications. *Clinical Psychology Review, 7*, 77-104.

Klinger, A. (1977). *Meaning and void: Inner experience and the incentives in people's lives*. Minneapolis: University of Minnesota Press.

Klinger, E. (1989). Goal orientation as psychological linchpin: A commentary on Cantor and Kihlstrom's social intelligence and cognitive assessment of personality. In R. S. Wyer & T. K. Srull, *Advances in social cognition, Volume II: Social intelligence and cognitive assessments of personality* (pp. 123-130). Hillsdale, NJ: Lawrence Erlbaum.

Kolb, D. A. (1985). *The learning style inventory*. Boston, MA: McBer.

Kopp, J. (1989). Self-observation: An empowerment strategy in assessment. *Social Casework, 70*, 276-284.

Kruzich, J., Van Soest, D., & Sullivan, M. (1990). *The role of personality characteristics and learning style in the field instruction process*. Paper presented at the Council on Social Work Education APM, Reno, NV.

Kutchins, H., & Kirk, S. A. (1986). The reliability of DSM-III: A critical review. *Social Work Research and Abstracts, 22*, 3-12.

Langer, E. J. (1989). *Mindfulness*. New York: Addison-Wesley.

Langer, E. J., & Piper, A. I. (1987). The prevention of mindlessness. *Journal of Personality and Social Psychology, 53*, 280-287.

Lauer, R. H., & Handel, W. H. (1983). *Social psychology: The theory and application of symbolic interactionism* (2nd ed.). Englewood Cliffs, NJ: Prentice-Hall.

Lazarus, R. S., & Folkman, S. (1984). *Stress, appraisal, and coping*. New York: Springer.

Lerner, M. J. (1980). *The belief in the just world: A fundamental delusion*. New York: Plenum.

Lewinsohn, P. M., Mischel, W., Chaplin, W., & Barton, R. (1980). Social competence and depression: The role of illusory self-perceptions. *Journal of Abnormal Psychology, 89*, 203-212.

Lieberman, M. A., Yalom, I. D., & Miles, M. B. (1973). *Encounter groups: First facts*. New York: Basic Books.

Linville, P. W., & Clark, L. F. (1989). Can production systems cope with coping? *Social Cognition, 7*, 195-236.

Locke, E. A. (1984). *Goal setting: A motivational technique that works!* Englewood Cliffs, NJ: Prentice-Hall.

Loftus, E. F. (1979). *Eyewitness testimony*. Cambridge, MA: Harvard University Press.

Loftus, E. F., & Ketcham, K. (1991). *Witness for the defense: The accused, the eyewitnesses, and the expert who puts memory on trial*. New York: St. Martin's Press.

Longres, J. F. (1990). *Human behavior in the social environment*. Itasca, IL: Peacock.

Mackelprang R., & Hepworth, D. H. (1987). Ecological factors in rehabilitation of patients with severe spinal cord injuries. *Social Work in Health Care, 13*, 23-38.

Maddux, J. E., Stoltenberg, C. D., & Rosenwein, S. (Eds.). (1987). *Social processes in clinical and counseling psychology*. New York: Springer-Verlag.

Magnusson, D. (Ed.). (1981). *Toward a psychology of situations. An interactional perspective*. Hillsdale, NJ: Lawrence Erlbaum.

Mahoney, M. J. (1991). *Human change processes: The scientific foundations of psychotherapy.* New York: Basic Books.

Maluccio, A. N. (Ed.). (1981). *Promoting competence in clients. A new/old approach to social work practice.* New York: Free Press.

Mandler, G. (1985). *Cognitive psychology.* Hillsdale, NJ: Lawrence Erlbaum.

Mann, J. (1973). *Time-limited psychotherapy.* Cambridge, MA: Harvard University Press.

Mann, J. (1981). The core of time-limited psychotherapy: Time and the central issue. In S. H. Budman (Ed.), *Forms of brief therapy* (pp. 25-43). New York: Guilford Press.

Markus, H. (1983). Self-knowledge: An expanded view. *Journal of Personality, 51,* 543-565.

Markus, H., & Nurius, P. (1986). Possible selves. *American Psychologist, 41,* 954-969.

Markus, H., & Ruvolo, A. (1989). Possible selves: Personalized representations of goals. In L. A. Pervin (Ed.), *Goal concepts in personality and social psychology.* Hillsdale, NJ: Lawrence Erlbaum.

Markus, H., & Wurf, E. (1987). The dynamic self-concept: A social psychological perspective. *Annual Review of Psychology, 38* (M. R. Rosenszweig & I. W. Porter, Eds.), 299-337.

Maruyama, M. (1968) The second cybernetics: Deviation-amplifying mutual causal processes. In W. Buckley (Ed.), *Modern systems research for the behavioral scientist.* Chicago: Aldine.

McCullough, L., Farrell, A. D., & Longabaugh, R. (1986). The development of a microcomputer-based mental health information system. *American Psychologist, 41,* 207-214.

McGuire, W. J., & McGuire, C. V. (1988). Content and process in the experience of self. *Advances in Experimental Social Psychology, 21,* 97-144.

Mead, G. H. (1934). *Mind, self, and society from the standpoint of a social behaviorist* (G. W. Morris, Ed.). Chicago: University of Chicago Press.

Mead, G. H. (1938). *The philosophy of the act.* Chicago: University of Chicago Press.

Meichenbaum, D. J. (1977). *Cognitive-behavior modification. An integrative approach.* New York: Plenum.

Merton, R. K. (1957). *Social theory and social structure.* Glencoe, IL: Free Press.

Meyer, C. H. (1970). *Social work practice: A response to the urban crisis.* New York: Free Press.

Meyer, C. H. (Ed.). (1983). *Clinical social work in the eco-systems perspective.* New York: Columbia University Press.

Miller, G. A. (1956). The magical number seven, plus or minus two: Some limits on our capacity for processing information. *Psychological Review, 63,* 81-97.

Milner, J. L. (1987). An ecological perspective on duration of foster care. *Child Welfare, 66*(2), 113-123.

Monroe, J. E. (1988). Generalization and maintenance in therapeutic systems: Analysis and proposal for change. *Professional Psychology: Research and Practice, 19,* 449-453.

Morris, R., & Anderson, D. (1975). Personal care services: An identity for social work. *Social Service Review, 49,* 157-174.

Myers, I. B., & McCaulley, M. (1985). *A guide to the development and use of the Meyers-Briggs Type Indicator.* Palo Alto, CA: Consulting Psychologists Press.

Natale, M., & Hantas, M. (1982). Effect of temporary mood states on selective memory about the self. *Journal of Personality and Social Psychology, 42,* 927-934.

Nisbett, R. E. & Ross, L. (1980). *Human inference: Strategies and shortcomings of social judgement.* Englewood Cliffs, NJ: Prentice-Hall.

Nurius, P. S. (1986). A reappraisal of the self-concept and implications for counseling. *Journal of Counseling Psychology, 33,* 429-438.

Nurius, P. S. (1989). Form and function of the self-concept: A social cognitive update. *Social Casework, 70,* 285-294.

Nurius, P. S. (1991). Possible selves and social support: Social cognitive resources for coping and striving. In J. Howard & P. Collero (Eds.), *The self-society dynamic: Cognition, emotion and action* (pp. 239-258). New York: Cambridge University Press.

Nurius, P. S. (1992). Practice evaluation methods: Practical variations on a theme. In C. W. LeCroy (Ed.), *A casebook for social work practice.* Belmont, CA: Wadsworth.

Nurius, P. S. (1993a). Human memory: A basis for better understanding the elusive self-concept. *Social Service Review, 67,* 261-278.

Nurius, P. S. (1993b). Assessing and changing self-concept: Guidelines from the memory system. *Social Work.*

Nurius, P. S., & Berlin, S. B. (1993). Negative self-concept and depression. In D. Granvold (Ed.), *Cognitive and behavioral treatment: Methods and applications.* Pacific Grove, CA: Brooks/Cole.

Nurius, P. S., & Gibson, J. W. (1991). Clinical inference, reasoning and judgement in social work: An update. *Social Work Research & Abstracts, 26,* 18-25.

Nurius, P. S., & Hudson, W. W. (1993). *Human services practice, evaluation and computers: A practical guide for today and beyond.* Pacific Grove, CA: Brooks/ Cole.

Nurius, P. S., Lovell, M., & Edgar, M. (1988). Self-appraisals of abusive parents: A contextual approach to study and treatment. *Journal of Interpersonal Violence, 3,* 458-470.

Nurius, P. S., & Majerus, D. (1988). Rethinking the self in self-talk: A theoretical note and case example. *Journal of Social and Clinical Psychology, 6,* 335-345.

Nurius, P. S., & Markus, H. (1990). Situational variability in the self-concept: Appraisals, expectancies, and asymmetries. *Journal of Social and Clinical Psychology, 9,* 316-333.

Nye, J. L., & Brower, A. M. (1994). Social cognition and small group behavior: What is "social" about social cognition. (Special Issue). *Small Group Research, 25*(2).

Offer, D., & Sabshin, M. (Eds.). (1984). *Normality and the life cycle. A critical review.* New York: Basic Books.

Pardes, H., & Pincus, H. A. (1981). Brief therapy in the context of national mental health issues. In S. H. Budman (Ed.), *Forms of brief therapy* (pp. 7-22). New York: Guilford Press.

Patti, R. J., Poertner, J., & Rapp, C. (Eds.). (1987). Special issue: Managing for service effectiveness in social welfare organizations. *Administration in Social Work, 11*(3/4).

Perlman, H. H. (1957). *Social casework: A problem-solving process.* Chicago: University of Chicago Press.

Pervin, L. A. (1989). Goal concepts in personality and social psychology: A historical introduction. In L. A. Pervin (Ed.), *Goal concepts in personality and social psychology.* Hillsdale, NJ: Lawrence Erlbaum.

Phillips, E. L. (1988). Length of psychotherapy and outcome: Observations stimulated by Howard, Kopta, Krause, and Orlinsky. *American Psychologist, 43,* 669-670.

Piaget, J. (1968). *Psychology of intelligence.* Totowa, NJ: Littlefield, Adams.

Pincus, A., & Minahan, A. (1973). *Social work practice: Model and method.* Itasca, IL: Peacock.

Rabinowitz, V. C., Zevon, M. A., & Karuza, J., Jr. (1988). Psychotherapy as helping: An attributional analysis. In L. Y. Abramson (Ed.), *Social cognition and clinical psychology.* New York: Guilford Press.

Reid, W. J. (1992). *Task strategies: An empirical approach to clinical social work.* New York: Columbia University.

Reid, W. J. (1978). *The task-centered system.* New York: Columbia University Press.

Reid, W. J., & Epstein, L. (1972). *Task-centered casework.* New York: Columbia University Press.

Reinoehl, R., & Shapiro, C. H. (1986). Interactive videodiscs: A linkage tool for social work education. *Journal of Social Work Education, 22,* 61-67.

Restak, R. M. (1988). *The mind.* New York: Bantam Books.

Richmond, M. (1917). *Social diagnosis.* New York: Russel Sage.

Rose, S. D. (1977). *Group therapy: A behavioral approach.* Englewood Cliffs, NJ: Prentice-Hall.

Rosen, A., & Proctor, E. K. (1981). Distinctions between treatment outcomes and their implications for treatment evaluation. *Journal of Consulting and Clinical Psychology, 49*(3), 418-425.

Rosenbaum, D. L., Salovey, P., & Hargis, K. (1981). The joys of helping: Focus of attention mediates the impact of positive affect on altruism. *Journal of Personality and Social Psychology, 40,* 899-905.

Rosenthal, D. (1955). Changes in some moral values following psychotherapy. *Journal of Consulting Psychology, 19,* 431-436.

Ross, L., Lepper, M. R., & Hubbard, M. (1975). Perseverance in self-perception and social-perception: Biased attribution processes in the debriefing paradigm. *Journal of Personality and Social Psychology, 32,* 880-892.

Ruehlman, L. S., West, S. G., & Pasahow, R. J. (1985). Depression and evaluative schemata. *Journal of Personality, 53,* 46-92.

Salovey, P. (1986). *The effects of mood and focus of attention on self-relevant thoughts and helping intention.* Unpublished dissertation, Yale University.

Salovey, P., & Rodin, J. (1985). Cognitions about the self: Connecting feeling states and social behavior. In P. Shaver (Ed.), *Self, situations, and social behavior.* Beverly Hills, CA: Sage.

Salovey, P., & Turk, D. C. (1988). Some effects of mood on clinician's memory. In D. C. Turk & P. Salovey (Eds.), *Reasoning, inference, and judgment in clinical psychology* (pp. 107-123). New York: Free Press.

Salovey, P., & Turk, D. C. (1990). Clinical judgment and decision making. In C. R. Snyder & D. R. Forsyth (Eds.), *Handbook of social and clinical psychology: The health perspective.* New York: Pergamon.

Sarbin, T. R., Taft, R., & Baily, D. E. (1960). *Clinical inference and cognitive theory.* New York: Holt, Rinehart & Winston.

Schwartz, W. B., Gorry, G. A., Kassirer, J. P., & Essig, A. (1973). Decision analysis and clinical judgment. *American Journal of Medicine, 55,* 459-472.

Segal, Z. V. (1988). Appraisal of the self-schema construct in cognitive models of depression. *Psychological Bulletin, 103,* 147-162.

Serban, G. (1982). *The tyranny of magical thinking. The child's world of belief and adult neurosis.* New York: E. P. Dutton.

Showers, C., & Cantor, N. (1985). Social cognition and individual differences. *Annual Review of Psychology, 36.*

Simon, B. K. (1970). Social casework theory: An overview. In R. W. Roberts & R. H. Nee (Eds.), *Theories of social casework.* Chicago: University of Chicago Press.

Simon, H. A. (1979). Information processing models of cognition. *Annual Review of Psychology, 30,* 363-396.

Singer, J. L. (1988). Reinterpreting the transference. In D. C. Turk & P. Salovey (Eds.), *Reasoning, inference, and judgment in clinical psychology.* New York: Free Press.

Slovic, P., & Lichtenstein, S. C. (1971). Comparison of Bayesian and regression approaches to the study of information processing in judgment. *Organizational Behavior and Human Performance, 6,* 659-744.

Snyder, M. (1980). Seek and ye shall find: Testing hypotheses about other people. In E. T. Higgins, C. P. Herman, & M. P. Zanna (Eds.), *Social cognition: The Ontario symposium.* Hillsdale, NJ: Lawrence Erlbaum.

Snyder, M. (1987). *Public appearances/private realities: The psychology of self-monitoring.* New York: Freeman.

Snyder, M. L., & Swann, W. B., Jr. (1978). Behavioral confirmation in social interaction: From social perception to social reality. *Journal of Experimental Social Psychology, 14,* 148-162.

Snyder, M., & Thompsen, C. J. (1988). Interactions between therapists nd clients: Hypothesis testing and behavioral confirmation. In D. C. Turk & P. Salovey (Eds.), *Reasoning, inference, and judgment in clinical psychology* (pp. 124-152). New York: Free Press.

Solomon, B. B. (1976). *Black empowerment: Social work in oppressed communities.* New York: Columbia University Press.

Sonne, J. L., & Janoff, D. S. (1982). Attributions and the maintenance of behavior change. In C. Antaki & C. Brewer (Eds.), *Attributions and psychological change.* London: Academic Press.

Spivak, G., Platt, J., & Shure, M. (1976). *The problem-solving approach to adjustment.* San Francisco: Jossey-Bass.

Stahler, G. J., & Rappaport, H. (1986). Do therapists bias their ratings of patient functioning under peer review? *Community Mental Health Journal, 22,* 265-274.

Straus, M. A., Gelles, R. J., & Steinmetz, S. (1980). *Behind closed doors: Violence in the American family* Garden City, NY: Archer/Doubleday.

Strauss, J. S. (1989). Subjective experiences of schizophrenia: Toward a new dynamic psychiatry—II. *Schizophrenia Bulletin, 15*(2), 179-187.

Strean, H. S. (Ed.). (1982). *Controversy in psychotherapy.* Metuchen, NJ: Scarecrow Press.

Stensrud, R., & Stensrud, K. (1981). Counseling may be hazardous to your health: How we teach people to feel powerless. *Personnel and Guidance Journal, 59,* 300-304.

Sternberg, R. J., & Kolligian, J., Jr. (Eds.). (1990). *Competence considered.* New Haven, CT: Yale University Press.

Sternberg, R. J., & Wagner, R. K. (Eds.). (1986). *Practical intelligence: Nature and origins of competence in the everyday world.* New York: Cambridge University Press.

Swift, C., & Levin, G. (1987). Empowerment: An emerging mental health technology. *Journal of Primary Prevention, 8,* 71-94.

Taylor, S. E. (1986). *Health psychology.* New York: Random House.

Taylor, S. E. & Brown, J. D. (1988). Illusion and well-being: A social psychological perspective on mental health. *Psychological Bulletin, 103,* 193-210.

Taylor, S. E., & Schneider, S. K. (1989). Coping and the simulation of events. *Social Cognition, 7,* 174-194.

Thompson, W. C., Cowan, C. L., & Rosenbaum, D. L. (1980). Focus of attention mediates the impact of negative affect on altruism. *Journal of Personality and Social Psychology, 38*, 291-300.

Tropp, E. (1977). Social group work: The developmental approach. *Encyclopedia of social work* (pp. 1321-1327). New York: National Association of Social Workers.

Turner, R. J. (1983). Direct, indirect, and moderating effects of social support on psychological distress and associated conditions. In H. B. Kaplan (Ed.), *Psychological stress: Trends in theory and research.* New York: Academic Press.

Tversky, A., & Kahneman, D. (1973). Availability: A heuristic for judging frequency probability. *Cognitive Psychology, 5*, 207-232.

Tversky, A., & Kahneman, D. (1974). Judgment under uncertainty: Heuristics and biases. *Science, 185*, 1124-1131.

Unger, R. K., Draper, R. D., & Pendergrass, M. L. (1986). Personal epistemology and personal experience. *Journal of Social Issues, 42*(12), 67-69.

von Bertalanffy, L. V. (1969). *General systems theory: Foundations, development, applications.* New York: George Braziller.

Wachtel, P. (1977). *Psychoanalysis and behavior therapy: Toward Integration.* New York: Basic Books.

Watson, D. L., & Tharp, R. G. (1989). *Self-directed behavior* (5th ed.). Pacific Grove, CA: Brooks/Cole.

Welkowitz, J., Cohen, J., & Ortmeyer, D. (1967). Value system similarity: Investigation of patient-therapist dyads. *Journal of Consulting Psychology, 31*, 48-55.

Wells, R., & Whittaker, J. (1989). Integrating research and agency-based practice: Approaches, problems, and possibilities. In E. A. Balcerzak (Ed.), *Group care of children: Transition toward the year 2000* (pp. 351-367). Washington, DC: Child Welfare League of America.

Whittaker, J. K., Schinke, S. D., & Gilchrist, L. D. (1986) The ecological paradigm in child, youth, and family services: Implications for policy and practice. *Social Service Review, 60*(4), 483-503.

Wiggins, N., & Hoffman, P. J. (1968). Three models of clinical judgment. *Journal of Abnormal Psychology, 73*, 70-77.

Williams, R. L., & Long, J. D. (1988). *Toward a self-managed life-style* (4th ed.). Boston: Houghton Mifflin.

Wills, T. A. (1982). The study of helping relationships. In T. A. Wills (Ed.), *Basic processes in helping relationships.* New York: Academic Press.

Winfrey, P. L., & Goldfried, M. R. (1986). Information processing and the human change process. In R. E. Ingram (Ed.), *Information processing approaches to clinical psychology.* New York: Academic Press.

Worchel, S., Cooper, J., & Goethals, G. R. (1988). *Understanding social psychology* (4th ed.). Chicago: Dorsey.

Wylie, R. (1979). *The self-concept* (Vol. 2). Lincoln: University of Nebraska Press.

Yalom, I. D. (1980). *Existential psychotherapy.* New York: Basic Books.

Yeaton, W. H., & Sechrest, L. (1981). Critical dimensions in the choice and maintenance of successful treatments: Strength, integrity, and effectiveness. *Journal of Consulting and Clinical Psychology, 49*, 156-168.

Zaro, J., Barack, R., Nedelman, D, & Dreiblatt, I. (1982). *A guide for beginning psychotherapists.* Cambridge: Oxford University Press.

Zimbardo, P. G. (1979). *Psychology and life* (10th ed.). Glenview, IL: Scott, Foresman.

AUTHOR INDEX

SUBJECT INDEX

ABOUT THE AUTHORS

AARON M. BROWER received his M.S.W., A.M. in psychology, and his Ph.D. in social work and psychology from the University of Michigan. Since 1985 he has been on the faculty of the University of Wisconsin-Madison School of Social Work, where he teaches beginning and advanced practice and practice research courses. His professional practice focuses on the coping and striving of adolescents and young adults. His current research explores differences between various cultural groups in their educational attainment and life course decision making, and on the roles played by goals and self-appraisals in meeting educational and developmental transitions. He has published widely in professional journals and is the associate editor for the interdisciplinary journal, *Small Group Research*. In addition to *Social Cognition and Individual Change*, he has also co-edited *Advances in Group Work Research* and is co-editor of the forthcoming book, *What's Social About Social Cognition?* Using the cognitive-ecological model, he has consulted with and supervised mental health students and professionals in the United States, Canada, and Hong Kong.

PAULA S. NURIUS received her M.S.W. from the University of Hawaii and her M.A. in psychology and Ph.D. in social work and psychology from the University of Michigan. She is currently Associate Professor at the University of Washington School of Social Work, where she directs the doctoral program and teaches research and practice courses. Her background is in women's issues and mental health, focusing on trauma and victimization. Her current areas of research include self-concept and the role of cognitive appraisal in coping and striving, particularly as they apply to self-concept change and to violence against women. She has been active in editorial consultation for journals, and in developing educational innovations related to critical thinking and clinical reasoning as well as the use of computers to support direct practice. In addition to this book, she has co-authored *Human Services Practice, Evaluation, and Computers: A Guide for Today and Beyond,* has co-edited *Controversial Issues in Social Work Research,* and has published extensively in the professional literature.